What have you got to lose?
just my dignity pride
and self respect
oh

RES
plays

DATE DUE			

by Joanne Klein

Making Pictures:
The Pinter Screenplays

Ohio State University Press: Columbus

Extracts from F. Scott Fitzgerald, *The Last Tycoon*. Copyright 1941 Charles Scribner's Sons; copyright renewed. Reprinted with the permission of Charles Scribner's Sons.

Extracts from John Fowles, *The French Lieutenant's Woman*. Copyright © 1969 by John Fowles. By permission of Little, Brown and Company.

Extracts from Harold Pinter, *The French Lieutenant's Woman: A Screenplay*. Copyright © 1982 by United Artists Corporation and Copyright © 1982 by J. R. Fowles, Ltd.

Extracts from L. P. Hartley, *The Go-Between*. Copyright © 1954 and 1981 by L. P. Hartley. Reprinted with permission of Stein and Day Publishers.

Extracts from Penelope Mortimer, *The Pumpkin Eater*. © 1963 by Penelope Mortimer. Reprinted by permission of the Harold Matson Company, Inc.

Extracts from Nicholas Mosley, *Accident*. Copyright © 1965 by Nicholas Mosley. Reprinted by permission of Hodder and Stoughton Limited.

Library of Congress Cataloging in Publication Data
Klein, Joanne, 1949–
Making pictures.
Bibliography: p.
Includes index.
1. Pinter, Harold, 1930–   —Moving-picture plays.
I. Title.
PR6066.I53Z713 1985   822'.914   85-326
Cloth: ISBN 0-8142-0378-7
Paper: ISBN 0-8142-0400-7

for William I. Oliver

Contents

Acknowledgments

Throughout the preparation of this book, I have been nourished by the assistance and encouragement of others, and I am grateful for the opportunity to thank them for their contributions. The incisive comments and illuminating exhortations of William I. Oliver have enriched this project from start to finish. His faith and fomentations, together with innumerable perusals of manuscript drafts, have inspired this study and made its writing a joy. For their helpful criticisms of various drafts, I wish also to thank George House, William Nestrick, Charles R. Lyons, and Ernest Callenbach, each of whom advised distinct revisions that have enhanced the final version of this study. Weldon A. Kefauver, the Editorial Board of the Ohio State University Press, and their readers have provided generous support and advice, for which I am grateful as well.

The process of researching and preparing this book has been indispensably facilitated by an Andrew W. Mellon Postdoctoral Fellowship at Stanford University and by faculty research grants from Middlebury College and the University of Denver. I am pleased to acknowledge their investment in this book, which has profited also from the hospitality of the American Film Institute in Los Angeles and the Pacific Film Archives in Berkeley.

Grateful acknowledgment is made to the following for permission to reprint from their publications: Associated Book Publishers; The Bodley Head; British Film Institute; Corporate Trust N.V.; Grove Press, Inc.; Hamish Hamilton Limited; Harlan Kennedy; Methuen London Ltd.; Random House, Inc.; Stein and Day Publishers; and Anthony Sheil Associates Ltd.

Finally, I wish to express my gratitude to Mark A. Rhoda, whose patience, generosity, keen eye, and hard work have contributed liberally to the production of this text. His devotion and labor have served me immeasurably in this task and in others.

Chronology of Pinter's Writing for Stage and Screen

1
Media

Harold Pinter's reputation as a playwright precedes and surpasses his work in the cinematic medium. His screenplays, however, have proliferated steadily to dominate his later career, in terms both of quantity and celebrity. Although studies of Pinter's work as a playwright have reached epidemic proportions in published criticism, scholars have generally neglected his career as a screenwriter. To date, the screenplays have received only superficial attention through reviews, in narrowly focused articles, or as obligatory and often cursory portions of Pinter monographs. The need for a closer examination of these film scripts has arisen from their prominence, their quality, and their utility as illuminations of Pinter's dramaturgical practices. Furthermore, since all of Pinter's screenplays are adaptations of material written originally for other media, analysis of his screenwriting process will promote generic distinctions among the various media implicated in their development.

The material for Pinter's screen adaptations originates in one of two sources: his own stage plays (*The Caretaker*, *The Birthday Party*, *The Homecoming*, *Betrayal*) or novels written by other authors. The present study will address exclusively this latter category of adaptations, thereby limiting itself to evaluation of narrative discourse peculiar to the novel and film media. Those distinctions between the medium of stage and that of screen which emerge from examining Pinter's film adaptations of his own work will remain prospects for a subsequent study. Because Pinter's adaptations of the novels provide a capital basis for revealing certain aspects of his original dramaturgy, however, the exegeses in this study are intended partly for that purpose. His personal aesthetic and technique become clear through comparison of the adaptations to their original sources. Where unilateral studies of Pinter's stage plays have sometimes found them mystifying and unyielding, scrutiny of his method as an adapter may facilitate comprehension of his practices as a dramatist. Thus, although this volume will serve primarily as an explication of his screenplays as adaptations of the novels, it will also yield certain insights into the less accessible dimensions of Pinter's work for the stage and trace correspondences between his writings for each medium.

Fundamental similarities exist between Pinter's original work and his eight adaptations. These resemblances occur due partly to Pinter's idiosyncratic manipulations of the source material, but due chiefly to the novels' ideological and methodological consonance with Pinter's own evolving precepts. When questioned, during his work on *The Proust Screenplay*, about his method of selecting the novels, Pinter replied: "They've been proposed to me. . . . It's always been Joe Losey who's given me the books to read. But of course I have been asked to do many other things and declined. These are quite rare items. I've chosen them because I thought something sparked."[1] The eight novels promulgate, or at least accommodate, a view of perception that allows Pinter to deploy his own approach to phenomenological complexity in the screen adaptations. Because Pinter's artistic biases figure prominently in both his selection and revision of the novels, a summary of his characteristic practices will prove helpful at this juncture.

Obfuscation has become Pinter's trademark. His habit of obscuring motives and situations has provoked innumerable tempers and inspired a broad spectrum of extravagant criticism. Bert O. States exemplifies this frustration when he defines Pinter's mystique as "a peculiar activity of mind. We have invented special words for this activity ('Pintercourse,' 'Pinterism,' 'Pinterotic,' etc.), which Pinter understandably detests, but it seems we have needed them as semantic consolation for his having hidden from us the thing they refer to."[2] Typically, misconstruances of Pinter's work arise when critics offer their perplexities to extrinsic formulas for resolution.[3] Since the impact of his drama depends on certain carefully developed doubts, these misguided efforts to decipher puzzlements by imposing patterns from outside the plays yield distorted impressions of the action. Designs of certitude and incertitude in the scripts contrive to engender special recognitions by the audience, and any importation of accessory perspectives, however well-intentioned, upsets this balance.

The preponderance of exotic interpretations of his plays has contributed to Pinter's valuation of the film medium. The advantages of film over stage, he claims, lie in its increased possibilities for articulating reality. He describes these advantages in the following two statements, which refer to the filming of *The Caretaker* and are taken from different sources.

What I'm very pleased about myself is that in the film, as opposed to the play, we see a real house and real snow outside, dirty snow and the streets. We don't see them very often but they're there, the backs of houses and windows, attics in the distance. There is actually sky as well, a dirty one, and these characters move in the context of a real world—as I believe they do.[4]

. . . (the play) got taken out of its natural place which was a room in a house in a street in a town in the world, so I was very glad of the opportunity to go outside and just show that people did come in, when they came in the door they had come in from the street you know and also there was a garden when in the play the man said " . . . all that wood under that tarpaulin in the yard" when given there to build his shed, there was wood under a tarpaulin.[5]

In both quotes Pinter stresses the cardinal familiarity of his fictional world, urging against any inclination to abstract the plays from ordinary and meticulous reality. His works, however affected by personal milieu, neither invoke nor depend on any system other than their own: that which is contained and apparent within them.

The disconcerting qualities in Pinter's work emerge not from its chimerical dislocation but from its literal replication of ordinary reality. His writing records the surface of life with an opacity and indifference that seem uniquely suited to the capacities of the camera. Form exists everywhere without certifiable substance. The replication is undeniable; the facts are inscrutable. In several of Pinter's stage plays, photographs become significant thematic vehicles; in *Night School* the central problem of identity turns on recognition of a photograph that fixes its subject in an unfamiliar image, and in *No Man's Land*, the photograph collection serves as a key metaphoric characterization of the past. Profoundly incapable of conveying any information beyond surface configuration, the photograph expresses the prevailing sensibilities of Pinter's work. He has, in fact, credited his photographic disposition, his fascination with image as signifier, as a source of inspiration for his writing. "I went into a room and saw one person standing up and one person sitting down, and a few weeks later I wrote *The Room*. I went into another room and saw two people sitting down, and a few years later I wrote *The Birthday Party*. I looked through a door into a third room, and saw two people standing up and I wrote *The Caretaker*."[6]

The opaque properties of observation inform Pinter's scripts much as the intermediate device of the camera confers precision and detachment on its subject. By making the surface of life impenetrable and its invisible components unverifiable, Pinter tries to weld each scene of his work to an obscure, inarticulate plane of reality. The inaccessibility of certain details never totally obfuscates the significant; rather it tends to bring the actual subject into sharper focus. Similar to a photographic image, Pinter's fiction merely records the superficial manifestations of its complement, allowing the mysterious counterpoint to emerge, in all its ambiguity, on its own.

In Pinter's adaptation of F. Scott Fitzgerald's *The Last Tycoon*, Monroe Stahr's formula for moviemaking receives emphatic restatement. Stahr's insistence that an effective screenwriter simply "makes pictures" occurs twice in Pinter's screenplay, again signaling Pinter's allegiance to this practice of surface inventories. This reliance on the legibility of photographic reality introduces a collection of thematic concerns prominent in Pinter's writing. Point of view, an intrinsic and restrictive property of pictures, obtains paramount significance in both stage and screen plays. Whether it involves the characters' perceptions of themselves, each other, the past, or the present, or our own perceptions of these depictions, point of view becomes problematic. Pinter's characters suffer from chronically fixed and unreliable angles of vision, an ailment that he intends to lend to us. Like the camera Pinter manipulates not reality, but the mechanisms through which we glimpse it. The imperfections of these mechanisms receive frequent accentuation by various emblems in Pinter's work; the incidence of blindness, eyeglasses, and telescopes, for example, signifies both a desire and a failure to yield the secrets in our picture of the world.

The extensive failure of photographic reality to account for experiential reality persists as a corollary theme in Pinter's writing, drawing him instinctively to the challenge of the cinema. For all its suggestion of familiarity and intrigue, the photograph does not yield its secrets; it yields only our own. Replications reproduce gaps between what we understand and what actually exists: our understanding amounts to hallucination. The camera shares with Pinter an invocation of artifice, opacity, neutrality, and distortion. It succeeds, where the stage sometimes fails, in connecting all these qualities to our perception of ordinary reality. A photographic picture differs from a stage picture in that the former lacks inherent codification. Roland Barthes notes, "To ask whether a photograph is analogical or coded is not a good means of analysis. . . . From a phenomenological viewpoint, in the Photograph, the power of authentication exceeds the power of representation."[7] Elsewhere in *Camera Lucida*, Barthes postulates that the photograph is always invisible, a contingency that, unless it assumes a mask, lacks the capacity for signification. In this respect the photograph becomes a transparent referent and escapes the representational valuations of the stage. The inaccuracies and ambiguities also implicit in the nature of photography, however, transfer their ramifications to the condition of Pinter's world. Thus, the photographic image becomes for Pinter the ideal expression of the moment, fixing it in all its authenticity, obscurity, and isolation.

Cinematic language, however, includes not only the contents of image, but also the codifications of montage, the ordering of images in time. Because pictures are always primary over dialogue in film (except as sound merges inextricably with image),[8] montage inherits leading responsibility for the narrative. The evolution of the image in time necessitates a narrative articulation that is absent from the immobilized image of the photograph. In Christian Metz's discussion of this difference, he elucidates the process of designation involved in montage and advocates a semiotics of denotation to explicate these codes. Noting that the cinematic designation of a "house" occurs through a progression of partial views, Metz concludes, "Thus a kind of filmic *articulation* appears, which has no equivalent in photography: It is the denotation itself that is being constructed, organized, and to a certain extent codified."[9] Montage, therefore, partly relieves the simple photograph of its mute inaccessibility by enabling a contrived articulation of its significate. Unlike written texts, which organize material temporally, this articulation depends on a "dynamization of space" and a "spatialization of time" for intelligibility.[10] George Bluestone clarifies this procedure through his discussion of distinctions between the two media. "Both novel and film are time arts, but whereas the formative principle in the novel is time, the formative principle in the film is space. Where the novel takes its space for granted and forms its narrative in a complex of time values, the film takes its time for granted and forms its narrative in arrangements of space."[11] Consequently, Pinter's principal task as an adapter of novels for cinema consists in a conversion of temporal values into spatial counterparts.

Despite its increased capacity for manipulating and developing information, montage retains the "zero degree" qualities associated with the operation of the camera. In this respect film superficially resembles the non-omniscient neutrality of the *nouveau roman*, and it accommodates the narrative indifference peculiar to Pinter's aesthetic. The camera passes as an acceptably passive and omnipresent recorder of action, conferring a generic objectivity on its subject. Picture images, of course, can and do insinuate narrative bias, but they escape the mire of narrative explication almost indigenous to the novel. In his essay on the differences between narrativity in the novel and that in film, Robert Scholes is critical of modern writing that emulates cinematic inscrutability.

> Some movements in contemporary fiction can be seen as attempts to acquire a cinematic opacity and freedom from conceptual thinking. Alain Robbe-Grillet has tried very hard to be a camera and produced some interesting verbal *tours de force*. But these experiments in writing against the grain of

5

verbal narration are limited in their developmental possibilities. A writer who wants to be a camera should probably make a movie.[12]

Scholes also indicts films that "founder in seas of rhetoric," and encourages each medium to discover and exploit its appropriate narrativity. Regardless of its apparent impartiality, however, cinematic opacity actually substitutes its own sets of biases and artifices for those peculiar to the novel. As Scholes observes the reader supplies visualization for the printed text, where the spectator supplies a more categorial and abstract narrativity for the film. Pinter's treatment of *The French Lieutenant's Woman*, through its obtrusive attention to artifice, suggests not only that he recognizes the contrivance inherent in cinematic visualization but also that he intends to capitalize on its pretense of literal documentation. In this manner Pinter trades on film's capacity for opaque description while evoking its ability to deceive.

Cinematic adaptation of the novel involves the discovery of both spatial equivalents for time and perceptible equivalents for thought. The difficulty in translating thought from the page to the screen extends not only to the internal monologues of the characters but also to the descriptive, historical, and analytical commentary of the narrative. In his foreword to Pinter's screenplay for *The French Lieutenant's Woman*, John Fowles elucidates his awareness of film's inadequacies in these respects and confesses that he holds "strong and perhaps idiosyncratic views on the proper domains of the cinema and the novel."[13] Fowles cautions against screenwriters who try "to remain faithful to the book," observing that such efforts tend to result in prolix scripts that lack dramatic dialogue. Noting the simultaneous advents of film and psychoanalysis, Fowles hypothesizes a complementary relationship between these two methods of organizing experience; "It is not perhaps entirely chance that the invention of motion photography, this sudden great leap in our powers of exploring and imitating the outward of perception, coincided so exactly with the journey into inner space initiated by Freud and his compeers."[14] According to Fowles the novel belongs to the Freudian expedition because the role of language is to designate the invisible and because the concerns of the novel, as it has evolved, lie with "all those aspects of life and modes of feeling that can *never* be represented visually."[15] Where cinematic equivalents for the novelist's narrative do not exist, or where the narrative bulk proves too complex or unwieldy for cinematic legibility, the adapter must find some approach to editing the text for film. Ideally this reductive tack produces minimal distortion of the source work.

Significantly, each of the eight novels that Pinter has adapted for filming develops through the cinematically anathematic first-person narrative form. The stories evolve for us through the conspicuous contrivance of one person's eyes, one person's point of view. The authors have made no effort to disguise or to exempt the presence of bias and manipulation in the storytelling; they avoid suggesting that the yarns unfold in some third-person wonderland where all motives and actions are objectively manifest. The mind of the narrator presides over the tale. We see only what the narrators see, and only in the way that they see it. None of the eight authors indulges our penchant for omniscience, and none admits the practice into his or her own work. These eight fictions, however, go beyond assumption of the bold narrative device in their indictment of omniscience; each designates the unreliability of the narrator as a central theme of the piece. The narrators unanimously confess to incompetence at explaining themselves and their stories, and their frustrations in this matter contribute liberally to the substance of their tales.

The screenplays that Pinter concocts from the eight novels, however, discard the first-person narrative structure. He excises the device due primarily to two main considerations. In the first place, narrators make tedious devices in films. Their speeches lack genuine activity, becoming awkward and burdensome, and their persons violate the narrative conventions of omnipresence and immateriality when (or if) they become visible. We must question, in cases where the narrator becomes an objectified presence, whose eyes we then actually obtain; and ultimately, unless the narrator remains wholly invisible—a yet clumsier undertaking—the format renders itself improbable and dishonest. Pinter actually considered employing an absent narrator in his screenplay for *Remembrance of Things Past*, but he withdrew the idea due to technical worries along these lines.

> Naturally, we did have discussions, early on, about whether it was possible to have Marcel as the subjective camera. But I certainly felt that it becomes a device, it becomes a burden in itself, and you're not facing the fact . . . it's just too bloody. . . . So that was that. I just simply feel that if the film, in action as it were, was persuasive, then these particular problems of verisimilitude just would not be raised in the viewer's mind.[16]

Marcel's subjectivity and the subjectivities of the other seven narrators lie outside the effective capabilities of film. The viewpoints, however, are not only difficult but also unnecessary to sustain, as Pinter indicates in his statement, above. Because the camera has less responsibility to justification and explanation than does the writer, and because it permits a broader freedom of interpretation and a scantier volume of mandated signification, the self-deprecating narrator is deleted. Through its fundamental opacity and apparent impassivity, the camera is capable of (although certainly not limited to) describing while withholding insight. Thus, the problems of omniscience and narrative bias may be more gracefully eluded in the cinema than in the novel.

Although he omits the narrative device as such, Pinter's attraction to these eight novels certainly derives from a shared sensibility, and he does retain the subsuming tension between the narrative figure and his material. Since the nature of this tension varies among the novels, Pinter's articulation of it in the screenplays differs accordingly. We shall examine these treatments individually in the following explications of each script, but we can conclude here Pinter's apparent attraction to eight novels sharing this focus on narrative culpability, this rejection of authorial omniscience.

Beyond the bonds that exist between Pinter's original writing and the qualities inherent in both film and the eight adapted novels, a pattern of development emerges when we compare corresponding periods of his playwriting with his screenwriting. The themes and techniques of his work in both media describe a parallel evolution and appear generally to conform to three phases of this process, which involves shifts in focus from the dynamics between self and other, to the dynamics between self and self, to the dynamics between self and nothing. Each of these phases exhibits a range of distinctive characteristics, including most notably certain depictions of time and game-playing, which we shall identify in the screenplays and link with Pinter's stage plays of the same period.

In the discussions that follow, I have distinguished among three separate renditions of each narrative: the novel, the screenplay, and the film. Each of these versions merits consideration as a distinct, authentic entity and, despite the value and utility of comparative study, each requires ultimate appraisal as a fully synthesized, autonomous *texte*.[17] The relation between novel and screenplay is the primary subject of this study, however, and the films themselves receive direct attention only when they exhibit significant discrepancies, for better or worse, with Pinter's screenplays. The discussions address two questions for each screenplay: What in the source work captured Pinter's imagination? What modifications of the original does Pinter make in his version? Through deliberation of these issues, the individual chapters will amplify the observations stated in this introduction and will illuminate Pinter's working methods and concerns. The last chapter will include an exploration of correlations between the screen adaptations and Pinter's original playwriting as well as a provisional evaluation of his development as a screenwriter.

2

The Servant

This story is about Tony. Therefore I only want to introduce people whose actions affected Tony. I must resist the temptation to write of events which were important in my life during this period. . . . This suppression of events may possibly appear unlikely and eccentric and it may distort the account of my relationship with Tony, because it will seem as if he was more important in my life than he was in fact. It will seem as if I met and thought about no one else. Whereas during this period, although I was fond of him, our casual meetings were only pleasant interludes in the busy life we both led.[1]

Pinter's first screenplay excises the principal figure in the novel on which the story is based. Robin Maugham, who wrote the novel, develops it through the eyes of a third-party, first-person narrator, whom I have quoted above. The episodes of the novel thus depend on the experience and hearsay of an old military chum, Richard Merton. As a device for structuring and editing material, Maugham makes clever application of the narrating Merton. The gaps of time between Merton's encounters with Tony, or with news of Tony, provide striking contrast and a sensation of the rapidity and extremity of Tony's demise. The narrator serves to compress the expanse of Tony's story into a dozen vivid pictures of its progress. "Perhaps if I had seen him every month or so I would not have noticed the change in him and therefore could have done nothing to prevent it. Yet I was only six months in the Middle East that winter, and when he came to lunch with me the day after my return I noticed the difference. He had put on weight, and there was a coarse look about him which I had never seen before" (p. 18).

Merton plies other figures who have contact with Tony for information as well. The collection of viewpoints that finally make up the story includes those of Merton's housemaid, who provides a peer's-eye view of Barrett; Sally, who contributes a rival's view of the situation; and Vera, who casts a self-interested doubt over our previous impression of the affair. The third-party narrator and his informants protect the story from the conceit of author-omniscience and endow it with a stubborn untrustworthiness. Our perceptions of the bizarre relationship between Tony and his manservant Barrett never acquire the weight of fact; they are invariably filtered through the bias and happenstance of other characters. Furthermore, Maugham treats these factors of unreliability as an articulated subject of the novel. Several times, as the two previous quotes demonstrate, Merton warns of the peculiarities intrinsic in his perception of the tale. Vera's remarks late in the novel, although Merton apparently chooses to believe them, wax unreliable when she clearly betrays them as a seductive ploy. Ultimately, we possess a dozen impenetrable vignettes from dubitable points of view, from which we must make any conclusions we can, according to our own individual biases.

Maugham's narrator, however, assumes only a peripheral role in the action of the novel. He partakes directly in the plot only once, when he discovers Vera and Barrett together in Tony's bedroom. Otherwise, Merton functions merely to draw out the combatants, and to set their stories in print. In such a capacity, Merton poses certain problems of artifice and awkwardness, which Maugham does not manage to avoid. In several episodes Merton's voyeuristic style becomes conspicuous.

> At that moment a tide of passion swept over him, and the room turned black before his eyes. It was as if he had given his sight to increase his sense of touch, for he felt intensely aware in all his limbs. He felt his arms encircle her waist and crush her body to him. He felt his lips on her skin searching for the moist softness of her mouth. Then with a spasm of joy he felt her tongue sliding through his lips and her hands stroking his hair. They stumbled through the door to her little room. [P. 35]

> Then, one afternoon, or perhaps as he lay in bed at night, the animal would turn over uneasily. His heart would begin to beat faster as the creature stirred into consciousness. Until, finally awakened, desire stroked his guts and clawed at his heart and his head and throat took control over him so that his whole being was aflame with passion and he could scarcely stop himself clambering down the stairs and bursting into the room where lay the only object in the world into which he could plunge his pain and pour out its fierceness. [P. 39]

Merton's claim that he has "tried to piece the scene together from the halting phrases which Tony used when he told me about it six months later," hardly accounts for the luridness of these two descriptions. If the passages are not evidence that Maugham expects us to mistrust his narrator, then they certainly reveal the shortcomings of the third-party narrative device.

Pinter easily excludes Merton from his cinematic version of the story. The camera waives his need for a voyeuristic middleman, presenting the opaque vignettes directly to the viewer's own prejudice, and he readily substitutes other characters in the one instance of Merton's participation. Although Pinter consequently loses the qualities of viewpoint and ambiguity that the narrative device contributes to the novel, he eliminates the quantities of explication and justification that attend the literary form. Pinter makes the basis of Tony's attraction to Barrett implicit; Maugham supplies articulated analyses of Tony's childhood deprivations and weaknesses of character. "Tony was silent. I could guess some of the thoughts passing through his mind. Tony had left Cambridge, where he was reading law, to join our regiment as a trooper in August 1939. Both his parents were dead, and he was unmarried. The regiment had taken the place of a family in his life" (p. 9). Subsequently in the novel, Tony comments to Merton that Barrett "insulates me from a cold, drab world" (p. 31), and both Merton and Sally refer frequently to Tony's weakness for comfort and sloth, and to Barrett's ability to exploit it. Pinter captures all of this in oblique dialogue and pictures, projecting a different brand of inscrutability over the action.

Pinter's opening sequence of shots, our first glimpse of Barrett and Tony, predicts the dynamics of their relationship and condenses much of Maugham's explicated background information into pictorial equivalents. The camera follows Barrett as he approaches and then enters Tony's house, moving from room to room and finding no sign of occupation. Barrett's efficient and alert intrusion into the unfurnished vulnerability of Tony's home finds immediate contrast with Tony, as Barrett discovers him: "*Low down in an old deckchair lies a body.*"[2]

Interior. Conservatory. Day.
  BARRETT *approaches, stops a little way from the body, regards it. He bends over* TONY.
  BARRETT. Excuse me . . . (TONY *starts up*) My name's Barrett, sir.
  TONY *stares at him, clicks his fingers.*
  TONY. Oh God, of course. I'm so sorry, I fell asleep.
    We've got an appointment.
  BARRETT. Yes, sir.
  TONY. What time?
  BARRETT. Three o'clock sir.
  TONY. Well what time is it now?
  BARRETT. Three o'clock sir.
  TONY. Too many beers at lunch, that's what it is. Do you drink beer?
  BARRETT. No I don't, sir. [Pp. 3–4]

Tony is caught off guard; he is dozing and tipsy, and he explains too much. Barrett takes the upper hand immediately; he commands the time, and he does not drink beer. In their discussion of the Pinter-Losey collaboration, Beverle Houston and Marsha Kinder note that Barrett's punctuality in this opening sequence prevails over the time signature during the earlier portions of the film; "*The Servant* begins punctually with the appointed meeting between master and servant; it ends at some unlocatable time when the power relationships have been reversed."[3] Their observation of this patterned temporal dissolution might answer other objections that Pinter's control of filmic time goes awry near the end of the screenplay.[4] Time, which becomes an increasingly prominent and problematic element in Pinter's work, already assumes a tricky role in his first adaptation: it remains familiar and intact to the extent that other social artifices in the story retain these qualities, and it disintegrates as these societal conventions founder. Punctuality here operates as a foil for the final scenes of the film and as a ploy in Barrett's strategy for manipulating Tony. Barrett's ironic promise of order is merely a conceit intended to appeal to Tony's self-image and to invite Tony's dependence on the miscreant servant.

In an attempt to regain his superiority over Barrett, Tony rises after the preceding dialogue, leads Barrett to another room for interrogation, seats him in a chair, and remains standing himself through the next segment of the encounter. Pinter gives Barrett a more respectable past than the sordid one that Maugham attributes to the servant. Vera supplies the only description of Barrett's background in the novel, and she speaks vaguely of some shady seaside dealings he had with her father. Pinter's Barrett has (possibly) acted as "personal manservant to various members of the peerage" (p. 5). We grasp his background and a significant bit of Tony's in the following exchange.

BARRETT. I was with Viscount Barr until about five weeks ago.

TONY. Oh Lord Barr? My father knew him well. They died within a week of each other as a matter of fact. [P. 5]

From this brief remark, Pinter conveys that Tony issues from solid stock, and that he has, within the last five weeks, lost his father. Maugham's Merton contributes that Tony grew up as an orphan, but Pinter evinces a greater vulnerability of his character from this terse reference to his father's recent death. Additionally, this connection of their pasts implies the truth of Barrett's pretentious reference by subjecting it to ready verification.

Tony interviews Barrett manipulatively: he stares out the window at the square, his back toward Barrett, studying Barrett's reflection in the

glass. In two respects, the turned back and the observation of the un-
seen, Tony's posture represents an attempt to subordinate Barrett. The
lines of the battle for dominance form rapidly.

> TONY. Can you cook?
>
> BARRETT. Well it's . . . if I might put it this way, sir, cooking is something in
> which I take a great deal of pride.
>
> TONY. Any dish in particular?
>
> BARRETT. Well, my . . . my souffles have always received a great deal of praise
> in the past, sir.
>
> TONY. Do you know anything about Indian dishes?
>
> BARRETT. A little, sir.
>
> TONY. Well, I know a hell of a lot.
>
> TONY *sits in the other chair.*
>
> You'd have to do all the cooking here.
>
> BARRETT. That would give me great pleasure, sir. [P. 5]

Clearly, Barrett has Tony on the defensive over the beer-drinking inferiority of his background. Barrett has a natural edge of elegance and
savoir-faire, which Tony plainly lacks, but desires. The aspiring aristo-
crat questions his prospective manservant about the preparation of exotic dishes: a form of intimidation familiar from Pinter's earlier play,
The Dumb Waiter. When Barrett indicates pride and seems to gain an
edge, Tony tries to stump him, hotly and inarticulately announces his
own superiority, and then, at last, sits. Barrett assumes an ingratiating
air, instantly.

We next learn of Tony's natural aversion to women and of his incipient helplessness and dependency on Barrett.

> TONY. I could have got a housekeeper of course, to look after the place and run
> the kitchen, but quite honestly the thought of some old woman running about
> the house telling me what to do . . . rather put me off.
>
> BARRETT. Quite, sir.
>
> TONY. Now apart from the cooking, I'll need . . . well, everything . . . (*He
> laughs.*) General looking after . . . you know.
>
> BARRETT. Yes, I do, sir. [P. 6]

We are, indeed, prepared to believe that Barrett does. And the themes
of Tony's trouble with women, of Tony's impractical nature, and of
Barrett's inexhaustible capability dominate the following several
scenes.

The Sally of Maugham's novel has become the Susan of Pinter's
screenplay, and, although her character remains largely the same, she
stays in the game much longer, partly to compensate for the loss of
Merton as a foil for the Tony-Barrett relationship. Pinter introduces her

in the scene following Barrett's interview, where she and Tony are dining at a restaurant. Their conversation confirms our previous impression of Tony as an extravagant dreamer. He is describing his plans to clear the jungle in Brazil, build three cities, and stock them with peasants from Asia Minor. Twice, during the course of this scene and the one between them that follows in Tony's drawing room, Pinter drops clues that Susan is a drag on Tony's aspiring self-image.

HEAD WAITER. Sir?
TONY. I'll have another bottle, and by the way, this one's corked.
HEAD WAITER. I'm very sorry, sir.
SUSAN. You're corked. [P. 6]

TONY. Oh by the way, I forgot to tell you. I've found a manservant.
SUSAN. (*laughing*.) What? [P. 7]

Barrett offers Tony an opportunity to better his persona, but Susan constitutes a clear threat to Tony's self-delusions and designs.

In Maugham's version of the story, Tony rents his new home furnished. Pinter omits the furniture in order to depict Tony's initial vulnerability and the dynamics of the Barrett-Tony affair through interior decoration. This device of the perpetually transforming house replaces written descriptions of the struggle between the two with a pictorial gauge that derives clearly from Pinter's medley of playwriting symbols. The hyperbolic deployment of living quarters not only jibes with Pinter's earlier fascination by rooms as prospects for sanctuary (as in *The Room, The Dumb Waiter, The Birthday Party,* and *The Caretaker*), but also anticipates the significance of redecoration in his subsequent plays, *The Homecoming* and *The Basement.* Although Tony's stamp dominates the house initially through the presence of his parent's householdry (and the consequent retention of his connection with his past), Barrett dictates the remaining considerations, commands the work crews, and eventually expels or obscures Tony's familial artifacts altogether. His dealings with the work crews, in the scenes following those between Tony and Susan, expose the domineering side of Barrett's character by presenting another viewpoint. Susan and Barrett clash instantly over the style of the place; their oblique confrontation is thick with innuendo and jockeying for position.

Interior. Dining-room. Night.
   TONY *and* SUSAN *sitting at dinner.* BARRETT *with wine. He wears white cotton gloves.*
   SUSAN. The whole place needs brightening . . . more variety you know . . . colour.

TONY. Oh. Do you think so?

SUSAN. Yes, and tomorrow I'm going to organize a proper spice shelf for the kitchen.

BARRETT. Would you like to taste the wine, sir?

TONY. Thank you.

SUSAN. What ducky gloves.

TONY. Barrett's idea. I like it.

BARRETT. It's Italian, miss. They're used in Italy.

SUSAN. Who by?

TONY *tastes the wine.*

TONY. Excellent.

BARRETT. Just a Beaujolais sir, but a good bottler.

SUSAN. A good what?

TONY. Bottler.

BARRETT *slightly inclines his head and goes.* [P. 11]

Susan's incipient sensation of exclusion from the burgeoning coalition between Tony and Barrett leads her to adopt unfortunate weapons; she strives to undermine Barrett's sophisticated airs with vulgar naivete. This tack serves only to forge a stronger alliance between Tony and Barrett. In their chapter on Pinter's films, William Baker and Stephen Ely Tabachnick observe that, "the masculine bond based on rivalry . . . excludes women. . . . Barrett literally supplants her in all the feminine functions of decorating, cooking for, and comforting her lover."[5] The following scenes explicate this trend, as we observe Barrett removing Tony's wet shoes and socks and placing Tony's feet to soak in a bowl of warm salt water. When he uncannily interrupts Tony and Susan on the floor of the drawing room, Susan finally articulates her animosity, and leaves abruptly. After she has left, Tony attempts to upbraid his servant.

BARRETT. I do apologize for the intrusion, sir. I had no idea . . .

TONY. Don't do it again!

BARRETT. I did knock, sir.

TONY. Oh get to bed.

TONY *puts his hand to his head.*

Have you got an aspirin?

BARRETT. Yes, sir. I expect you caught a bit of a chill the other day in the rain, sir. [P. 15]

Pinter's incisive montage progresses toward a cumulative impression that Tony's growing dependency on Barrett's care, on Barrett's maintenance of an illusion of order and prestige, has rendered him powerless to oppose his menial.

Susan and Barrett subsequently line up in another skirmish, this one over some flowers she has brought to Tony that Barrett will not have in Tony's sickroom. The incident, like the previous one, derives from passing relations and references in Maugham's novel that Pinter, due partly to the novel's brevity (56 pages), is able to embellish. In his development of full-blown scenes from these items of gossip, Pinter adds characteristic wit and irony. As Susan departs after the flower confrontation, Barrett remarks: "I'm afraid it's not very encouraging, miss . . . the weather forecast" (p. 17).

The character Vera, whom Barrett introduces initially as his sister, appears at roughly this point in both the novel and screenplay. Pinter, however, in his elaboration of narrator Merton's scant hearsay, adds two scenes as a preamble to her arrival. In the first we see Barrett, fresh from his victory over Susan and the sickroom flowers, placing a call in a public phone box. As he places and executes his call to Vera, we watch him grit his teeth at a group of girls standing outside the booth. The girls giggle and chatter, and one girl's skirt repeatedly blows up in the wind. When Barrett evacuates the booth, the girl squeezes past him, causing him to jab at her and remark, "Get out of it, you filthy bitch" (p. 18). Thus, Pinter has invented another context, that of the public street and the girls, in which to develop and convey facets of Barrett's character. In the Maugham story, Barrett exhibits a sexual fetish for adolescent girls (indeed, Vera, in the original version, is a mere sixteen years old), and Pinter's interest in this trait may have inspired this brief scene. Apart from the teeth-gritting, however, and the fact of the scene itself, Pinter's script does not sustain Barrett's inclination toward teen-aged females. This episode rather suggests Barrett's disinclination toward women, and the screenplay tends generally to shift his character toward misogyny: a modification due probably to cinematic demand for simplicity and clarity. Pinter, through this change, strengthens the primary relationship between Barrett and Tony.

While Barrett meets his "sister" at the train station, Tony lunches with Susan at a restaurant in a motley scene that intersperses their dialogue with witty and cliched snatches of the conversations at other tables. Susan, apparently, has quit visiting Tony at home due to her animosity for Barrett. Over lunch, they bicker about his personality and merit, and finally reach some uneasy truce on the issue as the scene ends.

Except for a brief and ill-fated reconciliation that the narrator arranges, Pinter's retention of Susan has already exceeded Maugham's by one scene. Pinter will bring her into the action five more times, but her relationship with Tony has entered permanent decline. Susan's utility for the screenplay lies in her ability to elicit dimensions of Tony's character and metamorphosis that might otherwise be lost through the omission of Merton's narrative. Her later appearances in Pinter's version of the story serve not only to expose Tony's thoughts, but also to protract his dilemma and to exhibit his deterioration against the emblem of his original pretensions. Twice they visit Lord and Lady Mountset, a pair of aristocratic boors whom Pinter invents from a passing reference in the novel, in scenes of spectacular wealth and acid parody. These episodes contribute to Pinter's depiction of Tony's background and aspirations while they simultaneously measure Tony's growing disenchantment with and alienation from this world.

Tony's interest in Vera, however, which sparks immediately upon her arrival, which she encourages by wearing short skirts, and which is presumably supplied and orchestrated by Barrett, has assumed obsessive proportions. We find, also, that Tony's relationship with Barrett has developed a ring of equality in the bitchy tone of Tony's address to him.

> *Interior.* TONY'S *bedroom. Day.*
> *Close shot of silent valet.* BARRETT'S *hand taking jacket off it, helping* TONY *into it. Pause.*
> TONY. For God's sake look at this. That's not much good, Barrett.
> BARRETT. I beg your pardon, sir.
> BARRETT *brushes the jacket gently.*
> TONY. Pull your socks up now. Come on, come on, come on, give it a good brush, you won't hurt me.
> BARRETT. Perhaps you'd like to take the jacket off, sir?
> TONY. No, damn it. Do it on. I haven't got time to mess about.
> BARRETT *brushes vigorously.*
> BARRETT. Would you turn around sir.
> TONY. No. All right, all right. (*Sulkily.*) All right, It'll have to do. [Pp. 26–27]

After Tony has subsided, Barrett requests permission for himself and his sister to leave for the day and visit their seriously ill mother. Tony fusses over the prospect of a lost hot meal, and finally agrees to give the two servants the following day off, so that he has time to adjust to the idea of their absence.

When Tony has left for his appointment, we get wind that something off-color is in the works: our first hard glimpse behind the scenes. Barrett goes to fetch Vera from Tony's shower, occasioning the following dialogue.

> *Interior. Bathroom. Day.*
> BARRETT *and* VERA. VERA *in towel. He holds the bottle of cologne.*
> BARRETT. Who told you to take a bath in his bathroom? Who said you could use his bathroom? A gentleman doesn't want a naked girl bouncing all over his bathroom.
> VERA. You told me to, didn't you?

BARRETT. Me? Why would I tell you a thing like that?
He closes the door.
I'll tell you what I'm going to do now.
VERA. What?
BARRETT. I'm going to have a bath in his bathroom.
VERA *turns the tap.*
VERA. You're terrible.
He gives her the cologne.
BARRETT. And I want that . . . all over me.
He takes off his jacket. She watches him. The water boils into the bath. [Pp. 28–29]

Although the details of this scene issue entirely from Pinter's imagination, he develops this cinematically potent scenario from Vera's simply stated claim in the novel that "It was he who put me up to Tony" (p. 57).

The play-acting game that becomes apparent here, and again later when the two menials usurp Tony's bed during his temporary absence, invites comparison with Genet's play, *The Maids,* which develops a similar subject through similar devices and insights. In both works dominance and subservience occur as deceitful strategies in a game by which the two parties create, destroy, and exchange roles with each other. Genet's maids, who play compulsively at the game of being Madame, define themselves as much as their mistress according to their enactment of her. As Sartre has expressed their predicament: "These dream dwellers, pure reflections of a sleeping consciousness, use the little reality which this consciousness has given them to imagine that they are becoming the Master who imagines them. . . . they are dreams who dream of swallowing up their dreamer."[6] Like the maids Barrett and Vera lack authentic identity: in Tony's presence they fake servility, and in his absence they imitate him. Their success at the game of supplanting Tony by these tactics is accomplished through Tony's acceptance of their definition of him; his dependence on them for his identity equips them with the power to bring his ruin. The dynamics of worship and spite that incite the rituals of Genet's maids also effect the behavior of Barrett and Vera, who, in their game of deposing Tony, reveal love-hate ambivalences both in their relationship with Tony and in their exploitation of each other. Adoration fuses with animosity, and subservience operates as dominance. The vortex of disguises and pretenses that engulfs all circumstances also swallows up Tony, whose persona is an imposture: a contingency of other contingencies. Like all of Pinter's usurpers during this period (for example, Riley in *The Room,* Goldberg/McCann in *The Birthday Party,* and Mick in *The Caretaker*), Barrett insinuates his scheme by undermining the fabric of artifice that

affords Tony's image. In each case the usurpers participate in the creation of the victim's identity while retaining an inchoate, unpredictable
identity for themselves, and through these means, derive the power to
manipulate and overcome their prey.

While Barrett is away ministering to his mother, Tony wanders
aimlessly and dissipates rapidly. Pinter's montage depicts him listlessly
studying a menu in a coffee bar, then leaving before the waitress can get
to him. He returns home to drift about the halls and kitchen, throwing
down the mail without opening it (a characteristic symptom of withdrawal and malaise in Pinter's work, which he repeats in similar scenes
in *The Pumpkin Eater, Accident,* and *The Last Tycoon*). Suddenly, Vera
appears, stating that Barrett has told her to remain at the house because
she felt ill. Pinter retains Maugham's audiovisually sensual dripping
faucet (which director Joseph Losey captures brilliantly on film) and
adds the dilemma of an unanswered telephone (presumably Susan, who
phoned earlier) during this brief prologue to Tony's abrupt seduction of
Vera.

Barrett returns, efficiency incarnate, and moves straight to the mail,
examining it. He has clearly obtained the position where he holds
Tony's life together, providing all of its order and direction. Pinter
mines the subtext for all its worth during their first meeting after Tony's
fling with Vera.

> BARRETT. I hope she hasn't been any inconvenience to you.
> TONY. Oh not at all. No, she hasn't at all.
> BARRETT. Did she manage to do anything for you, sir?
> TONY *looks at him sharply.*
> TONY. I beg your pardon.
> BARRETT. I hope she was well enough to see to your meals.
> TONY. Oh yes, yes, we . . . I had lunch.
> BARRETT. I notice she didn't do the washing up.
> TONY. Still under the weather, I suppose.
> BARRETT. Under the what, sir?
> TONY. The weather.
> BARRETT. Oh yes. [P. 32]

Tony hastily sends Barrett out for beer, although they have plenty in the
house, so that he can quickly ravish Vera in the library and establish a
time to meet that night. When Vera leaves her room to meet him at
midnight, we clearly see Barrett left behind in her bed, *"reaching for a
newspaper"* (p. 35).

Over the next several scenes, the rapidity of Tony and Barrett's alternation in her favors is conspicuous and enlightening.

> *Interior. First landing. Day.*
> VERA *slips out of* TONY'S *door, flushed, and goes downstairs carrying the tray.*
> *Interior. Hall. Day.*
> VERA *comes downstairs, puts tray down on hall table and looks at herself in mirror. Suddenly* BARRETT'S *hands reach for her. He pulls her back out of sight. A sharp gasp from her, a grating "Aaaahhh" from him. A phone can be heard ringing off screen. Stay on empty hall.* [P. 36]

Barrett, perhaps even more clearly in retrospect, apparently thrives on the kinky sharing of the girl. Through the pandering of Vera, he manages not only to satisfy certain sexual appetites that later emerge directly in his relationship with Tony, but also to contaminate and undermine the fragile conceits of Tony's posture. The unanswered phone forecasts an incipient disintegration of order in favor of irrational ritual, and the camera's retention of "the empty hall" (a characteristic Pinter-Losey device, which we shall examine in their subsequent films) provides visual affirmation of the ascendancy of latent, invisible corruption.

From here, the situation rapidly escalates (or perhaps deteriorates) in all reaches of the plot. Susan arrives to redecorate the house, playing out a vicious scene with Barrett in the process. She and Tony leave for the second of their two trips to the Mountsets' estate, but decide to return early to the house in order to spend an impulsive and ill-fated night together in Tony's room. Again by capitalizing on a device familiar from his playwriting, Pinter loads the stakes in anticipation of the story's climactic turning point. His preoccupation with rooms as refuges builds with intensity through a montage of three quick scenes: first in Susan and Tony's comparison of individual room views at the Mountsets' and in their decision to return to Tony's room in London, then in their observation from the car of an inexplicable light in Tony's room, and finally in their discovery of the two servants, together in Tony's bed.

The speed and force with which Pinter establishes the nature of room as sanctuary, only to reveal its desecration, exemplify his skill at reshaping this material for cinematic impact. Although the novel contains both the cue and spirit for such a sequence, Pinter's instinct and aptitude for this particular motif of usurped sanctuary, which dominates his early playwriting, induce him to focus the process as an index of dynamics fundamental to the story. Similar uses of territory and intrusion occur throughout Pinter's original writing, including both his early plays (*The Room, The Birthday Party, The Dumb Waiter,* and *The Caretaker*), where the theme emerges directly from action, and his later plays (*The*

Homecoming, Old Times, No Man's Land, and *Betrayal*), where such matters become more abstract and complex. In all cases, theatrical and cinematic, the room symbol presents opportunities for rendering ideas visible, and Pinter exploits its capacity for translating time into space and language into image.

The discovery of Barrett and Vera in Tony's bedroom belonged, in the novel, to Merton, who subsequently reported his findings to Tony in a later episode. Lacking Merton and preferring the shock of firsthand confrontation, Pinter writes the scene for Tony, himself, and includes Susan to intensify the strain. When he understands the situation, Tony yells for Barrett to come down, and asks Susan to leave. She insists, however, on staying.

> TONY. Do you realize you've comitted a criminal offense?
> BARRETT. Criminal, sir?
> TONY. She's your sister, you bastard!
> BARRETT *looks at him.*
> BARRETT. She's not my sister, sir. (*Pause.*) And if I might say so we're in the same boat.
> *Silence.* BARRETT *looks at* SUSAN.
>   He knows precisely what I mean. . . .
> *She stares at* TONY.
> BARRETT. . . . In any case, apart from the error of being in your room I'm perfectly within my rights. Vera's my fiancee. [Pp. 41–42]

After Vera appears and corroborates this piece of news, further insinuating Tony's complicity in front of Susan as she does so, Tony throws them both out of the house and turns to Susan. "*Eventually* TONY *in a half-appeal, half-demand, whispers:* Come to bed" (p. 43). Susan abruptly leaves the house.

Again, in Barrett's absence, Tony rapidly goes to seed. He throws himself onto Vera's bed (a metaphoric statement of his own servitude to his servants) and staggers through half a dozen shots enumerating his dereliction and ineptitude. The condition of the house deteriorates radically, and Tony wanders through it in an alcoholic stupor. The period in Maugham's novel witnessed Tony's almost complete rehabilitation and reconciliation with Sally (Susan), but, in both novel and screenplay, the periods end when Tony encounters Barrett in a pub. Maugham gives us Barrett's story through Merton via a postcard from Tony recounting its details. Pinter lets Barrett speak for himself. In both versions, however, the account is largely the same. Barrett claims that Vera had exploited him, told him nothing of her affair with Tony until moments before the discovery, and left him immediately upon their expulsion for a "bookie." He manages to insinuate himself back into Tony's graces, adopting a lackey's humility and preying upon Tony's pity. The halting eloquence of this lie not only recalls Aston's recollection of shock treatment in *The Caretaker*, as Baker and Tabachnick observe,[7] but also anticipates Sarah's account of her affair with the French lieutenant in Pinter's much later screenplay. In this respect it exemplifies Pinter's skill at replicating the rhythms and manipulations of a liar, and it alerts us to possible instances of lying in his other works.

The artificial roles and barriers of the Tony-Barrett relationship have collapsed, however, due to their common use of Vera. After Tony agrees to reemploy Barrett, we discover, through yet another transformation of the battleground-house, an immediate change in their situation.

> *Interior. Hall. TONY's house. Day. The house is changed. It is airless, dark, oppressive. Curtains and blinds are almost constantly drawn. There are no longer any flowers. The log fire has been replaced by illuminated gas logs. The sleek television in the bedroom has been replaced by a heavy console, now in the drawing room. Cheap sex magazines replace the expensive monthlies. There is an overlay of BARRETT everywhere. Photos of footballers cellotaped to mirrors. Pornographic calendars. Nudes stuck in oil paintings. The furniture has subtly changed, the rooms no longer possess composition. Elegant pornographic books have been yanked from TONY's bookshelves and are strewn about. The bookshelves are left disordered and heavy with dust. BARRETT's brown paper obscene books are piled about, and cellophaned piles of photos. The ashtrays are crammed full, glasses half empty and empty beer bottles are on the liquor trolley. BARRETT is now dressed in a rough sweater, corduroy trousers and heavy boots.* [Pp. 46-47]

As the decor suggests, Barrett has clearly gained the upper hand in the struggle with his titular master. Their first dialogue in this new atmosphere has the character of a domestic spat. Tony is in his pajama jacket solving crossword puzzles, and Barrett is assailing him over the mess, always being in the way, not retaining a maid, and not having a job. "Look, why don't you get yourself a job instead of moping around here all day? Here I am scraping and skimping to make ends meet . . . getting worse and worse . . . and you're no bloody help . . . d'you know that butter's gone up twopence a pound" (p. 48)? The bitching and needling steadily worsen; they nag at each other and fight over the duties of their constantly shifting roles; their contact with the outside world dwindles to nothing.

Finally, Barrett and Tony resort to party games (a standard Pinter motif that operates in his plays and screenplays as a manifestation of competition on other levels of the action) as a way of determining momentary superiority and order. In a breather between games, the two have a conversation that recalls Tony's military background from Maugham's novel, but the dialogue takes an odd twist.

BARRETT. You know sometimes I get the feeling that we're old pals.
TONY. That's funny.
BARRETT. Why?
TONY. I get the same feeling myself.
Pause.
BARRETT. I've only had that same feeling once before.
TONY. When was that?
BARRETT. Once in the army.
TONY. That's funny. I had the same feeling myself there, too. Once. [P. 52]

The reiteration of the word "once" in this passage, particularly by Tony in the final line, suggests some hidden subject or reference in these lines. The all-male nature of the army, the already strongly sexual character of their relationship, and the repetition of the peculiar "once" imply that the real topic of this conversation consists in a testing out of each other's availability for homosexual activity. The subsequent party game marks a new shift in their relationship that tends to support this reading. The game is Hide and Seek; Tony is hiding and Barrett is seeking.

BARRETT. . . . Where's your little lair this time? Puss, puss, puss, puss, pussy, puss, puss, puss, puss, puss.
. . . I'm getting warm! You're hiding but you'll be caught. You've got a guilty secret, you've got a guilty secret, but you'll be caught. I'm coming to get you, I'm creeping up on you.
. . . I'm getting warm, I can smell a rat, I can smell a rat . . .
TONY *shivers. The door bursts open.* BARRETT *charges in and confronts him.* BARRETT *utters a terrifying maniacal bellow.* TONY *faints.* [P. 53]

Their relationship has indeed acquired some extraordinary, private, and intense dimension. Barrett now refers to Tony as "Tone," and when Vera arrives to beg money from her ex-boss, Barrett ejects her from the house in the middle of her exposure of his mendacity. In both the novel, where Vera delivers this account to Merton, and the screenplay, Vera's motives suggest that she cannot be trusted. Tony's reaction of helplessness to her tale (conveyed to him by Merton in Maugham's version), which lays the apparent premise of his resumed relationship with Barrett open to suspicion, confirms his doom. As Baker and Tabachnick suggest, "Tony, in true Pinter fashion, has nothing left in his life except his relationship with Barrett, to which he must cling even as it destroys him. . . . Tony's early need for order has become an absolute desire to be commanded."[8]

At this point in the novel, Tony retires to the kitchen where Barrett and a female child await his participation in a sexual *ménage*. Pinter, who makes Barrett and his revamped sexual taste more respectable, brings Susan into the milieu for one final cut. The situation between her and Tony is hopeless, and a party is commencing in other rooms of the house as they attempt to talk. After trying to convince her to leave, Tony leads Susan into the bedroom, where Barrett and four women are drinking and playing a recording of Susan and Tony's "song": one that has played several times during their scenes together.

> Leave it alone
> It's all gone
> Leave it alone
> It's all gone
> Don't stay to see me
> Turn from your arms
> Leave it alone
> It's all gone
> Give me my death
> Close my mouth
> Give me my breath
> Close my mouth
> How can I bear
> The ghost of you here
> Can't love without you
> Must love without you
> Now while I love you alone. [P. 13]

As the song plays, the women converge on Tony. He lies on the bed, staring vacantly at Susan, as she moves to Barrett and kisses him. Barrett's ascendancy, certified even by Susan's recognition, is now complete. Tony smashes the record player and commands from the floor, "*(in a sudden dazed childish horror, in a monotone)* Get out, get out. Get 'em all out" (p. 59). Barrett clears the house, recovering his composure to incline his head to Susan as she leaves the house after hitting him in the face with her closed fist. In our last view of them, Tony crawls onto the landing and sits in a corner, as Barrett mounts the stairs, his hand trailing along the banister. (The film adds the plainly visible figure of Vera to this final image, effecting a clearer sense of her continued complicity with Barrett and of Tony's deposal.)

Pinter's screen adaptation (1962) of Maugham's sinister tale of the intricate and almost incomprehensible relationship between Tony and Barrett contributes a heightened menace to the proceedings. Because Maugham's novel is short and consists largely of narrative discourse that the screenplay omits, Pinter is free to embellish incidents where, elsewhere in his adaptations, he works chiefly to condense and edit material. His skill at reshaping the piecemeal plot for cinematic impact and at capturing its subtextual dynamics in pictorial images is evident throughout his revisions of the novel.

He capitalizes, in the first place, on the struggles for dominance and insularity that are present both in the novel and in his original writing of this general period (*The Room*, 1957; *The Birthday Party*, 1957; *The Dumb Waiter*, 1957; and *The Caretaker*, 1959), and he accentuates these through such devices as the party game and the perpetually redecorated house. Examples in the plays of these struggles and devices are both numerous and conspicuous: Rose, Stanley, Gus, and Davies all fail in their efforts to secure territory because they manage to assert authority over neither others nor place. Party games achieve prominence in Goldberg and McCann's strategy for overpowering Stanley in *The Birthday Party*, while explicit and implicit games of manipulation account for much of the interaction in all of these plays.[9] In each case, during this early period of Pinter's writing, the games occur as techniques for protecting or interrupting routines that are closely associated with territory. The eruption of the contest between Tony and Barrett into coups of sport and decor may illumine similar patterns in the stage plays wherever these are obscure, as the screenplay shares the characteristics of Pinter's early dramaturgy while revealing these more clearly, perhaps, through their derivative process. Pinter's emphasis, for example, on Barrett's skill at conforming milieu to his taste and expedience contrasts sharply with the domestic inefficacies not only of Tony, but also of Stanley, Gus, and Davies, each of whom reveals an impotence at this task which forecasts his eventual expulsion. Although the notion of redecoration finds expression only in the dialogue of the plays that precede *The Servant* (most notably in *The Caretaker*), the introduction of material changes in the settings of succeeding plays, such as *The Homecoming*, in which Jessie's absence presides over the action through an architectural hiatus in the set, and *The Basement*, in which a duel for supremacy is waged through fickle interior design, suggests Pinter's enthusiasm for this device.

Above all, Pinter's screenplay for *The Servant* exploits the opaque and objectified communicative facility of cinematic expression; due to relative impartiality of the camera's eye, he retains the inaccessible, mysterious, and incredible levels of the action without elucidating them or necessarily subjecting them to narrative apologies. These disclaimers by Merton in the novel tend themselves to reduce and resolve the inexplicable developments of the story. Pinter, by virtue of his reliance on cinematic impassivity and of his attunement to subtextual contours, preserves the inscrutability of the story, the fallibility of perception, without recourse to obvious negations of omniscience or to the alternative perspectives that Merton implies. The simultaneous close scrutiny and analytic indifference of the camera exempt Pinter from the need for such a device while generically focusing the dilemma that the device serves. Consequently, we, as audience, suffer the frustrations mandated by viewpoint without the awkward, and explicative, nods to inexplicability that the narrator entails.

3

The Pumpkin Eater

I have tried to be honest with you, although I suppose that you would really have been more interested in my not being honest. Some of these things happened, and some were dreams. They are all true, as I understood truth. They are all real, as I understood reality.[1]

In *The Pumpkin Eater,* Pinter's battleground shifts somewhat toward internal climes, consistent with a trend in his playwriting, already initiated in the intrapersonal frictions of *A Slight Ache* and *The Homecoming,* and extending throughout his subsequent work. Penelope Mortimer's novel, on which the screenplay is based, describes the circumstances surrounding a woman's emotional breakdown from her own point of view. Her final statement in the novel, quoted above, tallies with the volatile mood of the work, which consists in a collection of apparently unrelated, nonsequential, and noncreditable scenes. The narrator suffers a certifiable rupture from "reality." We meet her thirteen years into her fourth marriage, with a brood of uncounted (uncountable?) children. Mainly through the device of psychoanalysis, we learn that her previous marriages had landed her in happy poverty, but that her present husband, Jake, has become a wealthy screenwriting sensation. The trappings of success have undone our narrator (who goes nameless in the novel), as Jake's expanding circles of activity parallel a constricting pattern in her own. Her talents for homemaking, organizing, rallying, and reproducing go unheeded. Payrolled employees have rendered her obsolete, proliferating comforts have eroded her usefulness, and professional worries and attachments have apparently undermined Jake's affection for her. She recedes further and further from the nurse-dominated world of her innumerable children and from the clique-dominated world of her inaccessible husband, into her own world of doubting.

By nature and circumstance, our narrator remains chronically incapable of discerning the truth about her own situation and about those of the others in the story. She prevents us from discovering the facts as well. Neither of us can afford to trust the few conclusions she manages to make. "Things happen. I look. I'm miserable, or frightened, or angry. But up here, in my head, I do not know what it *is* that's happening. I can't *believe* what is happening. . . . I believe it, but I don't believe in it. It's not really happening, I kept saying to myself. It's not really true" (pp. 186–87). And nowhere do we get *the* story; everywhere we get *her* story.

The spoils of ambiguity infest the novel at all levels. Time sequences jumble, collapse, and expand, leaving us uncertain of the order, relationship, and duration of events. We seldom know what caused what or how long it has been going on. Motives become impossible to determine, and even the narrator concludes that their divination is a waste of time. When she is confronted, after her abortion/hysterectomy, with the pregnancy of Jake's mistress, she capitulates. "How can you tell about anything? It's what you do that matters, the reason is just . . . nothing. The reason why Jake and Beth Conway went to bed together—whether it was good or bad, it couldn't matter less. Reasons don't have consequences, only actions. She's pregnant and I'm sterile . . . and who cares if it's justified or unjustified" (pp. 189–90).

According to the narrator's perspective, we are condemned to watching and guessing. Life around us promises no more accessibility than a still photograph, frozen forever in its fleeting mystery. The existences of others elude us: "I always found it hard to believe in the actuality of other people's lives" (p. 213). Our own pasts slip away: "I waited in the car for two hours till you came back. I remember it, but it's like remembering seeing a woman sitting in a car" (p. 187). Our selves disintegrate with them: "All this, and more, I saw myself perform in my children's memories, but although I knew at one time it was so, I could not recognize myself" (p. 214).

The narrator laments the predatory indifference of the infinite present that now envelops her in the absence of all other connections.

I seemed to be alone in the world. . . . I had found, or had created, a neutrality between the past that I had lost and the future that I feared: an interminable hour which passed under my feet like the shadow of moving stairs, each stair recurring again and again, flattening to meet the next, a perfect circle of isolation captive between yesterday and tomorrow, between two illusions. Yesterday had never been. Tomorrow would never come. [P. 212]

She relinquishes her quest for the elusive—her desire for verification, her scrutiny of motive, her visits to the psychoanalyst (whose very nature persists in the attempt to explain the present through the past, and who, in the novel, makes an obvious figure of ridicule)—but she does so only to inhabit a magnified stasis, an absence of life. Mortimer's physical metaphor for this process, the newly constructed, vacant house, into which the narrator moves at this point, hurls the novel squarely into Pinter-land.

These themes and situations come tailor-made to Pinter. He provides the narrator with a name, Jo, and describes her situation in the cinematic language of fact. Previous studies that have wondered at the relevance of Mortimer's themes to Pinter's milieu seem to be confounded either by the novel or by the released film.[2]

Jack Clayton, who directed the film, misapprehended Pinter's reworking of the material, and ruined or cut some of its finest moments. He violated the script by retaining from the novel some of Jo's disorientation as an excuse for fancy camera work in the mode of grotesque subjective viewpoint. Consequently, he dislocated Pinter's re-routing of the signifiers of ambiguity, returning the blame to the narrator rather than attributing it to inescapable condition as Pinter had intended. Although their argument runs almost contrary to mine in this respect, and they attribute Clayton's mishandling of the script to his "cool camera technique," Baker and Tabachnick also sense the director's inappropriateness for this material. "Jack Clayton . . . contradicts . . . the point of the story by attempting to present what we see as in fact truth. Pinter's early fears about the 'bastardising' tendency of the film industry find partial justification when it comes to this film. The limitations of the writer working in a medium only partially under his power to control become clear here."[3] Clayton corrupted the script in his cautiousness as well as in his boldness, by cutting and reordering it to alleviate Pinter's confused temporal scheme. Hopelessly out of synchronization with his material, Clayton finally invented a happy ending, disfiguring Pinter's finest contribution to the story, and rendering the entire film incongruously sentimental. Thus, in this discussion more than the others, I discount the filmed product and restrict my analysis exclusively to the screenplay text.

In Pinter's script (Clayton has altered this sequence to ensure a smoother "continuity") the early scenes comprise a temporal patchwork that juxtaposes Jo's past circumstances with her present condition. Here, in a fast-paced series of vignettes alternating the chaotic exuberance of the past with the antiseptic malaise of the present, Pinter delineates the horns of Jo's dilemma. We glimpse Jo alone, with tea laid for one, staring out the window. "*Reflected in the window pane demolition of buildings, tall skeletons of new constructions.*"[4] Again, we note the indictment of perceptual modes implicit in Pinter's indication that Jo's view of things is a reflected one, manipulated and occluded by the windows of her own world. The subject of this reflection, a radical encroachment on the old by the new, keynotes the prevailing theme of Pinter's adaptation, and he will repeat the idea in various forms throughout the screenplay.

Jo drifts without interest through the signs of the absent: glinting automobiles, overturned scooters, pools of petrol, untouched mail, sounds of water running elsewhere, expensive furniture, dark corners of the garage. From this study of alienation, Pinter cuts immediately to the past.

> *Interior. Barn. Day.* TEN YEARS EARLIER. *A large room, sub-divided by numerous home-made partitions. It is sparsely furnished but crowded with children. JO is at a table making pastry. Some of the children are playing on the floor with train sets and home-made constructions of roads and stations. The smallest girl apart, examining a doll's house.* [P. 65]

The scene that transpires here depicts Jo's first encounter with Jake in a maelstrom of children's exigencies and domestic toil. Pinter traces the progress of their relationship in two contiguous thumbnail scenes, first with Jake's father and then with Jo's, seeking permission for their marriage. Both of these figures from the past have died or will die during the ambiguous present time of the story. From the scene with Jo's father, Pinter cuts to the following sequence.

> *Interior. Kitchen—St. John's Woods. House. Day.* PRESENT DAY. *Close on tray. With tea being set on draining board, with a sharp sound.*
> *Another angle:* JO *stands, does not touch crockery.*
> *Another angle: at window.*
> *Glimpses of demolition through window.*
> *Another angle:* JO
> *She turns away, clutching her arms, walks vaguely about the kitchen, her heels clicking on the tiled floor. An immaculate, gleaming modern kitchen, spotless, nothing out of place.*
> *Another angle:* JO
> *As she moves, we see: new dishwasher, new refrigerator, new washing machine and spin dryer, new eleric oven, racks of gleaming crockery, photograph on teak wood wall, a large photo pinned from a magazine of* MR JAKE ARMITAGE, MRS ARMITAGE *and their* CHILDREN. [P. 69]

The schism that Pinter focuses between the past and the present suggests, with distinct economy and force, an incipient clash between the forces of chaos and those of order. Through this striking montage, juxtaposing kitchen past and kitchen present, Jo's dilemma emerges.

Jo's marriage to Jake has necessitated a "shedding of the load," as

Jo's father states it. The eldest of the brood are bustled off to boarding school, never actually to return to the clan. In Mortimer's novel three children, two girls and a boy, suffer the expulsion. Pinter, however, amends the composition of this group to two boys, and, although the shed children never reappear in the novel, he incorporates two scenes that stress the consequent estrangement of these boys from Jo. They have grown into things apart, being alien from her, and their masculine sex underscores the insuperable distance between themselves and their mother. The male/female gulf mirrors the second active schism of the conflict, occurring primarily between Jake and Jo. In the two scenes with the oldest boys, only the most vacuous pleasantries are exchanged with Jo, and she acknowledges the two only vaguely.

PETE. Hullo, Mum.
JO. Hullo.
JACK. Hullo.
JO. Hullo.
Pause . . . .
JO. (to boys). What do you think of your sister?
JACK. Pretty good.
Pause.
JO. Are you . . . everything all right?
JACK. Fine.
Pause.
PETE. Yes. Fine.
Pause.
JO. Good. [Pp. 107–8]

Thus ends the first of the two scenes. The second merely elaborates the rupture, the irreversible hardening of child against parent. Even the compulsive production of beings from her own flesh provides Jo no respite from her increasing solitude and exclusion.

After a brief sequence of shots depicting the early days of Jo's marriage to Jake (Pinter includes an original scene here that predicates a masterful episode, also of Pinter's invention, at the conclusion of the script), Pinter develops her gradual suspicions of an affair between Jake and the movie-groupie house guest, Philpot. These scenes he lifts practically intact, in all their unrelenting obfuscation, from the novel. Jo can neither confirm nor assuage her fears.

JO. Do you like sitting between two women? Does that thrill you?
JAKE. Yes it does. It really does. What do you think I should do about it? What shall I do, go and see a psychiatrist about it?
He sits. Pause.

JO. All right, what—

JAKE. Look. Listen.

Pause.

It was nothing, nothing. Don't you understand?

JO. What do you mean, it was nothing?

Pause.

What do you mean, nothing?

JAKE. What do you think I mean?

JO. What did you catch her for?

JAKE. I didn't catch her!

JO. She fainted.

JAKE. What does it matter if I caught her or not? I didn't catch her, it doesn't matter, can't you understand? Who cares?

JO. I care.

JAKE. What about? What's it all about? [Pp. 78–79]

In the second of these scenes, Jo returns to this Philpot issue after she hears that Jake has involved himself in an affair with an actress, Beth Conway. This interrogation further confounds the facts of the alleged tryst, as Jake alternately confirms and denies identical accusations.

JO. Did you sleep with Philpot?

JAKE. Oh, Christ, it's years ago, it's gone—

JO. Did you?

JAKE. Yes, of course I did.

JO. You told me you hadn't.

JAKE. I lied. So what? What else did you expect me to do?

JO. Here? In the house?

JAKE. I don't remember. Yes.

JO. Often?

JAKE. As often as we could. What's the point? What the hell does it matter?

JO. What about all the others?

JAKE. What others?

JO. The others.

JAKE. There weren't any others.

JO. How many?

JAKE. Half a dozen. A dozen. I don't know. What does the number matter?

JO. When you were away, or when you were here?

JAKE. When I was away! Is that what you want me to say?

JO. If it's true.

JAKE. Then it was while I was away.

Pause.

You live in a dream world, do you know that? [Pp. 120–21]

The scene continues for another full page, eliciting and then withdrawing the answers Jo demands. Its basic substance derives from the novel, but Pinter has sharpened the dialogue to achieve characteristic economy and terseness.

The initial development of Philpot, an episode Pinter places five years past, is interspersed with scenes in the present time, tracing Jo's emotional breakdown in Harrod's and her subsequent submission to psychiatric treatment. This portion of the script includes some excellent examples of Pinter's consideration for the potentialities of actors and of a largely visual medium. Himself an experienced actor,[5] Pinter possesses a highly developed ability to write dialogue that teems with actor's subtext. The following two examples of communication between characters, comparing Mortimer's dialogue with that of Pinter, exhibits his skill at erecting such smokescreens. In Mortimer's version the narrator overhears this snatch of dialogue between Jake and her physician following her collapse at Harrod's.

> "Perhaps she ought to go away?" Jake said.
> "Could you go with her?"
> "I'm afraid not. I'm off to North Africa for a couple of weeks and I've got a hell of a lot to get through before then."
> "Why not take her to North Africa?"
> "She wouldn't want to go."
> "Are you sure of that?"
> "I've asked her. She hates going on location. You know, there's nothing for her to do, she just sits about and gets in the way—she feels she gets in the way." [Pp. 53–54]

Pinter seizes the innuendo present in this scene, particularly in Jake's hasty rephrasing in the last speech, and rewrites the dialogue to occur between Jake and Jo during a roughly similar, but unspecified, period of time.

> JAKE. We've finished the script.
> *Pause.*
> We're going . . . to Morocco for a couple of weeks.
> JO. Mmm-hmm.
> *Pause.*
> JAKE. Would you like to come?
> *Pause.*
> I mean . . .
> JO. Oh, I . . .
> *Pause.*
> JAKE. It'd mean living in tents and all that . . . but . . . if you felt like it . . .
> JO. Couldn't just . . . sit in a tent . . .

JAKE. You wouldn't have to stay in the tent.

Silence. [Pp. 84–85]

In this lean exchange, Jake conveys, and Jo grasps, his unwillingness to have her along, and he exhibits undeniable, if unconfirmable, clarity of intention.

Pinter's artful knack for insinuating raw objectives into processed verbal subterfuge appears also in a scene with the psychiatrist. In Mortimer's work the narrator becomes outraged when she learns that her doctor is about to abandon her for an extended skiing vacation in the mountains. She plainly articulates her anger to the psychiatrist in a direct and lengthy diatribe (pp. 107–8). Pinter disguises Jo's alarm at this situation and unleashes it on an oblique target.

INGRAM. Oh, I'm sorry, haven't I told you? We're off to Gstaadt on Friday for a spot of skiing. It's my great passion, I'm afraid.

JO. Skiing?

INGRAM. Oh, and cut down on liquids as much as you can. Can we make an appointment for the . . . 19th?

JO. Can't make it. No . . . can't make the 19th.

INGRAM. The 20th?

JO. Can't make it.

INGRAM. Oh come now . . .

JO. What liquids?

INGRAM. Liquids.

JO. Yes, but what liquids? Listen, why are you going to Gstaadt? Why don't you go to Cortina? Why Gstaadt? Why the hell don't you go to Cortina? Or Kitzbuhel? [P. 91]

Although the reference to liquids appears in the novel, Mortimer never takes up the idea again. Pinter, however, capitalizes on its mysterious ring. In the next scene, at the hairdressers, Jo is besieged by a fellow customer who claims inexplicably to be "off liquids" when Jo inquires whether she would like some tea. (Clayton cuts this dialogue in order to serve them the tea anyway.) Pinter invents this scene from a letter that the narrator receives in the novel. The content of the letter is completely harmless, although Pinter's scene contains a heavy dose of menace, and the narrator's response to it introduces a poorly integrated "feminist unity" theme into the novel. Its author, an apparently lower-class housewife, describes her lower-class housewife predicament, and the narrator identifies with it. For Pinter, the incident contains capital visual promise, and he evolves an entire scene, set in the hairdressers, from it. The scene, in which the strange woman accosts Jo under the hairdryers, at first with cautious admiration and then with abrupt viciousness, is both savage and funny.

WOMAN. . . . I can see your grace and your sweetness just sitting here. What does your husband think of you, eh? Does he find you attractive? Eh, I've been wondering, do you think your husband would find me desirable? Eh?

JO. Look . . . I don't actually feel very . . .

WOMAN. I'd show him some tricks. I'd show him some tricks. Hah! You want to bet? . . . I'd show him a few things I bet you don't know. My love. My little darling. Anyone ever clawed your skin off? You see these claws? Ever had your skin clawed off?

An ASSISTANT *comes to the women. She looks curiously at them both.*

You going to give me two curls there this time? Over the ears, two curls, one either side, two lovely curls at each side, are you? Are you? [P. 93]

This scene and others, such as Jo's breakdown in Harrod's, demonstrate Pinter's flair for translating pages of narrative into a few spare, taut situational pictures. In Katherine Burkman's brief discussion of *The Pumpkin Eater,* she notes the banality of these surface milieux and contrasts them with the savage instincts they both conceal and reveal. "Once again the veneer of the sexual rituals of parties, shopping tours, and so on, works in counterpoint with primitive undercurrents, which erupt finally into a savage physical fight between husband and wife."[6] Pinter swiftly turns the narrator's vague mental landscapes into a reality, simultaneously too familiar and too strange, that we can neither claim nor reject. His apparent objectivity recreates Jo's affliction in us, as audience.

Pinter uses the camera to intensify our awareness of Jo's individual viewpoint, however, as well. When Jake arrives from North Africa, we experience the children's welcome for him first from an objective camera angle, and then we hear the identical dialogue repeated as the camera focuses Jo, alone in the "silent, empty" sitting room (pp. 93–94). We gain an immediate sensation of the disparities inherent in view, paralleling the major obstacles in the storyline. Although Pinter's script identifies the problems of verification with the human condition rather than with Jo's condition, she does represent the chief protagonist/victim of the theme in both versions. Either way, she remains incapable of discovering the facts of her situation, and she must make her choices, somehow, without them.

The pregnancy ritual insulates Jo on several levels against the need for choice; it provides a "natural" (and, for her, habitual) course of action, it promises two years of full-time occupation, and it actualizes the ever-evaporating bonds between herself and her family. Jo's sense of well-being derives exclusively from the ritual patterns of living that accompany child-rearing. Each pregnancy dispels the urgency of decision-making, temporarily; she keeps her routines intact. Her semiconscious despair over Jake's impatience with her astronomical brood awakens in her a craving for security, and this craving translates invariably and ironically into her desire for another child.

When Jo does manage to become pregnant in the "present-time" of the story action, she must conceal her condition and gratification from her husband. In the novel the narrator writes to Jake of her latest pregnancy from a desk by her father's deathbed. The timing and pathetic nature of the letter signal her anxiety over Jake's response to the news of her pregnancy. Partly to intensify her anxiety, and partly to exploit his medium, Pinter discards the letter device and substitutes for it a scene in which Jo's mother unthinkingly betrays the secret to Jake in her distress over her lost husband. Both novel and screenplay include scenes depicting Jo in the attic, hiding among items of infant paraphernalia until prospective intruders pass. Ultimately, Jo's desperation over her dilemma, coupled with Jake's urging, result in her decision to undergo an abortion and simultaneous hysterectomy. Mortimer's Jake seduces the narrator into her decision by listing plans he entertains for the two of them which the expected infant would spoil. Pinter's Jake persuades Jo with inarticulate platitudes.

> I don't want it. That's why. (*Pause.*) I wanted us to change. Now we can't change. You see? It's my fault. It's because of me, I know that. But I thought we could change . . . branch out . . . be free. (*Pause.*) Now there's no chance. (*Pause.*) We're back where we were.
> *She goes to him, holds him.*
> I'm not blaming you, I'm blaming myself. It's my fault, I know that. We haven't . . . lived together. But it's just that I've suddenly realized . . . that we could lead a more sensible life. It was possible. We haven't lived. (*Pause.*) We don't need it. It'll kill us. We could begin, you see, we could really begin . . . I know it . . . you know, too. . . . You know what I mean. I mean there is a world, there is a world apart from birth, there's a world apart from . . . we don't want any more . . . how can we have any more?
> *Silence.*
> I know the idea of abortion is repellent to you, I know that. It is to me, too. You must admit I've never suggested it.
> *Silence.*
> It's ghastly, the idea of abortion, I know that. Ghastly. (*Silence.*) I wouldn't dream of suggesting it. (*Silence.*) But after all, it would be perfectly legal, you've just been treated for depression, I mean the Doctor said . . . there wouldn't be anything underhand about it. [Pp. 110–11]

Although Jake's strongly implied threat to withdraw his love clearly motivates Jo's termination of her child-bearing capabilities, both versions of the story emphasize her authorship and ownership of the choice. When her sole option for security acquires simultaneous consequences of insecurity, Jo is trapped. Her realization that this pregnancy will rupture rather than cement her bonds to the family forces her decision to submit to surgery.

Significant differences exist between the two treatments of the story's main crisis. Mortimer's narrator learns of Jake's affair with Beth Conway by reading his mail while she is recovering in the hospital from her operation. Her desires for revenge against Jake and for an end to the liaison prompt her to divulge her information to Beth's husband. Pinter, however, invents a simpler and more ironic twist for this development. His adaptation puts Bob Conway in first possession of the news. While the narrator confronts Conway with her proof in a teashop, Conway confronts Jo with his story at the zoo. The caged animals provide a striking background for Conway's monstrous assault on Jo, as he springs the news of Jake's infidelity on her after two pages of maliciously sweet chit-chat and one unsuccessful sexual advance. Following his disclosure Conway harasses Jo with a derisive assessment of Jake's character and sexual performance. Most of the material for Pinter's dialogue here derives from the novel, but his relocation and restructuring of the scene lend it dynamic visualization while they enlarge the dimensions of Jo's calamity.

Jo, in both versions, next confronts Jake with her accusations, producing the earlier cited dialogue recalling Philpot. Jake frustrates all of her lines of inquiry, alternately admitting and denying identical allegations. At this point in Mortimer's story, the narrator fills three pages with introspection, elucidating her alienation and solitude. She complains, "I wanted to go home, but now my father was dead there was no home to go to, only a house where my mother mourned and thanked goodness that I had at last seen reason" (p. 173). Pinter spells out this thought in cinematic language: in the screenplay she does return home here to confront the permanent grief of her mother and her own lost rapport with the two "shed" boys.

During her visit to her mother, Jo also encounters the expanding threat of the demolition crews, a restatement of the theme from the opening sequence of shots. Apparently, construction corporations are pressuring to develop the land of her father's garden, but her mother has made some weak stand against them. The heavy mood of hopelessness and helplessness that permeates this scene evokes recollections of Madam Ranevsky and her fated cherry orchard, and it introduces (or rather reintroduces) the theme that Pinter will develop into a resolution of the piece. Jo's world has become a single, sustained chord of remorse and attenuation.

Pinter combines two episodes from the novel to craft the stunning scene in which Jo learns of Beth Conway's pregnancy. In the novel Bob

Conway's phone call, announcing this news, interrupts an interview of the narrator by an insidious magazine reporter. After the narrator hears Conway's vicious message, she flees to Giles, a previous husband, and attempts to retrieve their relationship. Her effort, of course, fails, but in the course of her stay with him, she tells Giles the ominous story of a mystic Jamaican who visited her recently. The strange figure claimed to be the new King of Israel and asked, in a prolonged, bizarre pitch, for money to build a radio station in Jerusalem. The narrator employs the incident as a format for self-analysis, concluding:

> He didn't seem like a maniac. I'm not saying he was sane. But neither was I. I'm not saying he even believed in himself, but neither did I. He got five shillings from me and I . . . I was comforted. I told you I don't know who I am or what I'm like, but I know there aren't any rules—perhaps the kind of person I am believes in Yahweh. Perhaps that Jamaican King of Judah and I need the same thing. [P. 194]

Pinter, however, elucidates a scene from this material and locates Conway's phone call in the middle of it. The Jamaican appears at the door when Jo is alone, drinking. He gains entry after his introduction of himself as "the new King of Israel, appointed by Yahweh, the Eternal Lord God. I have come to give you my blessing." Once inside he continues his mesmerizing spiel, promising Jo redemption and droning liturgical platitudes. The phone interrupts their conversation. Conway's poisonous diatribe, drawn mainly from the novel, inspires Pinter's final ironic twist in this scene. When Jo recognizes Conway's voice, and claims to be someone other than herself, Conway, knowing, asks her to convey the message of Beth's pregnancy to Jo.

> CONWAY'S VOICE. Tell her my wife's going to have this kid in a public ward, and if there's any way of stopping her getting a whiff of gas I'll find it.
>
> JO. She can't have it.
>
> CONWAY'S VOICE. She's going to have it all right. She's going to wipe its bottom and stare at its ugly mug for the rest of her life. No more gay life for my little Beth. This kid's going to make her curse Jake Armitage until she's dead . . . I'm going to grind the slime out of her. I'm going to see her oozing in her own slime. Until she's dead. She's going to hate that kid almost as much as I will. I'm going to see that she bleeds to death in Jake Armitage's dirt.
>
> *Another angle to include* MAN. JO *puts the phone down. She turns, looks at the* MAN. *He smiles.*
>
> MAN. You will be blessed for this. [P. 127]

Although Mortimer exposes a villainy in Giles during the next sequence of episodes that repels the narrator and causes her to abandon him, Pinter keeps Giles's motives apparently pure, allowing Jo's effort at reclamation to fail of its own accord. Both writers have Jo leaving

Giles to attend the funeral of Jake's father, but, in Mortimer's version, Giles had attempted to hide his death from the narrator to prevent her leaving. The funeral scene, for both authors, buries another section of past and chronicles the widening rift between the protagonist and her husband. Mortimer follows it with rumors of Conway's dissipation, and Pinter interjects a sinister scene between Jake and Conway, both drunk and ruined, in a bar. Jo, in both versions, retreats to the isolation and emptiness of the new house. She endures there, according to both stories, for an undefined period of time. Pinter describes her experience in a two-page sequence of shots (which Clayton discarded), the tone of which materializes in these first two directions.

> Interior. Main room of the new house. . . . The rooms are empty except for isolated pieces of furniture. JO pauses for a moment, then locks all the doors.
> Interior. Kitchen of the new house.
> JO wanders in. No food. No sign of life. Empty. Unused. Bare. [P. 133]

This vague period of vacuous solitude ends, according to novel and screenplay, in the convergence of Jake and the children on the new house. For Mortimer, Jake remains behind, purchasing goods, and the narrator observes him, at the end of the story, as he ascends the hill toward her. Pinter brings Jake and his chaos of groceries into the house with the mob of children, and he concludes the story with a remarkable idea (and one that is totally absent from the film): as Jo stands apart from the domestic bustle, Dinah, the eldest child, seems to have taken over control of the family. "Let me do it," she says to Jake. "Put all the paper in the bin," she orders the children.

Previously in this chapter, I referred to an earlier bit of dialogue that figures significantly in the final moments of the screenplay. The earlier scene, between Jo and Jake, includes the following exchange and business with beer cans.

> JAKE, with a grimace, opens can. It spurts over the wall, where we can already see the stains from previous moments of this kind.
> JAKE. Want one?
> JO. Yes, I'll have one.
> He hands her opened can. She takes it. JAKE opens second can. It also spurts over wall.
> JAKE. Aaahh!
> JO. It's all right, it'll wipe off. . . . Do you want turnips or swedes?
> JAKE. Turnips or swedes?
> JO. Yes. Or both if you like.
> He looks at her blankly.
> JAKE. (with sudden concentration). Turnips or swedes.
> Wait a minute. Just a minute. Let me think about it. [Pp. 72–73]

The last moments of the screenplay echo this scene, except that the children have usurped Jo's words and place.

> DINAH *hands opener to* JAKE.
> DINAH. Here you are. Do you want cabbage or carrots?
> JAKE *opens beer can. It spurts.* CHILDREN *react noisily.*
> I'll wipe it.
> CHILD FOUR. I'll do it. [P. 135]

The story ends as Jo accepts a can of beer from Jake. She has made a passive capitulation to the persistence of ambiguity and disorder in her world; she has outlived her passion to resolve them. The signs of fertility and ongoing life that invade the sterile and alien house—the spurting beer, the clamoring brood, the grocery bags—serve only to focus Jo's helpless attentuation. Like the house, the clean-scraped pumpkin shell, she suffers an estrangement from living and purpose. The house provides both a metaphor and an environment for Jo's condition; she represents and inhabits the pumpkin shell. The tide of children has ascended to supplant her.

Both the title and the conclusion of *The Pumpkin Eater* (1965) seem to indicate the familiar mechanism of Pinter's emblematic "room" as a factor in this adaptation. Clayton's modifications of the screenplay plainly subscribe to a traditional "Pinteresque" view of the room as a prospect for refuge. By omitting Pinter's lengthy articulations of the antiseptic qualities in Jo's present house, and by alleviating his intense juxtaposition of these qualities with the happy pandemonium of her past, the film implies that her final inhabitation of the new house represents a remedial seclusion. For Clayton the pumpkin shell is plausible as a device for keeping one's wife content, and he alters Pinter's sour ending in order to affirm this view. Despite some patterns typical of Pinter in Jo's inclinations against the alien and toward the insular, however, Pinter's treatment of the "room" syndrome in this work marks a divergence from his earlier writing, in which characters in *The Room, The Dumb Waiter, The Birthday Party,* and *The Caretaker* sought to escape the vicissitudes of life through homemaking rituals, or characters in *The Servant* competed to assert their authority through interior decoration. The pumpkin shell is not, here, a symbol of comfort, security, or triumph: it is identified principally with the evacuated infertility of Jo's womb. The pronounced affinity between "room" and "womb" in Pinter's early work renders this new attitude even more distinct and compelling. At best, Pinter's depiction of Jo's final ensconcement in the new house reveals an ambivalence in his regard for the room's possibilities as a refuge. Where before the room was subjected mainly to the threat of intrusion, it now exhibits qualities that render it almost uninhabitable.

Similar qualities become apparent in the settings and tensions of Pinter's plays of this period. We have noted that in *The Homecoming* (1964) an architectural deletion serves to lament Jessie's absence and to proclaim a need to fill this vacancy. The design of this space operates to capture certain thematic ideas in the work, such as the simultaneous containment and erasure of the past by the present, the fracturing of old structures without recourse to new ones, the persistence of old forms despite assault and erosion, the sterile, alien nature of the present juxtaposed with the contrary implications of the almost obliterated past, and the urgent deprivation of something necessary for unity and completion of the situation. Although Jo's estrangement from the past, as announced by her final dissociation from its accoutrements, seems more extreme, the themes of the screenplay resemble those of the play and they become accessible through a similar use of place. In both works the settings codify a tension between generations that suggests the passage of old, unified systems into modern ones that sustain the old in attenuated fragments, integrate according to pragmatics rather than to wholeness, and lack internal designation of the past or future. Except for the temporal allusions of the set, however, *The Homecoming* conforms to a linear time scheme. Pinter's discovery of subjective, nonlinear structure as a device for exploring these themes occurs initially in his work for the film medium, and specifically in his adaptation of *The Pumpkin Eater.*

The antiseptic character of the room in *The Homecoming* (strikingly realized in the film of the play), which is inhabited exclusively by males, anticipates Pinter's depiction of Jo's pumpkin shell and defines his growing interest in the problem of effective seclusion. Previously, in *A Slight Ache* (1958), Pinter explored the dilemma of two characters whose apparent control over their milieu is so complete that they must invite (or possibly, since this play was originally written for radio broadcast and the third character is a nonspeaking role, invent) an intruder to generate vitality through opposition. Where Pinter's earlier characters forged identities through the struggle with others, his characters of this period wrestle unavailingly against the elusiveness of themselves. The accompanying transition in his view of the room, from sanctuary to empty hull, becomes increasingly significant in his later plays, such as *Old Times* and *No Man's Land,* where imagination must combat the monotony and sterility of this latter condition. Clayton's option for a conventionally "Pinteresque" approach to this theme obscures this crucial development in Pinter's attitude; the change, however, is conspicuous in the text of the screenplay.

4

The Quiller Memorandum

During Oktober's attempt to interrogate me under pressures induced by my fears for [Inga] while she was apparently being tortured in my presence . . . I was aware that (1) she was not in fact suffering distress but lending herself to a new method of inducing me to talk, (2) I must appear to believe that she was being tortured, and (3) I must get out of the corner without revealing that I knew her to be an agent, in case I could use her later as a source of information. (Reference Point 2: the moment I realized that Oktober had come to simulate a torture scene, I made myself believe in it, so that all my subsequent actions should appear consistent. This deliberate self-deception was an aid in throwing the faint.)[1]

Although Adam Hall adopts a first-person narrative structure for his novel, *The Quiller Memorandum*, the perceptual difficulties he explores through this form differ from those of the other novels that Pinter has adapted. In this text the problems of observation intrude between the narrator's character and his experiences, rather than between the narrator's viewpoint and the story. The game of interpretation comprises the fabric of the plot, but its implications never reach explicitly beyond the internal action of the novel. Instead, the narrator Quiller confronts a series of impenetrably ambiguous situations that he must interpret correctly, since one misstep will cost him his life and bring global disaster. Quiller must choose and act rapidly according to his instincts and calculations, but his data is neither verifiable nor sufficient. Although the reader shares this handicap, the limitations of viewpoint complicate the novel's narrativity in an exclusively implicit manner. Unlike *The Servant*, where the narrator's fabrication is emphatic, or *The Pumpkin Eater*, where the narrator's perception is flawed, this novel describes the efforts of a candid, incisive narrator to render a recondite situation in the present time. The excerpt above, for example, necessitates a retrospective revision of the episode it annotates; because Quiller's original description of Inga's torture issued from his contrived point of view, it produced a false impression of the incident, requiring the reader to reevaluate this episode, and others, as succeeding perspectives qualify it.

The urgency for guesswork in impregnably mysterious circumstances commends this novel to Pinter as a suitable exercise for his aesthetic. His adaptation, however, deviates radically and necessarily from the source: more so than any other of his screenplays. As constituted, Hall's novel is virtually impossible to render cinematic, due to its indispensably interior nature. Although the novel abounds with action, the intrigue is enormously complex and entirely private, existing exclusively within the mind of Quiller. In order to draw the conflict to the surface and convey it through cinematic language, Pinter overhauls even the fundamental premises of the story. Without resorting to the clumsy, trite device of voiceover narration, Quiller's extreme reticence and solitude must somehow yield their secrets. To achieve this revelation, Pinter liberally adds, subtracts, and changes characters and situations. Hall's "I" emerges as an obscure accumulation of his own calculations and impressions, remaining chronically elusive and subjective throughout the novel. Pinter, therefore, must invent Quiller's outward, objective personality which, for purposes of cinematic legibility, seems more aggressive, congenial, and debonair than the furtive, amorphous figure in Hall's story. The screenplay substantially diminishes the atmosphere of silence and strain that pervades the novel. Not only does the material Quiller acquire the characteristics of a playboy, he also is forced to tolerate the nuisance of accomplices, which he so scrupulously avoids in the novel. Both of these devices, Quiller's new affability and his provision with foils, serve to externalize the involuted complications of the intrigue.

Even so, Pinter's adaptation grossly simplifies and reorganizes the novel's plot, shifting the story's emphasis from its thematic network to its surface action. The intricacies of Nazi and neo-Nazi activities disappear from the screenplay to reveal a simpler story of thrills and suspense. Pinter, for example, radically alters the role of Inga (which he spells "Inge"), whose complexity and mystery dominate the novel. For Hall, the significance of Inga's psychology, appeal, and betrayal is paramount. The horrors of Hitler's aftermath have served only to exacerbate her neurotic obsession with the immolated Fuhrer, and through her dependancy on Nazi authority, Hall elucidates his contention that Germany, if allowed, will reproduce the Third Reich. Furthermore,

Inga's apparent frankness and self-incriminations, coupled with her impervious androgyny (the casting of Senta Berger in this role, consistent or not with Pinter's intentions for it, removes the character in the film itself even further from its counterpart in the novel), challenge Quiller and pose the most devious of the opposition's traps. Her ambivalent posture as a double agent provides a rigorous test of Quiller's cunning, since his belief in her wavers. Ultimately, her attempted betrayal of him and his treacherous rejection of her become the novel's chief statements of omnipresent deception and threat.

All of these circumstances, however, are absent from the screenplay, where Inge becomes a schoolteacher whose affiliations remain relatively speculative and impotent. Although her death or arrest may be presumed from the final action of the novel, Pinter stipulates her exemption from the raid, preserving her ambiguity into the final scene of the screenplay where, surrounded by her students, she bids Quiller an inscrutable goodbye. Martin Esslin captures their relationship in his reference to "the scenes between Quiller and the German girl, where we sense that he knows that she is not what she pretends to be, and that she knows that he knows, and that he knows that too, while yet carrying on as though neither of them suspected anything beneath the surface of what looks like an ordinary love affair."[2] Our sense of her complicity and of the vertigo of deceptions it produces, however, derives from the slightest evidence in Pinter's script. Although Berger's performance in the film contains rather broad indications of secretive subtext, the screenplay tends to incriminate Inge only in her inexplicable release by the neo-Nazis which results in her survival of the raid. Quiller's provision of Inge with an incorrect telephone number, an idea that Pinter retains from the novel, serves also, through its suggestion of Quiller's mistrust, to implicate her; but Pinter's characteristic penchant for ambiguity emerges conspicuously in his revision of Inga's role.

Extensive differences between the novelistic and cinematic versions of the story preclude rigorous comparison of the two works. Pinter's initial deviation from the novel occurs in the opening sequence of the screenplay: the murder of Kenneth Lindsay Jones. In both accounts this incident triggers the subsequent action, since Quiller assumes the operations of the deceased KLJ, but the episode precedes Hall's entry into the narrative and emerges only through cumulative reference. Pinter sacrifices the mysterious, less cinematically communicable, circumstances of this murder in order to exploit its value as an indication of tone and as a harbinger of later images. By establishing this sequence of images and associating it with the murder, the screenplay's subsequent repetition of this montage approximates the climactic recognition by

Hall's narrator that he is tracing the fatal footsteps of KLJ. The significant difference in the function of this incident as it operates structurally in the screenplay as opposed to the novel, however, lies in Pinter's use of it to effect *our*, rather than Quiller's, recognition of this duplication and threat.

Succeeding episodes of the screenplay develop this pattern of divergence from the novel. Immediately following Pinter's dramatization of the KLJ murder, the screenplay includes a conversation between Rushington and Gibbs: two characters of Pinter's invention who materialize a minor theme from the novel suggesting the imperious indifference of the executive echelon. Rushington and Gibbs appear twice during the screenplay (but only once in the film), contributing exposition and juxtaposing their idle dinner banter with preceding scenes of extraordinary tension and violence.

In accordance with his campaign to render his protagonist cinematically accessible, Pinter next overhauls the initial meeting between Quiller and the liaison, Pol. Where Pol originally entraps Quiller into accepting the assignment, the screenplay changes the circumstances of their encounter and depicts Quiller as the aggressor in this matter. Thus, the reluctance of Hall's Quiller to undertake the mission transforms into the eagerness of Pinter's Quiller to replace KLJ. Quiller also agrees, at least initially, to cooperate with his cover men, although he refuses all cover in the novel (and many of the references to this situation were deleted from the film), so that Pinter may exploit their interaction to reveal Quiller's waggish sense of humor and otherwise unintelligible working strategy.

Although most of Pinter's modifications in the story produce externalizations of material which, in the novel, remains entirely cranial, some new episodes seem inspired either by the serendipitous discovery of interesting locations or by a cinematic requirement for pictorially conveyed suspense. Pol's initial meeting with Quiller, for example, transpires in Olympic Stadium: a change from the novel that seems explicable only as Pinter's response to the need for representation of undercurrents through images and setting. Consistent with Pinter's opportunistic choice of this location, the film adds a chorus of subliminal "Sieg Heils" to the sound track for this scene. The screenplay also depicts scenes in a bowling alley and swimming bath that have no basis in Hall's work except as a total reworking of Quiller's efforts to expose himself to adversary forces. Quiller's pursuit of KLJ's path, which leads him to the bowling alley and baths, is original in Pinter's version of the story, and it includes only one situation with any bearings in the novel. Although Pinter revamps the episode to introduce his version of Inga,

45

Quiller's visit to the school is liberally adapted from an incident in Hall's account. Since the common denominator between these school scenes consists in the presence of ex-Nazis on the teaching staffs, Pinter presumably wished to conserve the novel's suggestion of Nazi influence over German youth. Otherwise, no similarity exists between the two uses of the school setting.

Because Pinter's alterations are so inclusive, even those episodes he retains from the novel exhibit substantial differences from their source. Consequently, Pinter's account of Quiller's capture and interrogation by the Nazi Oktober shares little with that of Hall beyond its pattern of drug injections. Pinter changes both the circumstances and the interaction in this scene, which in the novel depends heavily on Quiller's unspoken perceptions of his situation. In both versions, however, Quiller's evasive divulgence of his passion for Inga/Inge serves to formulate succeeding Nazi strategy. According to Hall's account, the Nazis intrude when Quiller obeys their psychological forecast by going immediately to Inga, and they attempt to extract information from him by faking her torture. Pinter, however, deletes this episode, reserving Inge's jeopardy for a surrogate situation in a later scene. Since he eliminates the complexities of Quiller's dilemma and of the Nazis' operations, Pinter employs Inge's captivity in the Nazi headquarters as a source of suspense during the final sequence of action.

Despite bold deviations from the circumstances in the novel, the screenplay capitalizes on Hall's description of the tensions during the climactic developments of the story. Pol explains the situation to Quiller through a metaphor that Pinter preserves intact from the novel.

> You're on a delicate mission, Quiller. Perhaps you're beginning to appreciate that. Let me put it this way.
> *He takes two large cream cakes and arranges them on the table.*
> There are two opposing armies drawn up on the field. But there's a heavy fog. They can't see each other. They want to, of course, very much.
> *He takes a currant from a cake and sets it between the cakes.*
> You're in the gap between them. You can just see us, you can just see them. Your mission is to get near enough to see them and signal their position to us, so giving us the advantage. But if in signalling their position to us you inadvertently signal our position to them, then it will be they who will gain a very considerable advantage.
> *He points to the currant.*
> That's where you are, Quiller. In the gap.
> *He pops the currant in his mouth and eats it.*[3]

Pinter embellishes Pol's point here with both business and elucidation; in the novel this encounter is terse and outdoors. Although Pinter ridicules Pol's dalliance by stipulating the incongruous cream cake illustration, the metaphor retains its impact. Thus, the screenplay duplicates Hall's fascination with the activities of a figure who occupies this gap.

For both authors the climactic scenes occur after Inga/Inge (variously) leads Quiller to enemy headquarters, and Quiller endeavors to convey its location to his own bureau without detection. Quiller, released by the Nazis for reasons that differ in the two versions, must shake his tags and signal his knowledge to his organization before the opposition sacrifices as too risky its opportunity to learn the location of his bureau. Both accounts allow Quiller until dawn to accomplish this delicate task. Hall reveals Inga's complicity with the enemy during this action, but Pinter adds the threat of her murder to the consequences of Quiller's failure to satisfy the Nazis. Quiller does not manage, in either version, to lose his tags, but he escapes detection finally by pretending to fall victim to the bomb they have rigged in his automobile. Their presumption of his death allows him to go freely to his bureau and to file his report.

Quiller's success at outwitting the enemy leaves a different question for resolution by each medium; Hall's Quiller must ferret out the unapprehended Nazi officer who was the original object of his mission, and Pinter's Quiller must discover the final disposition of Inge. Where Quiller's accomplishment of the former objective tends to seal the novel in conclusive fashion, his ascertainment, in Pinter's version, of Inge's return to her students produces a more ominous conclusion of the action. As Burkman notes, this unsettling resolution robs Quiller (and us, as well) of his victory and squares the screenplay with Pinter's general interest in such victimized figures. "But if the gap of the isolated hero is closed at the book's end, it remains painfully open in the film. . . . A lesser work than *The Birthday Party* or *The Dumb Waiter*, *The Quiller Memorandum* is illuminating as a further exploration of man as the victim of forces which he cannot subdue, of man as victim even when he is victor."[4] Thus, despite the lighthearted tone that Pinter incurs through his simplification and externalization of Hall's narrative, the screenplay retrieves some of the novel's serious, complex quality by its inconclusive ending, which pictures the ambiguous, influential Inge surrounded by her class of eager youths.

Although Pinter's work on this screenplay (1965) tends to interrupt the pattern of temporal deformity and introverted conflict that emerges over the course of his writing career, these qualities are nonetheless present in Hall's novel, and we may presume that they attracted Pinter to the project. The disruptions of linear time, which result in the novel from Quiller's subjection to drugs, self-deceit, limited viewpoint, and continual revision of the apparent past, are consistent with Pinter's evolving interest in temporal manipulation and disintegration. Already, in *The Pumpkin Eater*, we have observed his deployment of a nonlinear time structure as a technique for revealing the subjective perceptions of his protagonist, and his playwriting of this period exhibits a similar trend. We have seen also that *The Homecoming* (1964) implicates the past in the present through an architectural detail that activates a certain relation between the two periods. Pinter's subsequent plays (*Landscape*, 1967; *Old Times*, 1970; *No Man's Land*, 1974; and *Betrayal*, 1978) will elevate temporal fusion to a pivotal role in the action. However we attribute Pinter's omissions of this theme and the theme of Quiller's game against himself from his screenplay for *The Quiller Memorandum*, whether he felt their manifestation might overwhelm the genre or whether he simply failed to find some way of rendering the confusion cinematic, we may at least postulate the novel's consonance with the pattern of his concerns.

Pinter's approach to the problematic complexity and introversion of Hall's narrative lacks the ingenuity of his other adaptations, where he finds appropriate conversions of similarly difficult material. Particularly in his subsequent adaptations, Pinter has managed to invent filmic surrogates for narrative involutions, and his conceits have produced fewer distortions of the original concerns while successfully transforming them into cinematic language. In comparison with Pinter's other screenplays, this adaptation exhibits signs of hack writing for popular markets; Baker and Tabachnick suggest he may have written it "for sheer technical exercise or perhaps simply for money."[5] Quiller's perceptions, however interior, of his situation might have emerged through a more innovative and faithful translation of Hall's story into the deceptive opacity of images. Because Quiller's predicament consists in his restriction to interpretations of an essentially superficial or filmic reality, Pinter might have discovered some cinematic exploitation of this condition. Contradictory impressions of experience, as they become available according to future qualifications and perspectives, are communicable through cinematic means. Numerous films in the detective fiction genre operate by implying and then subverting certain premises of their narratives. Francis Ford Coppola's film, *The Conversation*, for example, achieves precisely this effect in its pivotal capsizing of the tape recorded statement, "He'd kill us if he got the chance." Hall's novel and Coppola's film share a fascination with the mechanisms of mistaken and corrected impressions, and Coppola's cinematic presentation of this phenomenon reveals the facile nature of Pinter's rendering.

Although Hall's novel lacks the literary richness of Pinter's other sources, the screenplay lacks equivalents for the novel's most meritorious aspects. Pinter needed to devise some structural principle, as he has done in his later adaptations, capable of delivering Hall's dynamic of cumulative, modified, and contradictory perceptions. Such a rendering of the novel into film might have proved more satisfying and challenging than the relatively simplistic spy movie that Pinter has produced in this case.

5
Accident

I might always be writing of myself. Charlie might be writing this story. . . .

I have tried to explain all this. I want to say—this is the letter from Charlie, this the football game with William. There were other things at this time—driving in and out of Oxford, my pupils, the common room, going for walks under the willows by the river. But I have to say—This and that have a meaning. . . .

Charlie is the writer: he will write this book. But I wanted to say— This is the point of it. Remember it happy; the sun in your eyes.[1]

The screenplay for *Accident* also entails an intricate transformation of its source material, although the revisions are less extensive and less discordant than those in Pinter's script for *The Quiller Memorandum*. If author Nicholas Mosley's performance of a small role in the film constitutes his approbation, then he apparently found Pinter's broad liberties consistent in some way with his intentions for the novel. Mosley's narrative whirligig exceeds those of the preceding three source novels in its convolutions and ambiguities. In addition to invoking narrative disclaimers similar to those we have experienced in the novel versions of *The Servant* and *The Pumpkin Eater*, Mosley obscures the identity of his medium for the story until we cannot determine with any certainty which of the central figures in the story has relayed the tale. The last of the three quotes that introduce this chapter appears as the final statement of the novel, and although the identity of the narrator has been questioned before in the story (see first quote), we are left to ponder the suddent implications of authorship by Charlie, the retroactive imposition of his strong point of view, and the impossible question of to whom "I" refers. As before, Pinter has substituted the camera's noninterpretive record for the sensibilities of this technique. He shifts the ambiguities from device to condition, utilizing a flashback structure to evoke a subjectivity that remains, nonetheless, inaccessible.

Mosley's apparent narrator is Stephen Jervis, a professor of philosophy at St. Mark's College, Oxford. Repeatedly, in his narration Stephen notes the inherent fallaciousness of his endeavor, observing that he sees in others only what they care to exhibit to him, and that he then knows this only through the range of his own bias. "When she had gone, I stood with my arms on the ledge of the window and looked out on to the lawn. I thought—You never know a person; only what you put into them, their effects. A platitude. The shadow from the roof of the building made a line with two angles at the gutter and the ground. Once I had wanted to be an architect. Fitting things in: filling spaces" (p. 17). Hence we discover the nature of his effort in this forthcoming account: to fit things in, to fill spaces. The burden of this responsibility on him becomes apparent in the second quote of the prefatory three, and in numerous other references to the fabricated nature of his conclusions.

In Stephen's view the assignment of meaning to experience perverts it; to see is to alter, to interpret, worse. "I am looking back on all this not to explain it, nor to describe it, but to say what it means. Incomprehensible. But what else? Choices" (p. 60). Stephen stresses the unreliability of memory itself, imputing a dozen pages of recollection to an "Angus MacSomething-or-other" who was "a procurer for my imagination" (p. 65) and ascribing the use of the past to the need for "colour, tolerance" (p. 67). He frequently laments the absence of "connections" and the indeterminacy of motives. Charlie describes the writer's process: "You take some things from real life, but you invent the story and all its connections and so on" (p. 72). Stephen remarks, "Motives are different from actions" (p. 32). The impenetrability and ambiguity of the consequent story, the characters' exertions against these conditions, attracted Pinter to the work.

> I do so hate the becauses of drama. Who are we to say that this happens because that happened, that one thing is a consequence of another? How do we know? What reason have we to suppose that life is so neat and tidy? The most we know for sure is that the things which have happened have happened in a certain order: any connections we think we see, or choose to make, are pure guesswork. Life is much more mysterious than plays make it out to be. And it is this mystery which fascinates me: what happens between the words, what happens when no words are spoken. . . . In this film everything happens, nothing is explained. It has all been pared down and down, all unnecessary words and actions are eliminated.[2]

The problems of verification in the novel extend to the natures of time, past, others, and self. Stephen claims to write in the present tense because "there seems something timeless about this scene." (p. 20). Time is vertical in the novel; its entire narrative journey is punctuated by the inciting and concluding incident of the car crash, which hovers over the ruminative temporal scheme. Mosley compresses the elapsed, horizontal time frame of the novel because his concern lies with the exploration of internal time: that nebulous expanse of the past that qualifies, enriches, and betrays the present moment. We know the past, however, only as it is sustained in the present, and the present seeks inevitably to erase it. Time reforms external reality, just as it reforms memory.

> I think Oxford is conducive to all this; a very old place there for the young— old men, buildings, ways, for something which has nothing to do with them, and which they can only deal with by defeating. What else can the old do to the young? Sometimes at Oxford you come across a scene of extraordinary beauty—deer in front of an eighteenth century facade, trees growing out of the water of the river—and you stop to watch; and all around you there is the roar of traffic, dim at first, then growing; the blossom and the grass and the traffic pressed tight around Oxford in a circle of smoking vehicles like an army. I do not know what one makes of all this—we understand now only workings and not meanings. The traffic is undermining the structure of the buildings and the buildings crumble. [P. 28]

As in Mortimer's novel, the themes of aging and the advancing young comprise a wistful refrain in the story. The old cherish the lifeless forms, and the young ascend to challenge and destroy them. For both parties, however, the meanings are nowhere available. Time operates not only to reform, but also to alienate. This inscrutability of the reified affects our impressions of others: "People are not characters but things moving occasionally in jumps and mostly in indiscernible slowness." (p. 46). It also prevents our perceptions of ourselves: "I remember this time of my life very well. But we change too much; its not ourselves that we remember" (p. 44), and: "If you look into your experience you find a succession of impressions of, for instance, thinking, desiring, hoping, fearing; but you don't have a continued impression of a self that thinks or desires or hopes or fears. So the description of the self as an enduring entity is again impossible" (p. 29).

Although Pinter excludes the self-conscious exacerbations of the narrator, he meticulously retains and focuses the ramifications of this tension between the perceiver and the perceived.

> At first we thought of perhaps trying to do it the way the book does, to find a direct film equivalent to the free-association, stream-of-consciousness style

of the novel. I tried a draft that way, but it just wouldn't work—anyway, I couldn't do it. You see, suppose a character is walking down a lane. . . . You could easily note down a stream of thought which might be perfectly accurate and believable, and then translate it into a series of images: road, field, hedge, grass, corn, wheat, ear, her ear on the pillow, tumbled hair, love, love years ago. . . . But when one's mind wanders and associates things in this way it's perfectly unselfconscious. Do exactly the same thing on film and the result is precious, self-conscious, over-elaborate—you're using absurdly complex means to convey something very simple. Instead, you should be able to convey the same sort of apprehension not by opening out, proliferating, but by closing in, looking closer and closer, harder and harder at things that are there before you.[3]

Pinter opens, as does Mosley, with the automobile accident involving two of Stephen's students, William and Anna. The montage preserves Mosley's opening mood of horror within a panoramic indifference. The camera initially remains focused on Stephen's "silent, dark" house while the sound track monitors the growing hum of a car, and then, *"closer but still distant, a sudden screech, grind, smash and splintering."*[4] As Stephen emerges from the house to run to the scene of the wreck, the camera picks out the shapes of animals, the play of trees, the stars in the sky, and moonlight on the fields. We are subjected also to Stephen's experience as he approaches the scene: the camera jolting down the lane, to the sound of footsteps running. It moves in suddenly for a close-up on the wreckage:

> *The smashed mass of the car, shooting at passenger seat front section, lying on camera.*
> *Broken metalwork, jagged shapes of glass.*
> *Two bodies heaped together, still, forming one shape.*
> *Silence but for the ticking of ignition.* [P. 220]

This shot cuts to a long shot, once again placing the tragedy in its context.

> *The car seen clearly lying on its side in the middle of the road. Mounds of earth rise at either side of the road, by the hedges.*
> *Trees stand sharply against the sky.*
> *Moonlight passes gently over glass of the car.* [P. 220]

Throughout Stephen's effort to administer to the bodies in the car, close shots alternate with long shots, producing a vacillation between intense involvement with and indifferent alienation from the situation. Pinter's reproduction of this clash of sentiments conveys masterfully the ruminations of Stephen's mind in the novel as he sifts through the disaster.

Pinter diverges from Mosley's story almost immediately in his treatments of Anna and of her interaction with Stephen. After three pages of

camera directions, and aside from his speaking once each of the victims' names, Stephen abruptly screams out the first line of the screenplay: "Don't! You're standing on his face!" (p. 222). Pinter's phrasing
here represents a shocking variation of Mosley's line, "You're standing
on him!" (p. 6). In both versions Anna in fact steps on William's face to
boost herself out of the automobile, but Pinter will carry through the
characterization of a more exploitative Anna which his phrasing implies. Both authors, for example, return Anna to the car to retrieve her
handbag as Stephen inspects the dead William, and both subsequently
portray her wiping off her face with a handkerchief. Pinter, however,
takes her self-concern beyond this business.

> ANNA *takes out a comb and combs her hair.*
> STEPHEN. (*looking down at her*). Can you walk?
> ANNA *quickly completes her combing, puts comb, mirror, handkerchief into
> bag, closes bag.*
> *She sits still.* [P. 223]

During this opening sequence, not only does Pinter paint in Anna
hints of some ambiguous complicity, but he increases Stephen's con-
federacy as well. In the novel Stephen leaves Anna by the wreck and
goes to phone the police. Although Anna follows him, appearing at the
door to Stephen's house after the call is completed, Mosley's Stephen
does not attempt in any way at this point to protect Anna from the law.
The "unplanned" nature of his ultimate protection of her from retribution becomes a major issue at the end of the novel. In Pinter's screenplay, however, Anna leads off toward the house with Stephen trailing
her, until he finally closes the distance between them.

> *Long shot.*
> *They walk slowly up the lane towards the house.* STEPHEN *is no longer
> following. He is equal with her, but* ANNA *keeps a distance between them.*
> [P. 224]

Although he returns to the developments of the novel for the next sequence of action, Pinter will veer sharply from the original at the conclusion of the script, redeeming this modified portrayal.

Once Stephen has completed his call to the police, in both texts he
tries to discover from Anna whether, in fact, she was driving the car, as
her position on the driver's side suggested. Although Mosley refers here
several times to Anna's lack of a driver's license, Pinter's script acknowledges this fact later and only briefly, during a dinner scene where
Anna volunteers to drive William home, causing Charlie to betray both
himself and Anna by remarking, "You haven't got a license" (p. 251).[5]
For Pinter, the motives and intricacies of Stephen's harboring of the girl

become subordinate to the fact and consequences of his doing it, so that the details of Anna's jeopardy go unmentioned for now. In this respect Pinter remains truer to the milieu of the novel than Mosley, who articulates a similar sensibility, but then violates it in practice with too much rationalization. In Pinter's script the motivational information exists, but it no longer controls the organization and presentation of the material. He allocates these functions to the patterning of surface images and situations, and to the subjective properties of Stephen's memory.

In both versions Anna does not respond to Stephen's interrogation, and in both he serves her tea now, as he awaits the arrival of the police. Apparently Mosley's Stephen leaves her there and goes to meet the police at the scene of the crash. (We learn this in retrospect, however, as Mosley's time scheme exists in difficult convolutions, frequently lurching abruptly into the future and then describing broken circles into the past to return to its starting point, as reflected in the overall structure of the novel. In this instance he cuts abruptly to Stephen, who is sitting where Anna had been and talking to a policeman, having already returned from a second visit to the site.) Pinter's Stephen steps out the door to greet the police when he hears the sound of their car drawing up to the house. Cleverly, Pinter has added a second policeman to this scene; the configuration of two against one intensifies Stephen's vulnerability as he attempts to conceal certain facts from the pair of officers. The widely recognizable syndrome of the two-cop interrogation team contributes liberally to the sensation of threat and imminent exposure in Pinter's rendition. Like Mosley, Pinter cuts abruptly to an interior scene in which Stephen responds to the officers' questions from the chair where he last saw Anna. Both authors, by this ploy, pose the question of what has become of the girl; and both Stephens remain innocent of the answer.

After the policeman has left, Mosley's Stephen finally discovers Anna in the spare room, "lying on the bed with shoes off and her skirt in the air, no stockings" (p. 11). Taking his cue from the nature of these perceptions, Pinter locates Anna in Stephen and wife Rosalind's bedroom (a change that lends support to Tom Milne's insightful argument regarding the role of memory in creating a kind of "osmosis" among the various women in the film[6]), and alternates images of her sexuality with shots of Stephen's gradual approach to the bed. The final camera angle shows Anna's feet: *"One shoe is on. The other lying on the bedcover"* (p. 228). Pinter instantly articulates the previously undepicted image of Anna's brutality to William, and then cuts pointedly to the past in a striking series of juxtapositions involving contrasting views of Anna's shoe and of William's face.

> *Interior. Car.*
> ANNA'S *shoe, standing, digging into* WILLIAM'S *face.*
> STEPHEN'S *hands on her legs.*
> STEPHEN'S VOICE. Don't.
> *Close up.* WILLIAM'S *face. Dead.*
>
> *Interior.* STEPHEN'S *study, college.*
> *Morning.*
> WILLIAM'S *face, smiling.* [P. 228]

Mosley's work also shifts backwards into the past at approximately this point, but he omits the momentary recollection of Anna's shoe, and he concludes the opening scene with Stephen's phone call to Charlie, an incident that never occurs in Pinter's version of the story. Instead, Pinter invents a transition into the past that is cinematically effective as well as consonant with the manner in which the imagination organizes experience. The linkage among the images in the preceding montage suggests that Stephen's mind will preside over the subsequent narrative, and that its content and structure will be informed by his memory.

Pinter provides the character Charlie with a new spelling ("Charley") and a whole new background to accompany it. Mosley's Charlie exists as an endearing figure: an old school chum of Stephen's who writes unconventional works of literature with uneven success, lives some distance away with his wealthy wife and their three children, and invades Stephen's life at regular intervals with offbeat antics and welcomed affection. Pinter takes certain elements from this characterization, combines them with those of another figure in the novel, and invents from this hybrid a Charley who possesses a touch of the sinister, and who represents a head-on competitive threat to Stephen.

We know nothing of Charley's past relationship to Stephen from Pinter's script; he portrays them simply as well-acquainted colleagues on the faculty at Oxford. Charley apparently enjoys more popularity than Stephen; he dominates the scenes where the two mix with their peers or with students, and he hosts his own show on television. This last honor belongs to a minor character in the novel: another professor who occasionally appears on a telecast interview program; and whom Stephen bitterly envies. Both Pinter and Mosley feature Stephen's unsuccessful effort to gain a spot on this show later in the course of events. Pinter retains Charley's wife and three children, but he associates Charley with sexual mischievousness in our first glimpse of the character.

> CHARLEY. A statistical analysis of sexual intercourse among students at Colenso University, Milwaukee, showed that 70 per cent did it in the evening, 29.9 percent between two and four in the afternoon and 0.1 percent during a lecture on Aristotle. [P. 233]

These words derive directly from the novel, but Pinter alters their speaker in order to delineate Charley, and he invents the Provost's subsequent quip: "I'm surprised to hear Aristotle is on the syllabus in the state of Wisconsin." Pinter's adaptation of Charley's characterization provides a simplified representation of and focus for the complex network of fears and doubts that Stephen articulates in the novel. As Pinter described his method of attack on the source work, "In this film everything happens, nothing is explained. It has all been pared down and down."

Between novel and screenplay, the character of William and his relationship with Stephen also undergo modification. In the first place, Pinter has stripped Stephen's tutorials with William and Anna of all academic substance. Mosley parallels the prevailing themes of the story's action in the ongoing philosophical debates between Stephen and the students over empirical versus metaphysical sensibilities. Mosley's tutorial dialogues include consequent moments of stunning insight and irony, but Pinter deletes all of this in favor of straightforward and more filmic development of these themes in the action. The encounters between William and Stephen in Pinter's script become duels of wit and supremacy, so that William emerges more as Stephen's equal, and their relationship tends more toward the competitive. In their first scene together, William presses Stephen for information about Anna and introduces a hint of their sexual rivalry.

STEPHEN. You realize I'm her tutor?

WILLIAM. Naturally. I also realize you're my tutor.

STEPHEN. And that being her tutor, her moral welfare must be my first consideration.

WILLIAM . Ah. You mean besides being her tutor you are also her protector.

STEPHEN. I mean that I refuse to countenance or encourage male lust as directed against any of my woman students.

WILLIAM. Well said.

STEPHEN. Thank you. . . .

WILLIAM. Well, come on! What do you think of her?

STEPHEN. I don't think.

WILLIAM. I thought that was your job!

STEPHEN. Not about *that*.

WILLIAM. You're not past it, are you? Already? [Pp. 229-30]

Mosley's Stephen acknowledges bouts of this sort with William: "We used to talk like this, showing off, perhaps learning something from each other. . . . But I sometimes found myself almost flirting with William, which I afterwards hated" (p. 23). But in the novel Stephen's extensively elaborated pedagogical interests add a dimension to the relationship that we can only hypothesize, based on superficial configurations, in Pinter's screenplay.

The exclusive informality of the Stephen-William relationship in Pinter's adaptation also implies the intensity of Stephen's distress over William's death: a sentiment that Mosley establishes in dialogue and articulated thought, but one that obtains no outlet, otherwise, in Pinter's version. Pinter's characters rarely verbalize their real concerns: "What I'm interested in is emotion which is contained and felt very, very deeply. . . . But, perhaps, it is ultimately inexpressible. Because I think we express our emotions in so many small ways, all over the place—or can't express them in any other way.''[7] Our perception of the depth of Stephen's grief consequently depends on the nature of their relationship previous to the tragedy. When we take into account Stephen's apparent disregard for William following his death (and Pinter paradoxically exaggerates this repression or diversion of feeling as well, to the point of introducing a sex scene between Anna and Stephen on the night of William's death), we encounter a mystification of motives that actualizes the philosophical ruminations of the novel.

The elaborate intellectual substance of Stephen's appointments with Anna has been still further "pared down." I quote their first meeting in its entirety.

> *Interior. Study.*
> ANNA *sitting, knees together, with notebook.*
> *Her face, listening.*
> STEPHEN'S VOICE.Philosophy is the product of enquiry only. It does not attempt to find specific answers to specific questions.
> *Close up. His face, looking at her.* [P. 230]

Despite his simplification of the philosophical and interpersonal stakes of the story, Pinter has not discounted Stephen's character through negligence or default; the screenplay includes several deliberate inventions that shift Stephen in the direction of a "dirty old man" figure. The episode in which Anna, William, and Stephen glide down the river in a punt, which occasions a burst of lyric eloquence from Stephen in the novel, reduces to the following sequence of images on film.

> *Long shot of* STEPHEN *stepping into punt.*
> *The punt rocks.* WILLIAM *pushes off.* STEPHEN *squats by* ANNA.
> *The punt.*
> STEPHEN *settles into half-leaning, crouching position by* ANNA'S *legs.*
> *The punt.*
> WILLIAM'S *legs.*
> *Through them,* ANNA *sitting,* STEPHEN *reclining along punt, his head on the cushion by her hip.*

> *Her legs are bare, crossed.*
> *Vapour on her legs.*
> *Left foreground* STEPHEN'S *head. Above him* ANNA'S *back.*
> *Her hair glinting. Light in her hair.*
> *Beyond them* WILLIAM *standing, punting.*
> *Her arm, still.*
> *Her arm, moving.*
> *Her armpit, fuzzy hair.*
> *Hole at the side of her dress.*
> STEPHEN'S *body, stretched.*
> *Her hip. His head.*
> *Her eyes closed.*
> *The punt pole, dipping.* [P. 235]

I break the quote at this direction to underline its suggestive overtone. Through this sequence of contrapuntal images, Pinter manages to capture the fantastic flights of Stephen's mind that Mosley recounts during this trip down the river.

In both versions the outing ends in disaster for Stephen when he topples into the water. Mosley cleverly delays this information until a later scene, when Stephen's colleagues humiliate him over the incident. Pinter, however, includes the mishap as part of the sequence and capitalizes on its aftermath to stress Stephen's anxiety over his advancing age: "I'm getting old!" he complains to William. "Don't you understand? Old. My muscles. The muscles. . . . No judgement. No judgement of distance. It's all gone. Vanished!" (p. 236). Although the aging syndrome certainly contributes to Stephen's crisis in the novel, Pinter makes the issue more explicit and more central. We have already noted the presence of a contest between generations in *The Pumpkin Eater* and *The Homecoming,* and this rivalry recurs in *Accident.* Stephen's fascination with Anna in the screenplay becomes more urgent; Mosley's William manipulates Stephen into inviting himself and Anna over for a Sunday, but Pinter's Stephen initiates the idea on his own.

Stephen's wife, Rosalind, acquires through Pinter all of the manipulative guiles that Mosley describes, but fails to materialize, in her. Mosley's Stephen marks the existence of a kind of silent debriefing period after he reenters his house, during which his wife and children seem to exclude him from the animal unity. Each night a testing period, of a nonspecific nature, has to elapse before his belonging is truly recognized by them. Pinter makes a scene of these ruminations. Some of the dialogue derives from the novel, but Pinter has increased its surface tension and focused its undercurrents.

STEPHEN *standing at door.* ROSALIND *sitting,* CLARISSA *on her lap.* TED *(seven years old) lying on floor with book, looking up. The dog, asleep on the floor.*

Even the dog ignores his arrival!

Stephen's first words address the three-year-old Clarissa, and receive prompt deflation by his wife.

STEPHEN. She loves her Dad.
ROSALIND. She hasn't eaten anything today.

After some tentative monkey-business with the children, Stephen opens a conversation with Rosalind as she is sewing. (The two hiatuses in this quote involve brief activities with the children.)

STEPHEN. I've got a new pupil.
ROSALIND. Uh?
STEPHEN. She's an Austrian princess.
ROSALIND. *Is* she?
CLARISSA. A princess?
STEPHEN. (*whispering to* CLARISSA). I think so.
TED'S VOICE. I can't find the book!
ROSALIND. How do you know she's a princess?
STEPHEN. She's got a very long name.
ROSALIND. Has she got golden hair?
STEPHEN. Uuuh . . . No.
ROSALIND. Then she's a fake.

. . . .

STEPHEN. She's very sunburnt.
ROSALIND. Then she's definitely not a princess.
STEPHEN. Why not?
CLARISSA. She is!
ROSALIND. Princesses keep their skin . . . quite white.
STEPHEN. Your skin is quite white.
ROSALIND. I know it is.

. . . .

ROSALIND. Has she made advances to you?
STEPHEN. Oh no. I'm too old.
ROSALIND. You're not too old for me.
STEPHEN. I know that. (*To children.*) Now come on. Who's going to start?
ROSALIND *stands and moves across to them.*
CLARISSA. I'll start.
TED. She can't read!
ROSALIND *bends over him.*
ROSALIND. And I'm not too old for you. [Pp. 231-33]

At his mention of a new female student, Rosalind quickly, but guardedly, perks her ears. She maneuvers skillfully, using the children's interest and language as a format for her prying. Curious about Anna's looks, she asks about "golden hair." Anxious already to detract from her intuited rival, Rosalind denounces her twice as a fake when Anna's description fails to meet storybook standards. Only after she has forced Stephen into admitting his disqualification by age does Rosalind mellow in her victory and rise to greet him.

Later in the screenplay, when Rosalind learns that Charley is having an affair with Anna, she employs this same tactic with Stephen.

ROSALIND. He's sleeping with her, is he?
STEPHEN. Who?
ROSALIND. Charley. With Anna.
STEPHEN. Of course.
ROSALIND. How pathetic.
STEPHEN. What do you mean?
ROSALIND. Poor stupid old man.
STEPHEN. He's not old.
ROSALIND. Stupid bastard. [P. 267]

By working on Stephen's certain association of himself with Charley, Rosalind again slips him an oblique warning, and this time Stephen takes the bait. Rosalind's awareness of Stephen and his consciousness of her awareness of him prescribe a subtle dynamic between them. Their scenes together progress like the strategies of a fencing match.

Rosalind's pregnancy and his own nagging guilt make Stephen cautious around his wife. He broaches the subject of his Sunday invitation with painstaking care and phrasing.

He continues kissing her fingers.
STEPHEN. Oh, I've asked some people over on Sunday.
(*He looks at her.*) Is that all right? (*Pause.*) Mnnn?
ROSALIND. What people?
STEPHEN. Well . . . William . . . you know . . .
ROSALIND. Mnn-hmmn?
STEPHEN. And this Anna von Graz. (*Pause.*) You know, that girl—
ROSALIND. The Princess.
STEPHEN. Yes. She's William's girlfriend. (*Pause.*) What do you think? [P. 239]

Although Rosalind, after another page of maneuvering, finally agrees to the gathering, Stephen's unformulated hopes for the day dissipate when he realizes that Charley has "accidentally" turned up.[8] Apparently his professional opponent has already gained a foothold with Anna. When Stephen returns from a walk with the dog and his children,

Anna and Charley are standing on his drive, talking quietly by Charley's sports car. William has gone inside.

Pinter's chronicle of this day comprises the largest cohesive episode of the screenplay. With minor exceptions, primarily to expand or to reflect his modifications of the characters, Pinter draws the substance of the day's events directly from the novel. In its estrangement of motive from action, the novel suits Pinter's disposition handily, and he retains intact one of Mosley's finest scenes in this vein. The scene, which occurs between William and Charley on the lawn, addresses the process of writing, and could pass as Pinter's own description of his technique. As Charley explains it to William, "You just need a starting point, that's all" (p. 243). William's curiosity elicits this remarkable elaboration from Charley.

> CHARLEY. Here on this lawn. What are we up to?
> WILLIAM. I know what I'm up to.
> CHARLEY. What?
> WILLIAM. Anna and I were invited here for lunch. We've just had it.
> CHARLEY. Ah. [P. 243]

But we know plainly that William's designs for the day extend beyond this assumed naivete. Charley shatters the mood of reserve and intensifies the irony of this tack.

> CHARLEY. Describe what we're all doing.
> WILLIAM *looks about the garden.*
> WILLIAM. Rosalind's lying down. Stephen's weeding the garden. Anna's making a daisy chain. We're having this conversation.
> CHARLEY. Good. But then you could go further. Rosalind is pregnant. Stephen's having an affair with a girl at Oxford. He's reached the age when he can't keep his hands off girls at Oxford.
> WILLIAM. What?
> CHARLEY. But he feels guilty, of course. So he makes up a story.
> WILLIAM. What story?
> CHARLEY. This story,
> WILLIAM. What are you talking about? [P. 244]

At this point, in both novel and screenplay, Charley responds by swatting nonexistent flies. He shouts at Stephen to be sure that Stephen has overheard the conversation; and both Stephens reply with a simple "yes." Pinter, however, adds to this a shot of Rosalind, *"lying, eyes closed,"* and also commenting "yes" (pp. 244-45).

In both versions the dialogue between William and Charley drips with irony at several levels: Charley's projection is true about Stephen, at least in an imaginative sense; it derives special force from its implication of Anna, directed expressly at William, who is present because of his interest in her; by virtue of what we have observed already, it seems to describe accurately its speaker; and, by the conclusion of the story, we shall understand, by Charley's admission, that his affair with Anna had commenced before this dialogue, thus conferring a kind of retroactive irony on the moment. Pinter, through his alteration of both Charley and Stephen's characters, makes the statement a still more accurate assessment of the two men.

In the screenplay the diminished rapport between Stephen and Charley lends the day's developments an undercurrent of nastiness. Pinter describes an incisive shooting sequence for Mosley's afternoon tennis match, depicting various combinations of William, Charley, Stephen, and Anna caught in revealing game metaphors for their predicaments, as Rosalind initially looks on, and then disappears. Pinter seems to delight in focusing the concealed tensions of real life through game mechanisms, and he faithfully reproduces Mosley's paragraph of description in his outline for angles of *"William whipping the ball fiercely over the net," "Stephen serving, into the net,"* and Charley, barefoot, lobbing balls deliberately into Anna's backside (p. 245).

When Stephen does finally get Anna apart from the others for the walk that she declines with William, but accepts with him, Pinter remains generally faithful to Mosley's account of their hopeless, clichéd conversation. Tom Milne's perceptive discussion of this episode includes an example of Joseph Losey's sensitivity to Pinter's scripts. "By snubbing William and accepting Stephen's invitation to go for a walk, Anna has made her intentions as plain as she can. But Stephen is still held back by his inhibitions, and nothing happens. . . . And as they turn back to the house, the camera stays where it is, gazing at the empty landscape as though lamenting the end of the affair."[9] This "empty landscape" image recurs in various forms in Losey's films of Pinter's scripts, and we shall later note its accuracy as a revelation of Pinter's milieu. In this case the lingering camera does signify a coda in Stephen's "affair" with Anna, since his subsequent discoveries of her involvement with Charley and engagement to William reduce his romantic prospects to the anticlimactic rape.

Significantly, Pinter seizes the chance during this scene to embroider his ambivalence toward Anna when she and Stephen encounter a spider web, absent from Mosley's narrative.

STEPHEN. Mind. There's a spider's web.
ANNA *looks at him.*
ANNA. It won't hurt me. [P. 247]

For both writers Anna's thoughts are a mystery; her personality is utterly withdrawn, occluded by the perimeters of its own impenetrable world. Pinter evolves this tendency into a self-centered obliviousness in her; he underscores her trampling on William's face, he invents her subsequent business with the comb, he barges her through a spider's web, and he will portray her in a laughing embrace with Stephen immediately following William's death. Pinter has again embellished a strain from the novel that invokes the inscrutable nature of human activity. He subtracts from, rather than adds to, our understanding of Anna and of Stephen's fascination with her; or better, he frustrates our understanding as we habitually constitute it. By rendering Stephen's attraction to Anna incomprehensible through usual means, Pinter focuses two almost paradoxical phenomena: the undeniable surface truth of events and actions, and the inevitable distortion of interior truth by its reflection on the surface.

The obstinate inscrutability of the affair refers our efforts at comprehension back to Stephen's motives, and these, in fact, become the subject of the piece. No one, however, spells out his motives for us. Stephen claims repeatedly in the novel that he is incapable of doing so. If Charlie has written the novel, these insights are less creditable. The camera records the action impassively. We are abandoned with two simultaneous views: one that assiduously deprives and denies us, and one we are compelled to invent from our own experience in order to "fill in" the spaces in the story's architecture. Ultimately, we confront the omnipresent disfiguring of our own perceptual machinery, which the work addresses at the levels of plot and theme in its internal constitution, as well. We experience what Pinter has expressed in an early program note: "A thing is not necessarily either true or false; it can be both true and false."[10]

Except for the accelerating tensions between Stephen and Charley, the events of the day, in all their frustrations and disappointments for Stephen, proceed in Pinter's screenplay exactly as they do in the novel. William and Anna become too drunk to drive home and end by spending the night with Stephen and Rosalind. Charley stays as well, and he later claims to have slept the night with Anna. Stephen, after a momentary alcoholic delusion that he has discovered Anna in his bed (again consistent with Milne's "osmosis" theory), retires in resignation with his wife.

The night's conversation over dinner, aside from providing Pinter a format for delightful replication of drunken dialogue, elicits the news that Stephen has been invited to appear on Charley's television program. In Mosley's version Charlie invites Stephen on the show in a moment of inebriated comradeship. Pinter supplies the announcement with a less benevolent mood.

> STEPHEN. But he's more successful than me because he appears on television.
> ANNA. (*to* CHARLEY). Do you talk on television?
> CHARLEY. What do you think I do, play the flute?
> ANNA. What do you talk about?
> STEPHEN. He talks about history, zoology—
> CHARLEY. Anthropology, sociolog . . . sociologigy—
> STEPHEN. Sociology!
> CHARLEY. Codology.
> STEPHEN. And sex. In that order.
> ROSALIND. He suits the medium.
> STEPHEN. (*to* ROSALIND). Do you mean you don't think I would suit the medium?
> CHARLEY. They wouldn't let you within ten miles of the medium!
> STEPHEN *points a long arm across the table at* CHARLEY.
> STEPHEN. I have an appointment with *your* producer next week.
> CHARLEY. With *my* producer?
> STEPHEN. *Your* producer. [Pp. 250-51]

The scene that follows, delineating Stephen's failure, in fact, to book himself on the show, provides a heyday for Pinter. He apparently so relished the obnoxious mood of the scene that, in Losey's film of the screenplay, he took the role of the executive who obliviously evacuates Stephen's hopes. Mosley's hinted undercurrent of distraction translates into a form of bureaucratic hell in Pinter's adaptation. Ringing phones, efficient secretaries, massive paperwork, and intruding coworkers dominate Stephen's interview. The scene concludes abruptly and prematurely when the television executive flees the office with a coworker to visit at the hospital the man whom Stephen was supposed to see. In parting, the executive remarks (in both versions), "Give my love to Francesca," exhibiting his neglect of Stephen's previous response that he has not seen Francesca in some years, and presumably his indifference to everything else Stephen has said during the aborted interview.

Frustrated in all his efforts for rejuvenation and salvation as Anna and his television career recede into fantasy, Stephen conjures a retrieval of the past through Francesca. Mosley's Stephen experiences an agony of alienation during his attempt to relive his youth in the arms of his past lover. His mind drifts uncontrollably from the actual situations of the evening. Pinter contrives a stunning cinematic vehicle for this sensation by divorcing the soundtrack from the visual depiction of their meeting, dining, and lovemaking.

> *The following sequence with* FRANCESCA *is silent. The only sounds heard are the voices overlaid at stated points. The words are fragments of realistic conversation. They are not thoughts. Nor are they combined with any lip movement on the part of the actors. They are distributed over the sequence so as to act as a disembodied comment on the action.* [P. 256]

Francesca and Stephen invoke and relive the past in words, but the dialogue has no intrinsicality, no connection, in their witnessed actions. The experience serves only to confirm Stephen's dilemma: his occupation of a present life that sustains no retrievable meaning from its past nor exciting promise for its future. In an interview several years after adapting *Accident,* Pinter expressed a similar sentiment regarding his own life: "Well, it [the future] ought to be fanciful really. I know the future is simply going to be the same thing. It'll never end. You carry all the states with you until the end."[11]

Stephen's return home occasions the final blow. Having entered the house and ignored his pile of mail (Pinter's characteristic metaphor of despondency), he hears creaks upstairs and finally footsteps on the landing. Stephen endures his sudden recognition with typical reserve and guardedness, as first Charley and then Anna unexpectedly appear on the stairs.

CHARLEY. Hullo.
Pause.
STEPHEN. Hullo. I've just come from London.
CHARLEY. I know.
ANNA *appears at the top of the stairs. She is dressed in sweater and trousers. Bare feet.*
STEPHEN *stares up at her.*
Eventually his gaze drops to CHARLEY.
STEPHEN. To see the television people.
ANNA *remains still.*
Silence.
CHARLEY. Did you see them?
STEPHEN. I'm hungry. [P. 260]

Again we observe the simultaneous truth and falsehood of Stephen's response; it represents a true fact as it occurs, but a false one as we understand it. Stephen, in fact, cooks himself an omelette, in which Charley and Anna decline interest. As Stephen literally fries his eggs, Charley and Anna twist subtle and unsubtle psychological knives in each other (Pinter subdues the game from the novel, where Charlie relentlessly identifies her with the Nazis), and Charley opens and reads aloud a letter from his wife, Laura, to Stephen, in which she pleads pathetically for Stephen's help in discouraging Charley's affair with Anna. (Mosley's Charlie remains unaware of this letter, although it exists in the novel as well. In the novel Stephen finds and reads the letter after Charlie and Anna have left.) Then Charley adroitly devours half of Stephen's omelette.

Stephen leaves the kitchen and wanders through the house, noting the evidence of activity between his two uninvited guests. In the novel he makes an inarticulate effort to discuss things with Anna, but here he merely stops her from making the bed and offers to let them stay the night. In place of Stephen's scene with Anna, Pinter substitutes one with Charley, which appears in a later, unretained episode of the novel. Here Charley confesses to Stephen the length and depth of his affair with Anna, and Pinter makes only two significant alterations in the substance of the dialogue. The first one is difficult to characterize: either it signals a shift in Anna's character, a shift in Charley's impression of Anna's character, or a shift in the impression that Charley wants Stephen to have of Anna's character. In any case although Mosley's Charlie stresses that Anna was no virgin when he inherited her, Pinter's Charley insists, "She's not a whore" (p. 264). Probably this change results from all three shifts and certainly involves Charley's desire to emphasize the value of his prize. As a close friend of Stephen's, Mosley's Charlie can afford more candor than the competing Charley of Pinter's invention.

The second alteration in this scene, however, keynotes a more serious detour from the concluding concerns of the novel. In Mosley's story Stephen stakes everything on his purity of motive. He does nothing consciously to encourage the affair between Charlie and Anna, and he visits Charlie's wife, Laura, on several occasions to reassure her. Although he squirms over his inability to take the measures that Rosalind expects of him in this matter, he does not contribute actively to sustaining the relationship. The effort at self-vindication implicit in Stephen's stand echoes in his handling of Anna after the accident; he insists to Charlie that his actions shielding her were entirely spontaneous. Stephen is speaking:

> I said "No one saw her. I left her sitting in this room. Then when the policeman came she wasn't here, she'd gone upstairs. This is important."
> Charlie said "What is?"
> I said "I hadn't planned it." [P. 159]

The last several chapters of the novel, in fact, deal with Stephen's attempt to define his guilt, its consequences, and its expiation. Motives and actions, apparently, may be separated at the level of observation, but not ultimately at the level of efficacy. Chapters after Anna has been packed off to Austria, Stephen still suffers what he senses to be the effects of his complicity: Rosalind's pregnancy has gone awry, and the baby has been born with little chance for survival. Stephen's machinations surrounding his chasing and protection of Anna have prevented him from attending to Rosalind's needs. He expects to lose his position, and to face prosecution in a court of law. None of his dreads, however, materializes; the baby improves, his colleagues offer sympathy, and the judicial hearing is a farce. His doubts comprise the extent of his punishment. His final and only conclusion consists in the last words of the novel: "Remember it happy; the sun in your eyes."

Pinter begins here, in Stephen's discovery of Charley and Anna, to deviate radically from this path. In his conversation with Charley, Stephen invites him and Anna to use the house while he visits Rosalind at her mother's, where she has gone to relax during the last month of her pregnancy. He even presents Charley with a key to the house. But, while Stephen's degree of "sinning" becomes greater, his share of "punishment" becomes less; his visit to Rosalind is purely casual where, in the novel, her hemorrhaging necessitates it.

The shooting sequence for this segment of film alternates snatches of dialogue between Stephen and Rosalind with snatches between him and Laura. Both scenes occur in garden settings. The irony present in Stephen's situation clarifies in the juxtaposition of the two circumstances, which Pinter has carefully modified to resemble each other. For both women Stephen must explain and excuse the actions of his colleague, while he hides from them his own complicity in the affair and his envy of it. According to Milne, Pinter's reworking of this material corresponds with Stephen's confounding of the incidents in his memory, further implying an imaginative identification between the two women in their circumstances and reactions.[12] The scenes with Laura grind to a standstill of wordlessness, as the scenes with Rosalind intensify to a similar stalemate. In the final scene at Laura's, she stammers out inarticulate and ironic reassurance for Stephen's benefit, and in the penultimate and ultimate dialogues with Rosalind, the strain accelerates intolerably into protracted silence and then into an abrupt temporal twist.

Exterior. ROSALIND'S *mother's garden*.
ROSALIND. I've never heard of anything so bloody puerile, so banal.
STEPHEN. What's banal about it?
ROSALIND. That poor stupid bitch of a girl.

STEPHEN. You just keep calling everyone stupid, what's the use—?
ROSALIND. Well, they are. Except Laura. And she's stupid too.
Pause.
You chucked them out, I hope?

Exterior. Garden. LAURA'S *house*.
LAURA *and* STEPHEN *standing middle of lawn*.
LAURA. Well . . . don't worry about it.
STEPHEN. I'm not.
LAURA. Thanks for coming.

Exterior. ROSALIND'S *mother's garden*.
STEPHEN *and* ROSALIND *in the deckchairs, still*.
Silence.
STEPHEN. I think I'll pop in and see Laura. It's on my way.
ROSALIND. Give her my love. [Pp. 268-69]

Since it seems unlikely that Stephen would conceal an earlier visit to Laura from Rosalind (for what reason?), the alternated encounter with Laura would occur after his scene with Rosalind in real, as opposed to reel, chronology. Pinter has developed the two episodes simultaneously to capture a sense of the ironic counterpoint between the two and of Stephen's careening perceptual experience.

Aside from the dislocating effect of the unsynchronized scene between Stephen and Francesca and the overall scheme of the flashback, this particular montage contains the only evidence of nonsequential time in the screenplay. The significance of time as a theme in the script is manifest in such motifs as the frequent chiming of clocks and the ticking of the ignition. But, as Milne points out, both the structure and content of the screenplay indict conventional measurements of time, and "in this story, nothing can be defined or limited in this way."[13] In this montage, as in the previous one depicting Stephen and Francesca, Stephen's imagination emerges as a conspicuous instrument in characterization and organization of events. Milne's detection of evidence in the film that Stephen's subjectivity influences the portrayal of material is persuasive. Noting that the sequence between Stephen and Francesca, through its composition and gauzy tones, suggests Stephen's retrospective attempt to create an image of perfect romance, Milne cites further instances of the effects of Stephen's memory as it manipulates the television studio scene: an hysterical, two-dimensional grotesque.

In a way, of course, being Stephen's recollection, the whole film (with the exception, naturally, of the accident and last scene) is his fabrication, with

Charley being beastly, Anna provocative, Rosalind patient, and William callow. (It is interesting, in fact, to note the disparity between the dignified, hesitant Stephen of the flashbacks, and the man who virtually rapes Anna after the accident.)[14]

The nonlinear structure of the scenes with Laura and Rosalind likewise reflects the conjurings of Stephen's mind and, as Losey has noted, the capacity of the film medium to evoke multiple facets and layers of experience.

No stunt was intended at all, but simply two dialogues inter-cut in time and place; and at the end a deliberate sense that he is going to do—or is talking about doing—something he may already have done, which is part of his deception. If it seems a trick, then it is a failure; if it doesn't, then I think it's as much an extension of the medium as Picasso in his medium when he began to paint three or more aspects of the same face in one portrait.[15]

The tensions continue to build, and to deviate slightly from conventional experience, in the succeeding scene. Again, Pinter finds keen cinematic expression for Mosley's savage description of game dynamics. This game, waged by a gathering of aristocrats at William's estate, focuses and symbolizes the unspoken opposition between Stephen and William. A homicidal variation of football, the action pits Stephen against William in a series of vicious, bloody combats, which Pinter (and moreover Losey) characterizes in an almost expressionistic mood. The game serves metaphorically to elucidate Stephen's inescapable betrayal of William and his rising sensation of personal jeopardy. Both men fail ultimately in this rite of primitive brutality: Stephen falls to the ground, and William loses the ball. Pinter wickedly punctuates the contest with angles of the onlooking ladies, and finally cuts abruptly to the civility of the cricket field at Oxford, where William is *"hitting the ball savagely . . . immaculate in white"* (p. 272). The impenetrable deceit of life's surface prevails on all layers of the script.

Pinter strips Mosley's elaborate description of the cricket game scene to its bare essentials, adding somewhat to these by his incorporation of material from novel scenes that he has dropped entirely. Anna's announcement to Stephen of her engagement to William constitutes Pinter's major interpolation in this scene. In both versions Anna follows up her news with a blithe request that Stephen convey it to Charley. Mosley's Stephen, through several chapters of anxious rumination, insinuates his fear that Anna's request represents a sinister manipulation of Charlie through William. Pinter, however, reduces these protracted doubts to an angle of Stephen, looking at her, and interrupts the moment immediately by the appearance of William.

Significant differences also exist in the two authors' treatments of

William's announced desire for a conference with Stephen. Mosley's meeting time remains vague, some time later in the day, either in Stephen's office or later still at home; and Anna's inclusion in the meeting evolves ambiguously as a natural assumption by either Anna or William. In the screenplay William insists expressly on a "man to man talk," saying "I don't want her." Here, Stephen arranges Anna's presence, suggesting, "We can talk when she's in bed. She can sleep in the spare room" (p. 273). The three establish a meeting time to occur after a party that William and Anna plan to attend that evening. These two modifications of the original story possess strong ramifications; Anna's presence at the wheel of the fated vehicle and the post-party drunkenness of the two become direct results of Stephen's arrangements, amplifying his culpability in the disastrous outcome.

As Pinter shifts through a rapid sequence of shots recalling the accident (William's face dead, Anna's head emerging, Anna sitting on the bank, and Anna in Stephen's bed) and into the present time of Stephen's predicament, we discover no evidence of Mosley's pangs of conscience in Stephen. He does not contact Charley, as he does in the novel, where the subsequent scene between them elicits Stephen's agonized deliberations over the moral dilemma of protecting Anna from legal sanctions. This dilemma, indeed, remains entirely absent from Pinter's version, which plainly discounts the possibility of its existence. After brutally interrogating Anna about whether anyone knows of her presence at his house and receiving no decipherable response from her, Stephen suddenly kisses her. As an unanswered phone rings in the background (ringing telephones, usually proclaiming the urgencies of neglected affairs and usually ignored, occur almost invariably in Pinter's screenplays whenever characters attempt to suspend exigencies for the sake of indulgence), the camera concludes the scene with an angle of the two standing in dim light by the bed.

When the story picks up the next morning, a telephone call interrupts Stephen and Anna as they prepare to leave. From Stephen's end of the conversation, we learn that his wife is in some trouble ("But she's all right?") and that the hospital has been trying to reach him all night. Although Charlie returns Anna to her dormitory the same evening of the accident (without any sexual interaction between her and Stephen) in the novel, Pinter delegates this task to Stephen, whose execution of it smacks of morning-after strain and of his hospital-bound anxieties. He dully hoists her over the wall and grimly observes her disappear into the dormitory. The deadly mood of anticlimax and vague antagonism permeates the scene, insinuating our only hint of Stephen's guilt over his actions.

Pinter develops this motif of iniquity and retribution briefly in the two scenes that follow. The first describes a shot of the incubated infant as Stephen exits the room and omits the epiphanic glorification of life that accompanies Stephen's vision in the novel of the helpless baby. The entire theme of Stephen's magnified dependence on the child's survival escapes the screenplay. His subsequent dialogue with Rosalind reiterates his guilt ("They phoned you. You weren't there."), but Pinter terminates this situation without further elucidation. Whereas for Mosley Stephen's culpability remains minimal and his bad conscience becomes preponderant, for Pinter the inverse of this prevails: Stephen's complicity is amplified and his repentance is undetectable. Within the discrepant motive-action system of Pinter's milieu, we can predict Stephen's feeling of guilt, but we cannot ascertain it anywhere. We experience only the gap between what we know to exist and what irrefutably does exist, the two defiantly contradicting each other.

The final sequence of the film script confirms this theme of paramount indifference. After a rather long scene in which Stephen and Charley help Anna pack up in her room, where Stephen enjoys the bleak triumph of Charley's exclusion and of Anna's coldness to her bewildered ex-lover, Pinter snaps a masterful frame on the cinematic work. Over camera shots of Stephen's return to his usual existence, the sound track monitors, once again, the progression of the accident.

Note: *The following scenes until the end of the film are silent except for:*
The hum of a car growing on the soundtrack. The sound grows. It includes jamming gear changes and sharp braking.
The sound begins very quietly.

Exterior. Cloister. Day.
STEPHEN *walks through cloister towards his study slowly.*

Exterior. House. Day.
(Identical shot as at the beginning of the film.)
CLARISSA *and* TED *running over gravel towards front door.*
CLARISSA *falls, holds her leg, cries.*
The sound of the car draws closer.
STEPHEN *comes out of house, picks her up, comforts her, carries her into house, her arms around him,* TED *following. The dog runs after them.*
Camera slowly moves back to long shot outside the gate.
It comes to rest.
Sound of the car skidding.
A sudden screech, grind, smash and splintering.
Camera withdraws down the drive to the gate.
The house still, in the sunlight.
Silence.
Sound of ignition, ticking. [Pp. 283-284]

In this schism between sound and image, Pinter captures the pages of incomprehension that Stephen experiences in the novel as his life re-sumes its normal track. Like motives, desires, guilt, and all things invisible, the past slips with barely a trace from reality. Stephen's ac-tions in this sequence mirror the opening indifference of the environ-ment to the tragedy, at once framing the ordeal and sealing it from the present and future. As Milne explains it, "Seen in broad daylight (no moon, no horse, no shadows) the accident is simply an accident; and by implication the only fact of the . . . accident is that William dies."[16] The incident and its repercussions are absorbed into a final layer of opaque veneer.

Baker and Tabachnick observe that the dynamics of the "accidental" provide the unity of the piece. The ironic relationship between the surface of life and its invisible components prevails across the story's complexities. "Pinter teaches us that no pure 'accidents' occur in the world, that all events result from unspoken and uncomprehended needs and desires."[17] Similarly, Katherine Burkman states that the automobile accident "is in a sense no accident at all but an inevitable part of the ritual that patterns the film."[18] William's defeat (symbolizing the ob-solescent aristocracy), the crumbling buildings, the indifferent trees, the inexplicable lovemaking, the absence of consequence, all signify this consumption of meaning by the surface: this supremacy of accident in a world of indeterminate causation. Those who invest forms survive; those who invoke substance fall. Thus Mosley carries the self-depreca-tions of reluctant narration into the condition of the narrator's world: not only do his sensibilities impede the narrator in telling the story, but they also formulate the primary obstacle in his experience of the events. In both the form and content of his novel, Mosley negates omniscience and indicts perception, displacing the pansophic author by one who remains a victim of his perspectives and their fallibility. Painful description substitutes for glib insight, and "accident" becomes the final condition of incident.

These themes become increasingly pronounced in Pinter's original work as his career continues. In the context of his major plays, *Accident* (1967) follows *The Homecoming* (1964), an obfuscated anatomy of Ruth's decision to leave her husband and remain with his family. Pinter's depiction of this action exhibits the same fidelity to impervious surfaces that meticulously betray their resonant depths. In this play, a work relentlessly harnessed to external and internal verisimilitude, Pinter exorcises all tendencies toward lucid, artificial expression of the sorts that occur in his earlier characters. Only in the most surreptitious of activities and inactivities do we grasp the natures of the game and of its stakes, for self-exposure has become equivalent to self-annihilation in this domestic jungle, where every expression must contain the capacity to deny its meaning. Peter Hall, who directed the original production of *The Homecoming*, provides an amusing description of the game's format:

> The phrase always on our lips when we were doing this play was "Taking the piss." It's a Cockney phrase meaning getting the better of your opponent by mockery. This play doesn't take the piss in a light or flippant way. It takes the piss in a cruel and bitter way. The characters are all doing this to each other. They take the piss—this Cockneyism is central to the play. But of course one of the great factors about taking the piss is that if you're taking the piss satisfactorily the person whose piss is being taken must not be sure whether or not it is being taken.[19]

In *The Homecoming* the legitimate roles of familiar domestic structure appear only as tactics in an unrestricted game of exploitation that the characters wage against each other. Traditional valuations persist only as a pretext, and the characters contrive throughout the play to explain, conform, and conceal their objectives according to the superficial configurations of models and games. Teddy, who prefers to "operate on things and not in things,"[20] abandons Ruth the moment their marriage no longer projects the appearance he strives to transmit. Her decision, also explicable as preference for a winning game over a losing one, to remain with Teddy's family as a prostitute enables Teddy to forsake her as inconsistent with his marriage ideal. The shock of his departure is comprehensible only in terms of subtextual currents: the earlier games of antagonism between the two and the premiums inherent in the game of affecting appearance. The confounding of the literal and the figurative permits the incidents of the water glass and the cheese roll to acquire their own potencies, and the world of emblems and metaphors becomes equipped with its own consequential, if fragile, authority.

Thus, in the absence of alternative possibilities for interaction, the games in Pinter's work escalate, and their imperialism will be progressively manifest in his subsequent writing. The subjection of ulterior reality to the authority of the game, a shift in Pinter's work that occurs most notably in *The Homecoming*, facilitates the experimentation with time already prominent in his screenplay for *The Pumpkin Eater* and continued in his adaptation of *Accident*. Because of its capacity for temporal suspension and manipulation, the game, in its new omnipotence, provides Pinter a device for further exploration of time in its subjective mode. As a device particularly suited to the confusion of time on stage, the games will become increasingly significant and powerful in his upcoming plays, including *Landscape* (1967), *Old Times* (1970), and *No Man's Land* (1974).

In *The Homecoming* Ruth's widely discussed "underwear" speech serves as a conspicuous treatise on the subtextual, or possibly supertextual, mechanisms of *Accident*. She assumes a stance opposite to that of her credential-waving, intellectually-equilibrated husband, suggesting that significance often eludes its apparent form.

> Don't be too sure, though. You've forgotten something. Look at me. I . . . move my leg. That's all it is. But I wear . . . underwear . . . which moves with me . . . it . . . captures your attention. Perhaps you misinterpret. The action is simple. It's a leg . . . moving. My lips move. Why don't you restrict . . . your observations to that? Perhaps the fact that they move is more significant . . . than the words which come through them. You must bear that . . . possibility in mind.[21]

Even as she attacks conventional forms of meaning, though, Ruth merely substitutes alternative indices that, while subverting habitual modes of communication, rely still more exclusively on superficial signification. In Pinter's writing, as Ruth's speech suggests, articulation, motivation, justification, and designation fail to explain the truths of human action. Truth is sophisticated or disguised by the characters of *The Homecoming* in their contrived behavior, but it is revealed through a cognitive dissonance similar to the one which operates between our knowledge and our observations throughout *Accident*, and which abandons us, in both works, with two irreconcilable impressions of the same thing. The actions, apparently inexplicable and almost attributable to "accident," of Ruth and the other characters in this play derive from carefully plotted undercurrents that are detectable through patterns formed on the surface of the play.

The fascination and expertise Pinter brings to this parallax view of behavior suit him perfectly to the themes in *Accident*. Because his exclusion of narrative disparagement from the screenplay diminishes the role of inscrutability in the piece, Pinter reworks the characters and situations of the novel to produce a greater tension between implication and explication. This exacerbated tension, its resultant unanswered and unanswerable questions, states the narrator's dilemma through alternative means. Again, Pinter has exploited the reticence of the camera to instigate his perceptual agonies in us.

Since the vector of the past comprises a significant component of the inscrutable present, as the very structure of *Accident* implies, Pinter's emerging preoccupation with the past is a natural consequence of these earlier themes. Following his work on *Accident*, he wrote the stage plays *Landscape* and *Silence* (1968), adopting a view of the past that, in its subjectivity, ambiguity, and potency, is similar to the one in the screenplay. His growing interest in the ideas of the past, time, and memory, a thematic shift in his work which occurs most conspicuously with *Accident* and which, as we noted in the discussion of *The Pumpkin Eater*, seems to have been technically facilitated by his experience in film, is evident in all of his subsequent writing, original and adaptive, to date.

The Go-Between

To my mind's eye, my buried memories of Brandham Hall are like effects of chiaroscuro, patches of light and dark: it is only with an effort that I can see them in terms of colour. There are things I know, though I don't know how I know them, and things that I remember. Certain things are established in my mind as facts, but no picture attaches to them; on the other hand there are pictures unverified by any fact which recur obsessively, like the landscape of a dream.[1]

An old man's recollection of the summer that formed the turning point in his life comprises the principal narrative vehicle in *The Go-Between.* As the author of the novel, L. P. Hartley, develops the story, Leo Colston, the narrator, discovers his childhood diary for the year 1900 and endeavors to reconstruct his experience of that year through the information contained in the diary and through that which he retains in his mind. As the above quote suggests, the gaps and inconsistencies between these two sources of information describe a repeated (and metaphoric) tension in the work. Leo's memory has stored up the distorted impressions of a child: a chiaroscuro of horseshoe staircases, rustling silk skirts, and dilapidated outhouses. He laments now his lost image of the reputedly imposing southwest prospect of the Hall: "I laboriously transcribed into my diary a description of it that I found in a directory of Norfolk. . . . I can see the front of the house now, but through the eyes of the directory, not through my own" (pp. 32–33). The completion of this particular chink in Leo's memory occurs as the final statement, the final unity, of the novel when, as he revisits the place of his past, "the south-west prospect of the Hall, long hidden from my memory, sprang into view" (p. 311). We realize, however, that he confronts a spectacle incapable of surrendering the secrets of his past, the object of his pilgrimage. The fifty intervening years have altered both the image itself and his mechanism for comprehending it, allowing the activated gap between memory and "fact" to survive the story unchallenged.

The mind of a child, both in its evasions and exaggerations of social codes, provides the perfect vehicle for Hartley's concerns. The peculiarities of Leo's perceptions underline the interdependency of experience and bias; his experience of the summer, now so frustrating for him, exists in images screened through a paradoxical filter of childish self-involvement and schoolboy codes. What Leo's life has become, "all dried up inside," as Marian describes it, remains an incontestable product of this pivotal summer, but actual substance of the period is forever lost. Leo's present enterprise serves only to confirm this loss at every level. The uncensored egocentricity of childhood's viewpoint and experience deprives Leo of the comprehension he now craves. His journal and memory lack the materials for assembling a total, objective, "adult" reconstruction because they consist resolutely in the perversions of his childhood view. Repeatedly during the account of his tale, the older Leo discounts his recollections as the invalid misunderstandings of his youth, but he can spell out no other version than the one which they prescribe.

The perceptual handicaps of Leo's childhood describe a metaphoric condition for all humankind. His experience, and his memories of it, depend not only on the egocentric notions of youth, but also on the simple functioning and storage capacity of his mind. The final episodes of the story are absent from the novel because the shock of its climactic event has deprived the narrator of these memories.

Hartley accentuates the gaps in his story and allows the shortcomings of his narrator to determine its scope and nature. One of the chief corollaries to emerge from this process consists in the locking and unlocking properties of codes. From the opening words of the work, in which the old Leo struggles to recall the lock combination of his diary, codes persist on all levels of the story. Leo's ruminations, as he fingers the ancient lock on the diary, establish three of the major themes of Hartley's work: in the first place, the diary's contents lie inaccessible without possession of its lock code; in the second, Leo can simulate spiritual divination of the code while actually cracking it by superficial techniques; and in the third, the lock's combination actually consists in the simultaneously meaningless and profound letters of his own name. Each of these circumstances operates to characterize the past as both essentially alien from and obscurely implicit in the present milieu.

The past is contained in codes on every plane of its existence. Once

Leo has satisfied the combination that produces a text of the past, he yet confronts the tasks of deciphering the schoolboy articulations of this text: "The last few entries are in code. . . . There are still two or three sentences that don't give up their secret. . . ." (p. 31) and of entering the alien experiential conventions it contains: "It is like knowing the figures in a sum without being able to add them up. At least, if I added them up, they wouldn't make a game of cricket as I used to know it" (p. 138). The permeation of the novel with references to schoolboy codes, honor codes, nonsense codes, game codes, lock codes, and incomprehensible messages echoes Leo's dilemma; he encounters the signs of his past, but nowhere discovers its substance, which exists in an investment of the codes that he can neither recover nor honestly reissue. As Sartre has suggested, all experience becomes alien and incomprehensible to those who do not share its conventions; knowledge and acceptance of the code are prerequisite to genuine participation.[2] When Leo attempts to review his past without complete knowledge of and belief in its codes, he can forge only a "series," rather than a "group," of actions and events; connections wax inscrutable, sequence becomes random. Absent codes hold the keys to understanding, and the codes of the past cannot be retrieved. We can guess at them, analyze them, and perhaps even decipher them, but we can never again invest them with our innocent belief. All experience occurs in codes, and simultaneously cancels them out.

Codes maintained with conviction retain the power to transform reality. Leo's childhood subscription to the zodiac and to the power of black magic symbolizes this phenomenon. He writes of his youthful belief in hierarchies and circles, of how in the past things possessed the properties of order and renewal; but we see clearly that his withdrawal of faith, rather than any alteration in the nature of things, has produced the change. Indeed, the significance of his summer of 1900 lies in its reversal of the code / reality paradigm, marking a new effort in Leo to translate reality into codes. As R. E. Pritchard has noted, "Leo composes fictions; and Hartley's fiction in turn parades its fictional devices and echoes, so that this almost seems the real subject: the fictionalisation of experience into art."[3]

Oppositions between planes of expression and planes of content are manifold in Hartley's novel, revealing Leo's fateful tendency to project experience into artifice. He develops an incessant reliance on the thermometer as an index of heat, he accepts fashion as a signal of his character, he acknowledges the letter of the law rather than its spirit, he invokes the contours of fact over the content of intention, and he forsakes Ted's earthy world for the emblematic world of Lord Trimingham.

Even his daily journal entries are consciously manipulated to reflect the grandiose pretensions of the art of writing, the turn of the century, and the decor of the diary. His worst mistake, however, consists in his attempt to exchange the figures of the zodiac for the figures of Brandham Hall: his effort to endow them with the deified perfection of mythical symbols leads inevitably to final disillusionment.

Young Leo's attempt to affix the static ideals of form and order to the fluid realities of life deprives him at once of his conviction and harmony in both realms of experience. His matured preference for emblem over content empties his living, and his misdirected assignment of content to emblem enervates his believing. Old Leo accuses his younger persona: "You flew too near to the sun, and you were scorched. This cindery creature is what you made me" (pp. 17-18). The figurative, like Icarus, cannot be issued with impunity into the milieu of the literal; the vicissitudes of life will not conform to art.

Thus Leo retains his ability to replicate experience, to invoke the past, by simulating its codes; he can trace the facts and images of the past with verisimilitude, but he can no longer provide these with understanding. The schism between the fixed and the fluid, between the past and the present, although irreducible, remains active. From Leo's recollection that the diary's lock combination consists in the letters of his name to his conviction that his past has determined what he has become, we see that the inscrutable retains potency. The past contains the key to us, but we possess no key to it. It has made us what we are: so altered that we become incapable of determining its effect on us or its nature, incapable of understanding ourselves in it.

As a "go-between," Leo has become permanently trapped in the no-man's-land between these various oppositions. He runs messages with no understanding of their origins, destinations, or contents. In his present enterprise, he performs as a liaison between the past and the present, and between the diary and its referent. In the diary's reality, he mediates between artifice and instinct, between the spiritual world and the real world, between childhood and adulthood, between the upper class and the lower class, and between the nineteenth century and the twentieth. For Pinter's purposes the themes of Leo's enterprise come tailor-made.

The first words of Hartley's novel become the first words of Pinter's screenplay: "The past is a foreign country. They do things differently there" (p. 3). This statement captures the essence of the past as Pinter habitually regards it: the past *is* rather than *was* ("do" not "did"), and it involves *others* and never *ourselves* ("they" not "we"). Alive, but not real, the past exists as a property of the imagination, as a fictive rather than a factual phenomenon. Its inhabitants are strangers, and it bears no continuity with the present time or present self, existing as a product and origin of these, but neither part of nor apart from them.

By leading with this quote, Pinter signals his special interest in the relationship between the two disparate time periods that the novel treats. Pinter underlines this relationship immediately and throughout the script by utilizing the final episode of the novel, Leo's return to Brandham Hall, as the inciting incident of the screenplay. Hartley restricts present time developments to an opening and concluding frame for the novel, but Pinter intersperses present time sequences throughout the film, often overlapping time periods by separating sound and picture into independent eras. By moving the two periods forward in tandem, Pinter establishes their mutual exclusion and paradoxical interdependence with an economy impossible in the novel form, and he maneuvers the entire issue of time (replete with an emphasis on clocks and appointments, similar to this motif in *The Servant* and *Accident*) into a more conspicuous role in the story.

The opening sequence in Pinter's script provides an immediate example of simultaneity through audiovisual divorce. While the screen imagery depicts the English countryside of 1900, complete with pony carriage and antique horse-drawn farm machinery, the sound track amplifies the voice of elderly Leo making the statement from the novel cited above. As with his initial shots in *Accident*, Pinter focuses the imperviousness of humanity's environs to its passage, here keeping the camera still, monitoring the detail of the countryside, as Leo's carriage *"glimpsed only fragmentarily through the leaves . . . passes."*[4] Because of the double time scheme, however, Pinter materializes in this film a sentiment that has already occurred in *The Pumpkin Eater* and *Accident*, and that will recur emphatically in *The French Lieutenant's Woman*: that the efforts of humankind are steadily eroding the face of the earth, converting nature into a technocratic wasteland.

Pinter's second shot juxtaposes the previous flash of Leo's passage through the countryside with the countryside's fleeting passage through Leo's field of vision. From the viewpoint of the carriage, we catch a glimpse of Brandham Hall, as the carriage loses it in a descent downhill. These two initial shots together make a subtle and masterful statement of the work's central idea: that a kind of permanence and significance exists in things that human circumstance constrains us from ascertaining. This particular style of juxtaposition, the still view of an interior or exterior that precedes and succeeds the appearance of figures contrasted with a fluid view that trails the figures at the obtrusive expense of delineating their environs, recurs as characteristic technique in all of Pinter's screenplays. We have already noted the existence of a similar piece of camera work in *Accident*, during Stephen's walk with Anna. In that instance the image of empty landscape seems to have originated with Losey, but the device appears often in Pinter's scripts, as well. Its chief impact consists in an estrangement of human characters from their natural and manufactured surroundings and in a questioning of the consequences of viewpoint.

Pinter next sets about to draw a rapid contrast between the world of the children and that of the adults. In a sequence of brief shots that alternate the ennui of croquet and hammocks with the staircases and dog-greetings of Leo's arrival, Pinter establishes the groundwork of his situation. The thumbnail images introduce Leo's status as first-time guest at the house, his excitement at the prospect of such apparently unaccustomed grandness, his schoolboy relationship of mock rivalry with Marcus, and his adventurous, energetic, unrefined taste. Concurrently, Pinter develops an impression of the house, with its endless rooms and servants, and of its inhabitants, in their white-clad elegance and interminable leisure.

The recurring focus of this second group of camera angles consists in a female figure, not yet identifiable, who swings gently in a faded crimson canvas hammock, and who we later discover is Marcus's sister, Marian. Pinter invents this initial picture of Marian to represent with characteristic economy certain elaborations of her personality which the novel provides, but which he otherwise trims from his version. Her ensconcement in the red hammock at once establishes Marian's apartness from the others, her aloofness and indifference to their doings. Hartley makes Marian's distractedness, her absentminded self-centeredness, pronounced in her dealings with Leo, but Pinter paints her insular concerns in subtler strokes. As we have noted in *Accident*, Pinter tends to play off vividly developed situational demands against the veiled activities of his characters; what we witness perpetually belies what we know, and we are abandoned with two irreconcilable versions of truth. Pinter refuses to bend Marian's behavior toward what we can guess must be fact (although Hartley does so at length), allowing situations to enforce a mysterious incongruity.

While Hartley's Leo jealously guards his private discovery of the belladonna shrub in the outhouse, Pinter includes Marcus in this scene to excuse some dialogue necessary for clarification of the incident and its significance. Although Leo does not immediately recognize the plant, once Marcus has identified it as "deadly nightshade" Leo clearly has the botanical edge on him. "Atropa belladonna. It's poisonous. Every part of it is poison," Leo informs him (p. 290). For Pinter the extraordinary shrub remains primarily a visual metaphor for the sexual indulgence with which he later associates it, but Hartley articulates the parallel elaborately. In the novel Leo's initial response to the belladonna formulates a detailed prediction of his upcoming dilemma.

> It looked the picture of evil and also the picture of health, it was so glossy and strong and juicy-looking: I could almost see the sap rising to nourish it. It seemed to have found the place in all the world that suited it best.
>
> I knew that every part of it was poisonous, I knew too that it was beautiful, for did not my mother's botany book say so? I stood on the threshold, not daring to go in, staring at the button-bright berries and the dull, purplish, hairy, bell-shaped flowers reaching out towards me. I felt that the plant could poison me even if I didn't touch it, and that if I didn't eat it, it would eat me, it looked so hungry, in spite of all the nourishment it was getting.
>
> As if I had been caught looking at something I wasn't meant to see, I tiptoed away, wondering whether Mrs. Maudsley would think me interfering if I told her about it. But I didn't tell her. I couldn't bear to think of those lusty limbs withering on a rubbish heap or crackling in a fire: all that beauty being destroyed. Besides, I wanted to look at it again. [P. 38]

Leo's role in the Marian-Ted sexual affair and the impact of this affair on his life correspond precisely to this botanical forecast. Much of the 311-page novel consists in this kind of literary explication, which Pinter has deleted as unsuitable to the cinematic medium. Camera angles, visual images, and truncated dialogue chronicle the hyperbolic impact, proliferation, and deterioration of the plant, opaquely preempting Hartley's articulated elucidations. Here, the boys' horseplay becomes subjugated to the plant's preeminence: "MARCUS *runs through the outhouses*, LEO *following. The camera watches them with the bell-shaped flowers of the shrub in the foreground*" (p. 290). As Neil Sinyard argues, in his article on *The Go-Between*, the belladonna shrub, together with Leo's drying bathing suit, become principal emblems of the enticement-taboo rhythm of the text.[5]

Pinter does make occasional concessions to the film audience's taste for explicated clarity: despite Leo's conspicuous awe of his host's surroundings, a scene between Marcus and his mother, Mrs. Maudsley, original to the screenplay, reiterates his humble origins, confirming our observations even in its token retraction of verification.

MRS. MAUDSLEY. Didn't you say his mother is a widow, Marcus?

MARCUS. I think so. I don't really know very much about him.

MRS. MAUDSLEY. Seems to be a nice lad.

MARCUS. I do have an impression that he lives in rather a small house with his mother.

MRS. MAUDSLEY. Yes. He seems to be a very nice boy. [P. 291]

The point of this brief exchange, however, exceeds its informational face-value; Pinter is still laying the groundwork of his situation. Mar-

cus's practice of clandestine gossip sessions with his mother provides a
crucial link in the plot development and, although Hartley treats Leo's
suspicion of these in ruminant fashion, Pinter indicates their existence
by this vignette. Typically, Pinter adds a further dimension to this
exchange by focusing the camera not on Mrs. Maudsley and Marcus,
but on Leo, who eavesdrops anxiously at the door.

At dinner we learn of Leo's penchant for witchcraft through a playful
bit of dialogue that Pinter partly reproduces and partly interpolates from
the novel.

> MARCUS. His curses are fearful. He cast a fiendish spell on two boys at school.
> They fell off the roof and were severely mutilated.
> DENYS. Did they die?
> LEO. Oh no. They were just a little . . . you know . . . severely mutilated. [P. 292]

Leo answers their curiosity about this with a statement that later is
rebroadcast over the image of old Leo standing in the distance, looking
down a deserted present-time village street: "Well, it wasn't a killing
curse, you see. There are curses and curses. It depends on the curse."
Although Leo denies any intentions of practicing spells at Brandham,
Pinter alerts us to an ominous development of events.

Hartley's Leo dwells at length on the extraordinary heat of the summer and on the enigmatic taciturnity of Mr. Maudsley. Pinter summons
up both of these qualities in his next scene, which occurs by a thermometer on the wall of a disused game larder. (I note here that Pinter
has changed the time of the action from July to August, probably to
invoke the natural termination of the season.)

> MR. MAUDSLEY. Hello. Enjoying yourself?
> LEO. Yes sir.
> MR. MAUDSLEY. Good. Pretty warm. What does it say?
> LEO. Eighty-three.
> MR. MAUDSLEY. Warm.
> MR. MAUDSLEY *studies* LEO'S *clothes.*
>> Suit a little warm, is it?
> LEO. No sir.
> MR. MAUDSLEY *taps the thermometer.*
> MR. MAUDSLEY. Enjoying yourself?
> LEO. Yes thank you, sir.
> MR. MAUDSLEY. Good. [Pp. 292-93]

As she does in the novel, Marian moves quickly to Leo's rescue,
seeming initially to divine Leo's concealed embarrassment over his
apparel, but appearing in retrospect to have acted out of her own self-

interest. Marian spares Leo the agony of writing his mother to request nonexistent summer clothes by volunteering to purchase him a new outfit for his upcoming birthday. Coolly, she fences her mother's protestations and wins the opportunity to escort Leo to Norwich without the accompaniment of a Hugh Trimingham, who will arrive on Saturday. In scenes that follow, we observe that Marian meets an obscure male figure while shopping with Leo, and that she stands to make a profitable marriage with this Hugh Trimingham.

Leo's infatuation with Marian is underway, and it proceeds under a prediction of doom. As Marian and Leo trot into the distance on board the pony carriage, old Leo's voice murmurs on the sound track: "You flew too near the sun and you were scorched" (p. 295). The sequence of shots marking their shopping adventure includes the earlier noted present-time image, under the repeated explanation of the curse. Pinter notes in this direction that *"The sky is constantly overcast in all present-day shots"* (p. 296). Later, as the others admire his new clothes, Leo increases his complicity with Marian by concealing her hour-long abandonment of him to the Cathedral, after expressing a desire to do some shopping for herself.

> MRS. MAUDSLEY. You've chosen very well, Marian. Did you do any shopping for yourself?
>
> MARIAN. Oh no, Mama. That can wait.
>
> MRS. MAUDSLEY. It mustn't wait too long. You didn't see anyone in Norwich, I suppose?
>
> MARIAN. Not a soul. We were hard at it all the time, weren't we Leo?
>
> *Pause.*
>
> LEO. Yes, we were. [P. 298]

In the novel Leo stresses the rapidity of his avowal, here. Pinter, however, employs a pause to convey Leo's bewildered computation of the situation, his digestion of the two lies, and to signal the importance of the three lies, now including Leo's, to the audience. The pause usurps the function of several paragraphs that the novel devotes to deliberation of this conspiratorial leap.

Following the novel Pinter uses the bathing episode to introduce Ted Burgess and to further Leo's infatuation with Marian. The scene initiates via the audial portion exclusively, while the camera records the older Leo's arrival at the present-day train station. Over this image we hear that Leo will accompany the other bathers to the river despite his prohibition from swimming. The conjunction of these two ideas, audial and visual, accentuates the tension between taboo and temptation as a key to past mysteries and their impact on the present. As in *Accident* this patterning of time also implies the presidence of older Leo's memory over the tale through its suggestion of retrospective association, an artifice Pinter will explore further in *The Proust Screenplay*.

When the past regains the screen, we hear the unintelligible chatter of approaching voices, as we observe the emergence and dive of an unidentified male in "tight woolen trunks." The members of the bathing party decide against ordering the "cheeky trespasser" off their land when they recognize him as the neighboring tenant farmer, Ted Burgess. One of the women admires his build, but Marian discreetly avoids any observation, spoken or otherwise, of Ted. Pinter signals our attention to Ted, however, in accordance with the novel, by marking Leo's observation of Ted's sunning and by focusing upon Ted's hurried departure at the sound of Marian's voice. Later in the scene, Leo again comes forward to rescue Marian from disaster; he offers his dry bathing trunks to protect her dress from the dripping of her fallen hair.

The following morning brings two developments, both directly from the novel: the scarfaced Trimingham has arrived and become the center of attention, and Marcus has been stricken with measles, causing Leo's relocation to a private room. Returning from church, Trimingham strikes up a conversation with Leo, revealing himself to be a Viscount, and packing Leo off on an errand to Marian. Leo conveys Trimingham's message that Marian has left behind her prayer book, but Marian's response to the news is cool: "How careless. I forget everything. Please thank him for me" (p. 307). Pinter omits Trimingham's reaction to this message, however, which, in the novel, certifies the snub her words carry. Throughout the screenplay Marian's treatment of Trimingham proceeds much more guardedly than in Hartley's version, where she openly spurns and resents her aristocratic fiance. Pinter, again, relies on our perception of the situation to penetrate the facade of her behavior and never spells out Marian's feelings about Trimingham. Her dilemma communicates perfectly. And, as Sinyard has observed, her preference for Ted Burgess makes this Pinter's third screenplay that treats taboo relationships: ". . . between master and servant (in *The Servant*); between teacher and student (in *Accident*); and between aristocratic lady and farmer (in *The Go-Between*)."[6] Nazi-hunter Quiller, who enjoys an affair with a Nazi, may also quality for this category. In each of these cases, as in the case of Marian and Ted, the intrinsic appeal of the forbidden operates as a subtextual, presumable force on the otherwise often inscrutable actions of the characters.

Once Leo has obtained the safety of his own room, he unpacks his witchcraft paraphernalia, but leaves it to explore the countryside on his own. Eventually he discovers a strawstack in a strange farmyard and, sliding down it, injures his knee on a chopping block. Ted Burgess appears and, after recognizing Leo as a guest at Brandham Hall, invites him inside to dress the wound. When Ted has satisfied himself with Leo's trustworthiness, he presents Leo with a message for Marian, which he explains must be delivered or destroyed in absolute secrecy. Leo's career as a go-between begins as a matter of personal pride in his reliability as a confidant, and in his special favor with Marian.

Having thrust Ted's note up the sleeve of her dress, Marian showers her attention on Leo, absently endeavoring to bandage the wound she has already bandaged (salvaging Ted's handkerchief in the process), and enjoining Leo to secrecy. Pinter draws their words through a double twist of referents.

> MARIAN. You won't . . . tell anyone about this letter will you? You won't . . . will you?
> LEO. Of course I won't.
> MARIAN'S *hand smooths the stocking and touches the bandage. Close-up of* MARIAN *doing this.*
> MARIAN (*Softly*). There.
>
> *Exterior. Outhouses. The deadly nightshade. The camera is still, looking at it. It glistens.*
> VOICES HEARD OVER:
> COLSTON'S VOICE (*Older Leo*)
>   Of course I won't.
> MARIAN'S VOICE YOUNG (*softly*)
>   There. [Pp. 312-13]

By invoking the visual image of the belladonna and the aural impression of the future (present), Pinter explodes the dimensions of this exchange. The shrub's image expresses all of Leo's dread, ecstasy, and confusion, and it links the affair between Marian and Ted with the belladonna. Beyond this, the superimposed image implies Leo's association of sexuality with the nature of the vegetation, an idea that Hartley labors over throughout the novel.

The voice-overs of old Leo and young Marian similarly serve multiple purposes. That Leo repeats his vow from memory fifty years in the future underlines its significance to him, both at the time of its initial utterance and in the last years of his life. The youthful voice of Marian's reply suggests his fixation of her in his mind as she was then, his inability to project the figures of his past into any kind of future beyond his experience with them. Marian, for him, has become an inalterable figment of the past, a fixture of "they" rather than a possibility of "we." Hartley's Leo elaborates this point in the novel. "As to these 'others' of Brandham Hall, somehow I could not think of them as going on after I had stopped. They were like figures in a picture, the frame enclosed them, the two-fold frame of time and place, and they could not step outside it, they were imprisoned in Brandham Hall and the summmer of 1900. There let them stay, fixed in their two dimensions: I did not want to free them" (p.296). Pinter has focused all of Leo's reflections on this theme, in this passage and elsewhere in the source work, into this multiple-edged moment.

The potential for humor in Leo's situation does not escape Pinter's keen eye for ironic fun. Generally he restricts his jokes to those designed or implied by Hartley, but Pinter's mark unmistakably dominates their executions. Although Pinter's Marian maintains her equilibrium under stress with much greater success than Hartley's counterpart, Pinter cannot resist milking the false-alarm panic that attends Trimingham's dubbing of Leo as "Mercury."

TRIMINGHAM. Hello, there's Mercury!

MARIAN. Why do you call him Mercury?

TRIMINGHAM. Because he takes messages.

Over the back of MARIAN'S *head, rigid, to* TRIMINGHAM *and* LEO. MARIAN *turns away.*

You took a message for me, didn't you old chap? To this young lady, on the way from church. But it didn't fetch a very warm response.

MARIAN *laughs.*

Three shot. Relaxed.

MARIAN *laughing.*

(*to* LEO.) Do you know who Mercury was?

LEO. Mercury is the smallest of the planets.

TRIMINGHAM. Ah, but before that he was the messenger of the gods. He went to and fro between them. [Pp. 313-14]

The final portion of this dialogue, between Trimingham and Leo, touches two matters of chief importance to this work: the form and substance of Leo's reply contrast poignantly with the spiritual aim of Trimingham's question, focusing an icy turn in the concerns of humanity, and the supernatural function Trimingham's words assign to Leo plays directly into his obsession with sorcery. Leo becomes simultaneously cemented to his liaison role and symbolic of the rising tide: a herald of facts, figures, and signs. (Again, Hartley provides much more extensive treatments of both these points throughout the novel.)

As a first-person narration, much of Hartley's novel is expended on Leo's unspoken thoughts and impressions. Pinter captures some of this internal activity by reflecting Leo's states of mind in vistas seen from his vantage point. Thus, at the picnic outing that follows Trimingham's alarming proclamation of Mercury, Leo's pleasure upon overhearing what he construes to be Marian's concern for him (actually a ploy in her scheme to exploit his services as a message carrier) is manifest in the following vision.

> LEO *sits up.*
> *From his viewpoint on the grass:*
> *The carriages drawn up in the shade. Horses whisking their tails. The coachmen high up on their boxes, hats almost touching the branches.* [P. 314]

During the ride from the picnic, Pinter communicates Leo's frustration over his failure to comprehend the answers to urgent questions about Ted Burgess in a slightly different fashion.

> LEO. Do you know Ted Burgess?
> BUFF. Ted Burgess? We all know him. He's a bit of a lad, Ted Burgess.
> LEO. What do you mean by a lad? I should have said he was a full grown man.
> *The carriage has reached the top of a steep hill.*
> BUFF. Hold on, hold on. Here we go!
> *The descent begins, the coachman grinding the brakes, the horses' hindquarters sweating.* LEO *clutches the rail and turns sharply to look behind him up the hill. His face into the camera.* [P. 315]

Here, the isolation of Leo's face from the circumstance that immediately inspires its expression suggests the broader sources of his anguish. Curiously, Leo's reaction to the downhill peril in the novel consists in exhilaration and delight, a dreamy orgy of smells. Pinter's amendment of this is conspicuous, and suggests his practice of harmonizing the invisible dynamics of mood with the screen image. Although Hartley can explain away Leo's abrupt transition from exasperation to ecstasy here, Pinter must buy the obvious. But he buys it with style.

A back-and-forth montage of Leo's messenger adventures comprises the next stretch of film script. The sequence commences with Trimingham's request that Leo retrieve Marian "dead or alive" to make a fourth at croquet. Although Leo wanders aimlessly and cheerlessly along the cinder path to the outhouses, apparently without any faith that he can succeed in his mission, Marian materializes unexpectedly coming up the path from the decaying buildings. Hartley makes Leo's initial dejection and surprise upon discovering Marian clear in the text, but Pinter relates Leo's mood by activity: "LEO *wandering along, looking vaguely about, picks up a stone, throws it. Suddenly stops*" (p. 317). In both versions Leo's instinct for locating Marian is nonetheless notable, and both Marians react anxiously to his presence along the path, coolly to his message (Hartley's more so than Pinter's in this regard), and finally by packing him off with a message for Ted Burgess.

In three swift scenes, containing altogether only three lines of dialogue, Leo trades messages between Ted and Marian. Ted phrases two replies, the first in the midst of reaping cornfields ("Tell her it's all right"), and the second with hands bloodied from rabbit-shooting ("Tell her it's no go"). We witness Marian's receipt only of the first message, as she pauses in a long corridor to look at a painting and then walks silently away. After the second message from Ted, Marcus's recovery interrupts the sequence. Hartley's Leo makes much of the welcome release from his go-between duties he assumes Marcus's presence will necessitate, for his boyhood dread of wrongdoing had begun to rob the adventure of its relish. Pinter communicates Leo's situational and psychological crises here by following his immediate action with the camera: he runs down the back stairs, walks quickly down a passage, enters Marian's writing room abruptly, and attempts to blurt out his news, "Marian, Marcus is—" (p. 319). But the sound of the door latch interrupts him, and Marian has just time to slip him a letter as Trimingham intrudes on them to lead Marian away.

Leo's enthusiasm for his work has ebbed, however, and his curiosity and impatience have ascended to replace it. His participation in the affair is rising to a crisis, and his discovery that this letter is unsealed proves an irresistible goad. Leo's decision to read the letter, and his reaction to its romantic contents, represent matters of strict schoolboy code observation to Hartley. In the novel Leo tests his justification for reading the note against all the intricacies of boarding school convention and ultimately rules his guiltlessness according to a number of criteria. His disgust upon learning its ignoble message likewise conforms to peer scorn for "spooning." These attitudes, explicit in the source work, communicate only through their outward signs in the screenplay. Leo's reluctance to open the letter locates in his several aborted impulses to do so as he crosses the fields to Ted's farm. His amazed distaste for its message clarifies in an elaborate direction.

> *Close-up of* LEO, *his mouth open.*
> LEO *sits down by a tree.*
> *His expression is one of utter disappointment and disbelief.*
> *He leans on his elbow. He grimaces.*
> *He emits a number of short noises, grunts, and "hahs", hollow laughs. He sits baffled. Looks at the words again.*
> *He sighs, stands, seals the letter. He walks on, uttering further short noises. The loudest of these alarm some birds. They fly up.* [P. 321]

Instances of facial expression description are rare in Pinter's work (he claims that such reactions must be clear from an understanding of the dialogue and that he is "unable to write very explicit stage directions in the old sense''[7]), but even these permit latitude in our interpretation of Leo's response here. Pinter resists the awkward device of a monologue, which could clarify the nature of Leo's facemaking: whether it belongs to queasiness over sex, jealousy of Ted, loyalty to Trimingham, or a sense of his own abusedness. The quality of Leo's response, however, strikes Pinter as more significant than its motive, which he discounts as cheating in the terms of his medium. Leo's preoccupation, in any case, will clarify in the following scene.

With Ted, Leo finally gets an opportunity to explain his predicament: Marcus's recuperated presence will prevent Leo from carrying any further messages. Ted, however, rejects Leo's assessment and appeals to him for the sake of Marian's emotional well-being. When this conversation deadlocks, Ted temporarily changes the subject, and Leo seizes its potential.

> TED (*To himself*). I've been busy. Smiler's going to have a foal. She's ill.
> LEO. Why does she have it then if it makes her ill?
> TED. She hasn't much choice.
> LEO. What made her have one? [P. 322]

A page of dialogue ensues, as Leo pursues and Ted evades this line of questioning. Finally, Ted strikes up a bargain with Leo; he will provide the answers to Leo's inquiries if Leo will continue to "go on being our postman."

One of the central incidents of the novel consists in a cricket game between the townspeople and the members of Brandham Hall. The episode opens with Leo's explanation to Marian that he will participate as twelfth man. In the novel she quickly forgets this information in her selfish distraction, and Leo has to repeat it to her, painfully. Pinter describes her imperviousness to Leo and to his entire situation in a different fashion. After Leo explains to her that he will play only as first reserve, Marian, who is arranging flowers by a window, replies, "Ah. Well maybe someone will drop dead and then you can play. (*She pricks her finger on a thorn.*) Blast!" (p. 327). Her punishment for this heedlessness is swift and serves also to focus attention on the crime. Similarly, though for different purposes, Pinter softens Marian's snub of Trimingham's request (delivered by Leo) that she sing at the concert following the game. In both versions Marian agrees to sing if Trimingham will do likewise. Trimingham's crestfallen "But I don't sing," which elicits pangs of understanding and a white lie from Leo in the novel, is here broadcast remotely over a present-day image of old Leo crossing a street towards an unidentified young man. The sting of Marian's game is all but lost, as Pinter redirects the moment in order to exploit its value as an adumbration of future betrayals.

The events of the cricket game elucidate several situations. As we have noted in preceding chapters, Pinter seizes upon the metaphoric potentials of gameplaying, and he scripts this portion of the story with faithful alacrity. Ted's formidability on the cricket field dominates the conversational prelude to the festivities. The screen pictures and dialogue snatches delineate the tensions inherent in the situation: the elegance of the Hall's team versus the savagery of the townfolk, the grace of Trimingham versus the primitivity of Ted, the reserved etiquette of the ladies versus the physical exertions of the game, the determination of the older players versus the restraint of the young, and the impressiveness of Ted's triumphs versus the impassiveness of Marian's reaction. The game's final irony occurs when Leo goes to the field to substitute for an injured player. In a moment of ambivalent glory (Leo has earlier needed to cover his spontaneous applause of a spectacular hit by Ted), Leo catches Ted out. As the teams return to the pavilion, Leo apologizes miserably to him.

> LEO. I didn't really mean to catch you out.
> TED. It was a damn good catch. (*He laughs. Then murmurs.*) I never thought I'd be caught out by our postman. [P. 330]

Leo brings Ted's ruin, the graceful elegance of the Hall defeats the primitive appeal of the townspeople, and the day's events project a picture of what will come.

The concert that follows the game occasions three major developments. In a sequence that Pinter alters from the novel, Marian volunteers as a pianist when the scheduled one defers to illness. Hartley's Marian offers her services before the proceedings have commenced, but Pinter initiates her action after Ted has already moved to the stage, preparing to sing. Thus, in the film, although no observable communication passes between them during the performance, Marian's offer refers directly to Ted's need, while in the novel its origins are not specified. Pinter exhausts the situation of all its potential for tension, recording Mrs. Maudsley's watchful presence, Ted's awkward agony, and several overlaid images of present-time desolation. Subsequently, Leo's innocent rendition of a virginal hymn inspires a similar sequence of shots. Marcus's news on the way home, however, packs the greatest force of the sequence. Pinter exploits the occasion to convey the natures of the Hall's elitism and of schoolboy camaraderie.

> MARCUS. Well, thank goodness we've said good-bye to the village for a year. Did you notice the stink in that hall?
> LEO. No.

MARCUS. What a whiff! I suppose you were too busy mooing and rolling your eyes and sucking up the applause. Still, toadstool, I must admit you didn't do too badly.

LEO. Oh thank you.

MARCUS. Except that it was rather horrific to see your slimy serpent's tongue stuck to the roof of your mouth and your face like a sick cow.

LEO *seizes him.*

LEO. You pot-faced pot-bellied bed wetter!

MARCUS. Pax! I'll tell you a secret.

LEO. What?

MARCUS. Marian's engaged to marry Trimingham. It'll be announced after the ball. Are you glad?

LEO *lets him go.*

LEO. Yes, I am. I'm sure I am. [P. 334]

What we note here as Leo's hesitant ambivalence, due apparently to his mood of personal triumph, his anxiety over the secret letters, and his now clear fondness for Ted, Hartley explicates in detail along with a description of Leo's repeated relief upon expecting a cessation of the mysterious letters. Pinter holds the substance of Leo's thoughts for later clarification, monitoring Leo's observation of Marian and Trimingham together at croquet and his temporary abandonment by Marcus, until a scene along the cinder path brings Marian and Leo together alone. Here Leo's feelings surface irrepressibly when Marian presents him with a letter intended for Ted.

LEO. But I can't.

MARIAN. Can't? Why not?

Pause.

LEO. Because of Hugh.

MARIAN. Hugh? What has Hugh to do with it?

LEO. He . . . might be upset. [Pp. 335-36]

At this, Marian turns abruptly against Leo, abusing him viciously as a stupid, ungrateful wretch, and finally makes to pay him for his labors. Leo runs off with the letter, sobbing, as the screen image follows his journey to Ted's farm, "*a tiny figure in the landscape, walking, kicking a stone,*" and the sound track broadcasts the first substantial present-time dialogue, as if to explicate further the painful significance of this action to the older Leo.

MARIAN'S VOICE OLD (OVER)
So you met my grandson?
COLSTON'S VOICE (OVER)

Yes. I did.
MARIAN'S VOICE OLD (OVER)
Does he remind you of anyone?
COLSTON'S VOICE (OVER)
Of course. His grandfather.
MARIAN'S VOICE OLD (OVER)
That's it, that's it. He does. Yes, he does. [Pp. 336-37]

Although this bit of dialogue occurs again, intact, later in the film, it never reveals the intended identity of this "grandfather." Except for the conspicuous resemblance of the grandson to Ted, as the roles were cast in the film, we could construe their words to imply either Trimingham or Ted, as, conceivably, could either of the speakers.

When Leo arrives at Ted's, Pinter creates an image which appears almost casually in the novel, but which deals a shock on the screen.

> TED *is sitting alone holding a gun between his knees. His chest is naked. The barrel is pressed against it. The muzzle just below his mouth. He is peering down the barrel.*
> *The shot holds.*
> *Sound of a knock and a door opening.* [P. 337]

Leo's mind in Hartley's work is already racing with fears of a duel over Marian by the two men. His now reinforced association of Ted with firearms exacerbates his dread. (Trimingham, already scarred badly from war, bears a characteristic identification with military achievement.) Pinter's Leo will voice his fears in an upcoming scene, but for now the image contributes to our earthy and potent impression of Ted, and to our rising certainty of imminent disaster. The shot is a clear harbinger of the future's direction.

Ted attempts to placate the tear-stained Leo by offering him a shot at some rooks with the gun. Although Leo declines, he goes to watch Ted, who handily shoots down one of the birds. Leo is obsessed with one question; he presses Ted insistently for the facts of "spooning." Again, Ted eludes the questions, but both build to a peak of urgency that climaxes in Ted ordering Leo off the farm. The confrontation serves to provide Leo with even more questions than before, and he runs from the premises enriched by only one bit of hard information.

> TED. You'd like some tea, wouldn't you? I'm on my own to-day. My daily woman doesn't come on Sundays.
> LEO. Oh, do you have a woman every day?
> TED *looks at him.*
> TED. No. I told you she doesn't come on Sundays. [P. 338]

Although the basis for this exchange derives from the novel, Pinter develops a nasty payoff for it later in the script, when Leo corners Trimingham in the smoking-room. Frustrated by Ted's evasions, Leo attempts to pump the opposition for information, describing the hypothetical duel as a starting point for the interrogation. Mr. Maudsley's entrance interrupts their talk, however, before Trimingham has managed anything beyond confusing Leo with still more unfamiliar terminology. From Trimingham's conversation with Mr. Maudsley, Leo learns of the plan to hustle Ted off to the army, and, in the course of this dialogue concerning Ted, Pinter lands his punch.

MR. MAUDSLEY. They say he's got a woman up this way.

LEO. I know.

Close-up of MR MAUDSLEY.

MR MAUDSLEY, *in the act of pouring sherry, stops and looks over his shoulder at* LEO.

TRIMINGHAM *and* MR MAUDSLEY *looking at* LEO.

Close-up of LEO.

But she doesn't come on Sundays. [P. 347]

While he bides his time awaiting his mother's response to his freshly penned request to come home, Leo accompanies Marcus to check on the deadly nightshade's progress. As they walk Marcus mentions that his mother is ill in bed, but he does not know the nature of her malady. This bit of news derives from the novel, where Mrs. Maudsley's attacks of hysteria are well known to Marcus, who conveys the information to Leo, here. Pinter accomplishes almost the same purpose by keeping Marcus ignorant of the cause of his mother's disappearance, since illnesses kept from children usually imply something along this line. For both authors the grotesqueness of Mrs. Maudsley's hysteria will become crucial in the final scenes of the story.

Marcus also confides that Marian will leave for London tomorrow in order to shop for the ball and to purchase Leo a green bicycle for his birthday. He contributes that the bicycle will be green because Marian feels this to be Leo's true color. (Presumably, however, Marian takes more interest in the vehicle than in its color, since the bicycle will expedite Leo's missions as liaison.) Enraged by this teasing, Leo is goaded into almost betraying her confidence, and here Marcus's hotline to his mother becomes operative.

LEO (*violently*). Do you know where Marian is at this moment?

Two shot.

MARCUS *stops still.*

MARCUS. No. Do you?

LEO. Yes.
MARCUS. Where?
LEO. I don't tell little boys.
LEO *dances round* MARCUS.
    Little boy, little boy, wouldn't you like to know? [P. 343]

Their arrival at the deadly nightshade, however, interrupts Marcus's attempt to pry his sister's whereabouts from Leo. Pinter notes that "*It has grown out of its door, and spread. It emerges over the roofless wall. It is heavy, purple, oppressive.*" As the boys regard the transformed shrub, they suddenly hear the murmurs of first a man's and then a woman's voice. Marcus concludes that a couple must be spooning, suggests they "rout them out," and then announces his intentions to tell his mother. Leo successfully advises him against the first plan ("It will be too boring!"), but his success against the second seems unlikely.

In the two days remaining before his ill-fated birthday party, Leo wins apologies for their unseemly behavior from both Ted and Marian. He declines Ted's offer to explain about spooning, and volunteers, after learning of Ted's misery over Marian's engagement and his probable departure for the war, to take one more message. Hartley's Leo deliberately confuses this message when he delivers it to Marian in order to clear himself of any implication in what he suspects is wrongdoing. In the screenplay Leo repeats the message correctly, through the tears of his sudden understanding that Marian cannot possibly marry Ted and hence resolve her predicament, voicing concern only that she return in time for his cake-cutting party. She assures him that she will.

His strain compounded by the receipt of his mother's letter, denying his petition to return home, Leo ventures out at midnight to uproot some belladonna which he takes to his room. Chanting, crushing, mixing, and gesturing, Leo performs a rite of exorcism at his writing table, and then pours the mashed potion into the lavatory. Throughout this process Pinter refers variously by sound track and picture into the present time, recording old Leo's simultaneous memories and new adventures. As the story approaches its climactic scene, Pinter forges a rhythmic build from accelerated alternation between the two time periods, the present-time inter-cuts becoming more and more frequent.

Pinter increases the suspense by yet another episode, drawn as the others from the novel, but meticulously contrived to maximize the tension. The novel's faults of sogginess and overwriting vanish when subjected to the simplifying demands of Pinter and the cinema. As Sinyard has suggested, Pinter's revisions act almost as a critique of the novel, which he transforms from a love story into a mystery, relocating the tension between the present and the past, and rebuilding the plot to emphasize its suspense.[8] As a part of this program, Pinter sees clearly the value of Hartley's scene that runs Leo afoul of Mrs. Maudsley: the two must be armed and primed for battle; they must become aware of each other's advantage and strength.

The preclimax scrimmage between Leo and Mrs. Maudsley erupts when she spots him tussling with Marian in the garden. Marian skillfully covers the nature of their altercation, but Leo blunders and drops the letter, which he was resisting, onto the ground.

> LEO *looks sharply into camera.*
> MARIAN *remains composed.*
> *Close-up of* MRS MAUDSLEY.
> MRS. MAUDSLEY. Was that the bone of contention?
> *Three shot.*
> MARIAN *picks up the letter and puts it into* LEO'S *pocket.*
> MARIAN. Yes it was, Mama. I wanted him to take this note to Nanny Robson to tell her that I will go and see her some time this afternoon. And would you believe it, Leo didn't want to! He pretended he had something on with Marcus.
> LEO *looks at her.*
> Yes you did!
> MRS. MAUDSLEY. I shouldn't let it worry you, Marian. You say she often doesn't remember whether you've been or not. She is certainly growing old, poor Nanny Robson. I think it's about time Leo and I took a walk in the garden. (*She takes* LEO'S *hand.*) Come along Leo. I don't believe you've seen the garden properly, have you? (*She turns to* MARIAN.) You can spare Leo now, can't you Marian? [Pp. 355-56]

Mrs. Maudsley drags Leo into the garden and readily traps him in the lie. Discovering coyly that he does not know the way to Nanny Robson's, although he claims to have taken Marian's messages before, Mrs. Maudsley summons a gardener to deliver Leo's letter for him. In a panic Leo states he has lost the letter, but Mrs. Maudsley seems satisfied to have made her point and does not press him to produce the paper, although she clearly knows he has it.

> MRS. MAUDSLEY. I could ask you to turn your pockets out. But I won't do that. I'll just ask you one question. You say you have taken messages for Marian before?
> LEO. Well I—
> MRS. MAUDSLEY. I think you said so. If you don't take them to Nanny Robson—
>
> *Exterior. Village street. No cars. Day.*
> TIME NEUTRAL
> *Exterior. House. Garden. Long shot.*

> MRS MAUDSLEY *and* LEO *standing.*
> *Interior. House. Lavatory.*
> LEO *sitting on lavatory lid.*
> MRS MAUDSLEY'S VOICE (OVER)—to whom do you take them? [P. 358]

The temporal permutations of the screenplay are becoming marked. Several swift vacillations between past and present immediately follow this scene, culminating in the image of Leo in the lavatory as we hear a repetition of the "grandson-grandfather" dialogue between old Leo and old Marian. At this point (or perhaps before, if we are ingeniously observant), we become aware that the present-time scenes have been occurring in loops and jumbled order. Old Leo has been admitted by Marian's maid, visited with Marian, and appeared on the street in segments devoid of linear order. The repetition of this dialogue alerts us to the present-time warp, which in turn suggests the film's prevailing statement on the nature of time. Pinter develops this notion of time from the attitudes of the novel, but the time-matrix mechanism and its unique implications remain his own invention. Time for Pinter becomes indeed a fourth dimension, so that even present time is already acquiring dislocated characteristics of remembered time. Nothing happens once, but many times simultaneously and infinitely, perhaps altering or perhaps defying change, but never yielding its totality or its secret, always glimpsed through artifice and corrupted senses.

At the conclusion of the second "grandson-grandfather" dialogue, a new stretch of present-time conversation occurs in which, as Pinter notes, "*we see the faces of Colston and Marian old for the first time.*" Old Marian is pleading with old Leo to relate the story of the summer of 1900, the story we are witnessing, to her grandson.

> They tell me he wants to marry a girl—a nice girl—but he won't ask her . . . he feels . . . I think he feels . . . that he's under some sort of spell or curse, you see. That's just plain silly. Now this is where you come in. . . . You know the facts, you know what really happened. Tell him, tell him everything, just as it was. Every man should get married. You're all dried up inside, I can tell that. Don't you feel any need of love? Speak to him, tell him there's no spell or curse except an unloving heart. [Pp. 359-60]

Apart from Leo's endemic inability to discover the facts of his situation or of the affair between Marian and Ted, whatever insight or experience he could claim for the summer would hardly resemble Marian's golden memories. Pinter's particular placement of this present-time scene seems calculated to expose this discrepancy in views; and, as if to underline the agony of Leo's current straits at this moment in the past story, Pinter broadcasts old Marian's final line of this present-time dialogue ("Tell him that") over the image of Mrs. Maudsley descending the stairs as thunder sounds, ominously. Leo, "all dried up inside," and the environment, overcast and bankrupt, and the grandson, cursed and immobilized, represent the "facts" of the summer. Just as old Marian yet claims the fact of her title—"I was Lady Trimingham, you see. I still am. There is no other" (p. 366)—the facts are clear; there are no others. The disparities and obscurities endure without solution. Losey, who directed this film also, hints at this condition in a statement printed in a review of the film. "Perhaps the film is different from anything I've done in its period look, what some people may call 'romantic.' But I think there's a bitter core there for those who can taste worm."[9]

The bitter taste of worm worsens when we consider the pathetic quality of Marian's old-age prattle. An enigmatic figure in her youth, Marian becomes ridiculous when we learn the level of her perceptions. Whether the shallow selfishness of her garrulous old age derives from her present deterioration or her past mysteriousness, from aging distortions or youthful masks, its effect on Leo and on the audience remains equally dismaying. The insensitive self-aggrandizement of her present-time words suggests that Marian is nothing, really, but a bored and banal over-invested symbol for a twelve-year-old boy. Pinter secures this point most conspicuously during the scene that follows Leo's return from Ted's earlier outburst.

> *Interior. House. Tea. The silver teapot. The camera withdraws to find* MARIAN *presiding over tea.* TRIMINGHAM *sits beside* MARIAN, *on a low stool, half in shadow. She regards her guests with a smile, pouring milk in one cup, a slice of lemon in another and lumps of sugar into some. The cups and plates of cake are passed around. When it is* LEO'S *turn for tea* MARIAN *drops four lumps of sugar into his cup, giggling. This shot is silent. Over the shot we hear* MARIAN'S *voice as an old lady.*
>
> MARIAN'S VOICE (OLD)
> I rarely went to parties. People came to see me, of course, interesting people, artists and writers, not stuffy country neighbours. There *are* stuffy people, aren't there? No, no, interesting people came to see me. Artists and writers. Modern people with modern views. [Pp. 340-41]

The voice-over here painfully contrasts the enigmatic elegance of Marian's youth with the naked insipidity of her present. For the old Leo, the final illusion shatters; and yet it will remain intact.

Marian's failure to appear at Leo's birthday festivities (which may be compared to Stanley's fête in *The Birthday Party* in terms of their ironic consequences for their respective honorees) provokes the final and climactic incident of the past sequences. The scene builds through the tense silences of those around the table as they await Marian's presence to unveil the green bicycle. Leo's misery and Mrs. Maudsley's rising hysteria form an ironic counterpoint to the gay trappings of the occasion, and the irony increases as Mrs. Maudsley sends out a carriage to fetch Marian at Nanny Robson's. A storm dominates the proceedings. When a butler announces that the carriage has returned without Marian and that Marian has not been at Nanny Robson's all day, Mrs. Maudsley seizes Leo and drags him out into the rain, insisting that he show her the way to Marian. Apparently, however, she has already guessed Marian's whereabouts, and she leads the way through the gardens toward the outhouses in a crazy-quilt sequence of temporal overlays. As they approach the row of overgrown outbuildings, the camera holds momentarily on a stump of deadly nightshade lying on the path and then records the following shots.

> *Interior. Outhouse.*
> *A lantern on the ground.*
> *A shadow moving on the wall like an umbrella opening and closing.*
> *Close-up of* LEO *mystified.*
> *The shadow.*
> *Close-up of* MRS MAUDSLEY.
> *The shadow.*
> *Close-up of* MRS MAUDSLEY.
> *Her face contorts. She lets her breath out in a long exhalation and groan.*
> *The shadow ceasing to move.*
> *Close-up of* MRS MAUDSLEY. *Her face contorted. No sound.*
> *Close-up of* LEO.
> *The faces of* TED *and* MARIAN *on the ground.*
> *They are still.* TED'S *head is buried in* MARIAN'S *shoulder.*
> MARIAN *looks up through half-open eyes.* [P. 365]

This grotesque montage of images, which served in the novel to erase Leo's subsequent memories, leads also in the screenplay to a sealed, composite view of Marian, in all her irresolvable incongruity. Pinter accomplishes this duplication of Leo's final bewilderment through a double temporal dislocation, invoking, together with the preceding sequence, all three impressions of Marian in rapid succession: corrupt, innocent, banal.

> *Exterior. Lawn. Front of house. Day.*
> *In the foreground a shape of a girl lying in a hammock.*
> *The wide lawn falls away before the house on a gentle slope. Cedars, elms.*
> *The hammock, faded crimson canvas, swings gently. In background figures in white playing croquet. Over this* MARIAN'S *voice.*
> MARIAN'S VOICE (OLD)
> You came out of the blue to make us happy. And we made you happy, didn't we? We trusted you with our great treasure. You might never have known what it was, you might have gone through life without knowing. Isn't that so? [Pp. 365-66]

As Marian continues her deluded prattle, exhorting Leo to recount the "facts" of her affair to her grandson, the camera focuses first the image of "TED *dead. He is slumped in his chair, his gun against his leg. His shirt is bloody. His head cannot be seen*," and then the "*Car windscreen. Moving towards Brandham Hall*" (p. 366).

The final montage occurs in silence and consists in the south-west prospect of Brandham Hall: not the issue for Pinter that it had been for Hartley, but an ironic invocation of the opening shots of the screenplay, nonetheless.

> *The elms have been cut down.*
> *The car stops.*
> *Brandham Hall.*
> *A cloud of dust from the car slightly obscures the view.* [P. 367]

The view, still obscured, but now by dust rather than by leaves, at once encloses the work and symbolizes its themes. The imperious facade of Brandham Hall, so rich with its history and so inscrutable, so altered by time and so immutable, presides as the ultimate figuration of the relationship between past and present. Our final impression enlists yet another quirk of perspective, one which Pinter deleted from *Accident*, but which becomes fundamental in *The Proust Screenplay*: we leave the story on the verge of its telling. What we have witnessed has not just been told, but is about to be told, here to Marian's grandson. As Proust's Marcel expresses it, "It was time to begin."[10]

Pinter's cinematic manipulation of time and viewpoint has increased steadily over the course of his screenwriting career to dominate *The Go-Between* (1969) and his other recent film scripts. As narrative complaint against the fallibility of memory and perception has become more pronounced in his source literature, Pinter has developed and sophisticated an audiovisual expression of this tension between "author" and product that extracts the device of schizoid narration and substitutes a schism in the condition of perspective. His optical games with viewpoints and images refract against unsynchronized sound tracks to produce a sensation of contextual distortion that parallels the narrative agony in the novels; he shifts the perceptual liabilities of omniscience from a matter of content to a matter of form. Thus he invokes the themes of the narrator's suffering without recourse to the narrative device; he builds these tensions into the structure of his text.

Except for his adoption of linear time sequences for *The Servant*, *The Quiller Memorandum*, and *The Last Tycoon* and his adoption of a diachronic time scheme for *The French Lieutenant's Woman*, Pinter develops his screenplays across chaotic time circuits that travel a vertical

101

shaft into the past, and often span little or no time in the present. *The Servant*, a novice work and one that predates Pinter's shift toward cinematic manipulation of time, lacks this looped design, but *The Last Tycoon* escapes circularity through a surrogate subject matter; here the problem of discernment operates primarily on the present, and perceptual complications derive chiefly from the lure of overt fabrication rather than from the lure of the covert past. *Accident, The Pumpkin Eater, The Go-Between,* and *The Proust Screenplay*, however, describe virtual circles between their opening and closing scenes. Curiously, these bear further resemblances through their uniform initiation in an approach to a house that occupies a crucial role in the drama, and conclusion in a reprise of this image, sharpened by our altered perceptions.[11]

The Go-Between marks a new development in Pinter's progressive erosion of consensual reality. In the disparities of time and viewpoint that emerge from this screenplay, we find intrinsic flaws in the tasks of perception and recollection that will recur emphatically in Pinter's next two plays: *Old Times* (1970) and *No Man's Land* (1974). As the reliability of memory, always questionable in Pinter's writing, becomes increasingly doubtful and increasingly the subject of his work, Pinter's characters must confront the tricky business of inventing themselves through uncontested, or unsuccessfully contested, claims about their pasts. This new milieu, in which nothing exists except that which the characters manage to allege into being, evolves from the gradual alienation of experience that we have observed in Pinter's literature. A corollary theme in *The Pumpkin Eater* and *Accident*, this process becomes the subject of *The Go-Between*, in which Leo struggles hopelessly to understand the present through what he can make of the past. Unlike Teddy, who simply leaves the game when it threatens to defeat him, or Ruth, who believes she can play the game and win, Leo is condemned to a new kind of game in which both victory and desertion are impossible. A similar game will envelop the characters in *Old Times* and *No Man's Land*, as escape and triumph prove inaccessible except through fleeting manipulations of the game, which has now confiscated all of its alternatives for recourse. The characters in both of these plays have moved beyond the inconclusions of Leo, and into a world in which the past may be improvised according to the convenience of the present. In *The Proust Screenplay*, the central figure, Marcel, chooses to retreat altogether from living into the aesthetically manageable game of remembrances and their ceremonial invocation.

The Proust Screenplay

And so it is with our own past. It is a labour in vain to attempt to recapture it: all the efforts of our intellect must prove futile. The past is hidden somewhere outside the realm, beyond the reach of intellect, in some material object (in the sensation which that material object will give us) which we do not suspect. And as for that object, it depends on chance whether we come upon it or not before we ourselves must die.

How paradoxical it is to seek in reality for the pictures that are stored in one's memory, which must inevitably lose the charm that comes to them from memory itself and from their not being apprehended by the senses. The reality that I had known no longer existed. . . . The places that we have known belong now only to the little world of space on which we map them for our own convenience. No one of them was ever more than a thin slice, held between the contiguous impressions that composed our life at that time; remembrance of a particular form is but regret for a particular moment.[1]

The Proust Screenplay poses special problems in treatment here. Although preceding screenplays may contain compromises generated in filming, this script assumes plainly a "pure" form; it makes no concession to production exigencies because no film has evolved, to date, from the text. Joseph Losey commissioned Pinter to develop a screenplay from Marcel Proust's *À la recherche du temps perdu* in 1972, and Pinter completed the task over the following year. Losey, however, has been unable to raise money for filming the script, partly, Pinter suspects, due to its unusual length (estimated at three and a half hours). In 1977 Pinter published his adaptation as an autonomous work, but, in a *Village Voice* interview, he remained optimistic over its chances for eventual production: "Oddly enough, quite recently we've had a burst of activity and interest. We have had some rather—what appear to be—serious and concrete inquiries from America."[2] Hence, the uncompromised state of this screenplay may differ in nature from the scripts in preceding discussions.

Secondly, although more significantly, Proust's seven-volume masterwork demands labors of analysis beyond the scope of my focus here. As a strategy for avoiding overlong treatments of Proust and his interpreters, I shall delineate his concerns strictly in terms of the screenplay and omit any direct approach to the novels. This seems the only plausible approach to Pinter's adaptation, particularly since the need for cinematic distillation and transformation of material, in this case, is so overwhelming that only a general basis for comparison of themes and structure in the two versions materializes. Pinter's remarks in the *Village Voice* interview render a rudimentary grasp of his own tactics and misgivings with respect to this problem.

> I remember my first conversation with Joe Losey just after I'd finished the reading. I went to him and said, "Well, what the hell do I do?" We hadn't made any decisions whatsoever at that point. Nobody knew what was going to go or be sacrificed, or what form the thing could possibly take. Eventually, one day when I was in more than my usual despair, Joe said, "There's only one thing to do. Go home—tomorrow morning—and start. Just start."
>
> So what I was immediately plunged into was the question of what caught me—well, *everything* caught me, I was totally consumed—but what I was aware of in terms of film. I'm pretty sure that I suddenly went straight into images. I actually threw a lot of images down on paper and found myself left with them. And that's how I got started.
>
> I'm not fitting to write a masterpiece, but what I wanted to do was to try to express it in terms that would be true to it, so that the thing would work in itself and yet have a truth of a different nature.

In the introduction to his published script, Pinter elucidates some of the criteria that determined his final choices of material and presentation.

> The one thing of which I was certain was that it would be wrong to attempt to make a film centered around one or two volumes—*La Prisonnière* or *Sodome et Gomorrhe*, for example. If the thing was to be done at all, one would have to try to distill the whole work, to incorporate the major themes of the book into an integrated whole. With this Joe [Losey] and Barbara [Bray, a script editor and Proustian authority at BBC Radio who advised Pinter during this process] agreed. We decided that the architecture of the film should be based on two main and contrasting principles: one, a movement, chiefly narrative, toward disillusion, and the other, more intermittent, toward revelation, rising to where time that was lost is found, and fixed forever in art.
>
> . . . The relationship between the first volume and the last seemed to us the crucial one. The whole book is, as it were, contained in the last volume. When Marcel, in *Le Temps Retrouvé*, says that he is now able to start his

work, he has already written it. We have just read it. Somehow this remarkable conception had to be found again in another form.

. . . We evolved a working plan and I plunged in the deep end on the basis of it. The subject was Time. In *Le Temps Retrouvé*, Marcel, in his forties, hears again the garden bell of his childhood. His childhood, long forgotten, is suddenly present within him, but his consciousness of himself as a child, his memory of the experience, is more real, more acute than the experience itself.[3]

Stanley Kauffmann, who reviewed the screenplay soon after its publication, praised Pinter's success in this mission: "It's incomparably the best screen adaptation ever made of great work. . . . *I* would insist that this screenplay far surpasses anything conveyed by the term "adaptation" and becomes a re-composition in another art."[4] By working through the screenplay, we can clarify the mechanics of his adaptation and its relationship to Proust's work; we can identify the bias and craft of Pinter's interpretation in "another form."

Four of the images that persisted from Pinter's reading of Proust alternate with a yellow screen to form the first eight shots of the prospective film. Except for the first of these, which Pinter describes as *"Yellow screen. Sound of a garden gate bell,"* the sequence occurs in silence. Thus he materializes, with unpredictable success, Proust's notice of the heraldic bell. It summons Marcel's four epiphanic recollections, which Pinter lists as follows:

2. *Open countryside, a line of trees, seen from a railway carriage. The train is still. No sound. Quick fade out.*
4. *The sea, seen from a high window, a towel hanging on a towel rack in foreground. No sound. Quick fade out.*
6. *Venice. A window in a palazzo, seen from a gondola. No sound. Quick fade out.*
8. *The dining room at Balbec. No sound. Empty.* [P. 3]

Intervening shots each receive the same description: *"Momentary yellow screen."* The significance of this yellow screen lies in its invocation of synecdochical relationship, but we do not learn this until shot #22.

Yellow screen.
The camera pulls back to discover that the yellow screen is actually a patch of yellow wall in a painting. The painting is Vermeer's View of Delft. [Pp. 4-5]

In the relationship between these two views of Vermeer's painting, we have a metaphor for the central tension and technique of Proust's writing and for the prevailing concern and mechanism of the film. The discrepancy between detail and the overall view, the insistent return to the incomprehensible, but magnified, patch, focuses at once the attitude and impossibility of both authors' efforts. The relative insignificance of the wall to the statement of the full painting exacerbates this discrepancy, suggesting the pitfalls of describing an elephant by the nature of its tail. For Proust, however, in a passage strongly evocative of the older Leo's plight in *The Go-Between*, the restriction to detail proves endemic:

> . . . as though all Combray had consisted of but two floors joined by a slender staircase, and as though there had been no time there but seven o'clock at night. I must own that I could have assured any questioner that Combray did include other scenes and did exist at other hours than these. But since the facts which I should then have recalled would have been prompted only by an exercise of the will, by my intellectual memory, and since the pictures which that kind of memory shews us of the past preserve nothing of the past itself, I should never have had any wish to ponder over this residue of Combray. To me it was in reality all dead. [P. 33]

As Proust suggests again in the quote that opens this chapter, all of memory, all of perception, belong to elicitation of detail. Even detail, however, remains incapable of surrendering its substance, its secret, its meaning. For reasons similar to those encountered by Leo, the sum of all Proust's detail and intimacy will not yield the complete picture in all its parts, relationships, and contexts. Pinter, in the *Village Voice* interview, explains his adoption of this yellow screen device as a strategy for rendering the quality of Proust's immersion in detail: "There are only a handful of scenes (in the novel's entirety). It's more like the little patch in Vermeer, magnified many times."

The gradual expansion to the full picture from detail comprises a major structuring technique in the film script. As Enoch Brater has noted, "Pinter accomplishes pictorially what Proust accomplishes verbally: the wonder of a fragment which only slowly reveals itself as a small part of a far more comprehensive canvas."[5] Pinter introduces the themes, situations, and characters of his work in piecemeal fragments, which he often recognizably cues by some triggering event, such as the garden gate bell in the opening sequence, or the crackling napkin, which initiates the same sequence of images only a page afterwards. Each of the milieux depicted in this sequence will gain clarity through the accumulation of detail and context as the film progresses.

In a cinematic confusion of time periods similar to the one that Pinter developed for *The Go-Between*, the thirty-four shots that comprise the preamble to the film anchor in a series of "present-time" scenes at the Prince de Guermantes's, variously without sound, with sound, and with unrelated sound. From the middle of the sequence, the garden gate bell is again heard, "*becoming gently insistent*," and continuing irregularly

over the concluding shots. Several new images are introduced and repeated, including the three church steeples and the three trees, the
yellow screen returns once, with the music of Vinteuil tracked over it,
and the preamble terminates in a shot and note that Pinter states as
follows:

> 34. *Calm, still shot of the garden gate.*
> *The bell is slightly shaking but silent.*
> (NOTE: *In the preceding opening sequence, all scenes in the drawing
> room of the* PRINCE DE GUERMANTES'S *house are to be shot on
> colour stock in black and white.*) [P. 6]

In the *Village Voice* interview, Pinter outlined his intentions for this
unusual cinematic process: "It's a question of very old age and decrepitude. The manufactured faces . . . they *look* as if they're made up.
Proust describes it so vividly and remorselessly that it seemed to us that
we should employ all means available on film to make it as vivid and
remorseless." The significance of this technical draining of life from
image will become clear when we turn to the concluding statement of
the prospective film, since these "present-time" developments operate
as a frame for the work. For now, we note merely that they serve, much
like the overcast and desolate depiction of the present in *The Go-Between*, as a distinct and contrasting anchor situation at the commencement of the film, during the apparently random montage of recollected
images.

Even after the "story" gets underway, brief clips involving temporal
hiccups dominate the film script. The assembly of scenes amounts to a
pastiche of Proustian situations, viewed variously as fragments, wholes,
presciences, hindsights, from one viewpoint, and from another. The
introduction of Saint-Loup provides an example of how Pinter manipulates the piecemeal development of character and context. After a handful of articulated scenes that elucidate the character of Marcel's
childhood (his love for his mother, his estrangement from his father, his
fascination with Gilberte, his dread of lesbianism, and his interest in
writing) and alternate with adumbrative images, Pinter begins to insinuate Marcel's journey to Balbec. Our first glimpse, soundless, focuses
five girls (Proust's "little band"), "*strikingly dressed, quite distinct in
their carriage,*" on the promenade outside the Grand Hotel. The second
shot, contiguous with the first, receives the following description:

> 109. INT. DINING ROOM. BALBEC HOTEL. DAY. 1898.
> *Very hot afternoon. The curtains are drawn, although not fully, to shield
> the room from the glare.*
> *Through spaces between the curtains the sea flashes and in one of the*

> spaces SAINT-LOUP (20), *dressed in an almost white, very thin suit, is seen striding from the beach towards the hotel, his monocle dropping from his eye and being replaced.*
>
> *The camera shifts to look through the foyer to the glass front of the hotel, the bottom half of which is filled with sea,* SAINT-LOUP *in foreground striding towards a carriage and pair. He jumps onto the box seat and takes the reins from the groom. The hotel manager rushes out with a letter for him.* SAINT-LOUP *opens the letter and, starting the horses at the same time, drives off.*
>
> *No sound.* [P. 35]

This depiction, the first we have seen of Saint-Loup and the second of Balbec, gives way initially to a similarly mysterious and soundless portrait of the Baron de Charlus on the promenade and then to the compartment of a moving train, in which Marcel (18) and his grandmother (66) are discussing the health-oriented trip to Balbec. We learn that Marcel has become ill and has developed, as a technique for enduring the absence of his mother, a fondness for liquor. The train scenes, shot variously from Marcel's and objective points of view, precede a sequence of brief situations, some of these clarifying earlier image fragments, between Marcel and his grandmother as they settle in at Balbec. Eventually they lead to a second viewing of the Saint-Loup action.

119. INT. DINING ROOM. AFTERNOON.
> *The curtains are drawn.* MARCEL *sits alone with coffee. From his position he can see through the foyer to the glass front of the hotel.*
>
> *Against a background of sea,* SAINT-LOUP *strides towards a carriage and pair, jumps on the box seat, takes an envelope from the hotel manager, opens it, starts the horses, drives off.* [P. 40]

This altered context and viewpoint of Saint-Loup's departure cuts to a second viewing of the Baron de Charlus, situated identically to the initial shot of him except in close-up. The next shot provides a context for the Charlus fragments, and occurs against the same background as the two previous images of him.

121. EXT. THE PROMENADE. DAY.
> MARCEL, *feeling he is being watched, turns.*
>
> *From his P.O.V. sees* CHARLUS *in front of the playbill. He wears a dark suit, and slaps the leg of his trousers with a switch, staring at* MARCEL.
>
> *He turns abruptly to examine the playbill, takes out a notebook, makes a note, looks at his watch, pulls his straw hat over his eyes, looks up and down the front, sighs, walks quickly away.*
>
> MARCEL *stares after him.* [Pp. 40-41]

The succeeding scenes at Balbec, while introducing Albertine and Andree in similar cumulative fashion, clarify the relationships between

Marcel and Saint-Loup and between Marcel and Charlus in articulated vignettes with dialogue, sequence, and context attendant. Pinter's procedure for revealing significance here corresponds to his progression from the yellow screen to Vermeer's painting. The sensibility projected by these variously reduced and expanded frames also focuses the refractive operation of the spectator; it implies that events exist apart from and accompanied by witnessing, but that witnesses serve to alter and to contribute contexts of appreciation.

The patchwork of temporal fragments persists in this manner throughout the screenplay. They echo the mechanism of the magnified patch of yellow wall and formulate the philosophical disposition of the work. Often, temporally manipulated sequences include an isolated "future" shot amidst several from the past, suggesting a linkage among events similar to that inherent in the prophecies of Greek tragedy: the notion that the past contains a prediction of the future if we simply complete the paradigms that the past assumes, but that the relationships among events are generally teleological and inscrutable, cohering only as manipulated by the imposition of imagination. For example, Marcel's announcement to his mother that "it is absolutely necessary that I marry Albertine," whom he suspects of lesbian attachments, precedes a sequence of images from previously developed situations concerning Mlle. Vinteuil and Odette, all involving innuendos of dreaded and tragic lesbianism. The sequence initiates with a close-up of his mother's face, and culminates in the forecast circumstance of Albertine's fate.

275. MOTHER'S FACE.
276. MLLE. VINTEUIL RUNNING TO THE WINDOW TO CLOSE SHUTTERS.
277. ODETTE PLAYING VINTEUIL'S SONATA. SWANN LISTENING.
278. EXT. FIELD. DAY.
   A riderless horse gallops away from the camera. [P. 117]

Thus Pinter suggests another pattern in artificial organization of events that attacks notions of omniscience through substitution of ordering principles conspicuously native to perspective, subjectivity, and aesthetics. If the concept of fate generates from the hindsight of remembrance, then forecast merely represents a form of dishonest narrative inspired by a limited and biased impression of past and present experience. Such pretense of omniscient authorship, either of literature or of life, runs contrary to Pinter's (and Proust's) growing view of life and perception as the victims of endemic subjectivity, and he undermines all tendencies toward imposition of artificial designs on life by exposing and juxtaposing the false contrivance of their premises. Like Vermeer's painting Marcel's story is *fait accompli;* the part anticipates or unifies with the whole by virtue of completion, only. As Sartre expressed this idea, "Proust never discovered the homosexuality of Charlus, since he had decided upon it even before starting on his book."[6] The construct and significance of things become properties of projected or retrospective artifice.

Beyond establishing the thematic and procedural groundwork for the film, the yellow screen from the opening sequence serves as an emblem of the sympathy between Marcel and Charles Swann, whom Marcel invests as his spiritual father. Pinter articulates this symbol during the scene in which we learn that Swann will shortly die of a terminal illness. The immense pathos of this scene develops in the petty, banal chaos of the Duc and Duchesse de Guermantes's home, as they prepare to leave for a dinner engagement, and Marcel encounters Swann after a long period of separation.

> DUC. You're writing a book about Vermeer, aren't you?
>
> SWANN. Oh, hardly a book. . . . Just an article, about one painting.
>
> MARCEL. *View of Delft?*
>
> SWANN. Yes.
>
> MARCEL. That patch of yellow wall.
>
> SWANN. Yes.
>
> DUC. Patch? What patch?
>
> SWANN *suddenly recognizes* MARCEL.
> MARCEL *turns to the* DUC.
>
> MARCEL *(to the* DUC). I think it's the most beautiful painting in the world.
> [P. 89]

Marcel's identification of his own plight with that of Swann persists after Swann's death, occurring conspicuously during Marcel's misery over Albertine. As Marcel struggles to reconcile the death of the mysterious Albertine, Swann's image appears on the screen. The voiceover broadcast of Swann's epiphanic pronouncement accompanies, and according to the technical fracture dissociates itself from, this image, implying that this particular combination of image and sentiment is Marcel's retrospective formulation of Swann. "To think I have wasted years of my life, that I have longed for death, that the greatest love I have ever known has been for a woman who did not appeal to me, who was not my type" (p. 156). Only twenty shots into the future, during a reminiscence with the widowed Gilberte, Marcel will make a similar appraisal of his own life.

> GILBERTE. Why are you laughing?
>
> MARCEL. Because I didn't understand. I've understood very little. I've been too . . . preoccupied . . . with other matters. . . . To be honest, I have wasted my life. [P. 164]

Shortly after reviving this bond between Marcel and Swann through Odette's remark near the end of the screenplay, "Charles always intended to write himself, you know, but *(she giggles)* I think he was too much in love with me to find the time" (p. 175), Pinter will repeat the yellow image under the final words of the script: "It was time to begin."

The deployment of the opening sequence as a frame for the film serves multiple purposes. Some of these depend on specific developments in the action of the film, and these I shall table for later discussion. In bold terms, however, the "present-time" opening situation invents a context for what follows while it anticipates a context for itself. The completion, through intelligibility, of its conundrum will signal at once the unity, conclusion, and commencement of the story. This suggestion of beginning represents precisely what Pinter was striving for in his planning of the adaptation. Again, I quote from the *Village Voice* inteview: "Eventually, you see I got to the structure at the end . . . and I suddenly realized that that ('It was time to begin') was the crucial and absolutely essential sentence—in that, if we've just seen the damn thing, or read the damn thing, well, now he's going to do it, now he's going to write it." In the circularity of the film, in the reference to and containment of the end by the beginning, Pinter has managed to suggest through structure Marcel's final words. The last sequence repeats the first at the Guermantes's; we have at last come around to the beginning. Between the two the past forms a chaotic bridge, spanning identical moments of time: existing only in simultaneity with the present, leading always back to the start.

Although the past has no reality apart from coexistence with the present, Pinter suggests that experience of the two temporal worlds necessitates mutual exclusion. The screenplay makes the nature and cost of Marcel's options clear; he may remember, or he may live, but he must choose between the two. The silent or unsynchronized sound track that accompanies each of Marcel's adventures from the present into the remembered implies this withdrawal. The sounds of the present never penetrate the visions of the past, which themselves remain soundless until they obtain full maturity and dimension in memory. Returning to the point in the opening sequence at which the garden gate bell renews its ringing, we find this exemplary direction.

> 24. INT. THE DRAWING ROOM. THE PRINCE DE GUERMANTES'S HOUSE. 1921
> *No sound track.*
> *Old people chattering soundlessly.*
> MARCEL *stands detached from them.*
> *The sound of a garden gate bell heard, becoming gently insistent. [P. 5]*

Ten images from the past follow this shot in rapid succession, attended by the note, "*The tempo of the next sequence quickens, and the bell continues over it, irregularly,*" and culminating in the image of the shaking, silent bell. The fact of this choice, to partake or to recollect, derives from numerous references to this condition in Proust's work. In the first paragraph of *Swann's Way,* Marcel allows that his half-awake thoughts "lay like scales upon my eyes and prevented them from registering the fact that the candle was no longer burning" (p. 3). Then, as he regains consciousness, the autobiography that he was dreaming becomes remote.

> Then it would begin to seem unintelligible, as the thoughts of a former existence must be to a reincarnate spirit; the subject of my book would separate itself from me, leaving me free to choose whether I would form part of it or no; and at the same time my sight would return and I would be astonished to find myself in a state of darkness, pleasant and restful enough for the eyes, and even more, perhaps, for my mind, to which it appeared incomprehensible, without a cause, a matter dark indeed. [P. 3]

Marcel, then, suggests a preference for the world of fiction, of memory, due to a muteness in the world of the present, to its "darkness and incomprehensibility." He doubts, however, the validity of his escape world, because he recognizes it as an attempt to freeze the motion of life.

> Perhaps the immobility of things that surround us is forced upon them by our conviction that they are themselves, and not anything else, and by the immobility of our conceptions of them. For it always happened that when I awoke like this, and my mind struggled in an unsuccessful attempt to discover where I was, everything would be moving round me through the darkness: things, places, years. [P. 5]

Vice that it may be, Marcel returns over and over to his flight from the present, noting often, as in his attempt to travel backwards in time through the provocative combination of madeleines and tea, the necessary accompanying cessation of immediate experience. "I compel my mind to make one further effort, to follow and recapture once again the fleeting sensation. And that nothing may interrupt it in its course I shut out every obstacle, every extraneous idea, I stop my ears and inhibit all attention to the sounds which come from the next room" (p. 35).

His efforts to retreat from the motion of the present, to insulate himself in order to pursue the message of the sensation, resemble in Marcel's description the structural insinuation of Pinter's screenplay, accentuating its aptness. "The tea has called up in me, but does not itself understand, and can only repeat indefinitely with a gradual loss of strength, the same testimony; which I, too, cannot interpret, though I hope at least to call upon the tea for it again and to find it there presently, intact and at my disposal, for my final enlightenment" (p. 34). The insulating effect of the mechanism of recollection will figure richly in the final moments of the film, but its presence is consistent throughout and rooted firmly in Proust. The indulgence of memory, or art, is tantamount to denial of life: "Remembrance of a particular form is but regret for a particular moment." The regrets proliferate, the moments evaporate as Marcel spends less and less time in contact with the experience of living, more and more in the playground of imagination: "His memory of the experience is more real, more acute than the experience itself."

The madeleine episode, a Proustian cliche that Pinter deliberately excludes from the screenplay, introduces another quality of memory in keeping with Pinter's customary vision; the past remains malleable, and excursions into it may or may not re-create its original nature.

> It is for [the mind] to discover the truth. But how? What an abyss of uncertainty whenever the mind feels that some part of it has strayed beyond its own borders; when it, the seeker, is at once the dark region through which it must go seeking, where all its equipment will avail it nothing. Seek? More than that: create. It is face to face with something that does not so far exist, to which it alone can give reality and substance, which it alone can bring into the light of day. [P. 35]

The problem of uncertainty, which Marcel assigns to probes of the past here, dominates the present throughout the work of Pinter and Proust, and dictates the condition that challenges memory and perception. From early in both novel and screenplay, Marcel exerts himself without satisfaction against the unyielding obscurity of others, and he observes others in the same predicament. Marcel's doubts and curiosities compound due to his frustrations as an eavesdropper; he experiences life through an enforced alienation and a chronic lack of context. Remoteness, confusion, and impenetrability mark the condition of his experience and remembrance. In this regard Brater's allegation that Pinter obliterates "the security Proust was still able to find in his temple of art" through the screenplay's depiction of a "past that has now become fractured, unstable, and ultimately hazy," bereft of Marcel's "definitive narrative authority," seems ill-conceived.[7]

Marcel's quasi-invisibility, his machinations as an eavesdropper who sees and hears without detection by others, posed worries for Pinter. The presence of Marcel on film would require concrete dimensions of human corporality, and, without Proust's literary endowment of ethereal presence, Marcel's serendipitous position may appear contrived. Pinter considered and declined utilizing a "subjective camera," as we have noted in the first chapter, to establish Marcel's habit, because this technique, too, smacked of contrivance. Ultimately, Pinter deleted the omnipresent condition of eavesdropping from his adaptation, relying instead on sporadic suggestions of it and on his own skill at creating opaque situations that possess intrinsically the qualities of something overheard or glimpsed surreptitiously.

Marcel's frustrated efforts to discover the extent of the lesbian network that dominates the action of the screenplay provoke numerous scenes of this inscrutable nature. The early portion of the script, for example, develops Marcel's rising obsession with female homosexuality through his established overhearing of guarded innuendos by others, who refer in nebulous but sinister remarks to the activities of Odette, Mlle. Vinteuil, and others. These scenes transpire in barely decipherable order, interrupted at frequent intervals by "future" scenes that materialize mysterious images, later related to the lesbian theme, according to the associative patterning of memory. The supressed subject of this early sequence finally erupts in a confrontation between Swann and Odette, which proceeds without Marcel's conspicuous surveillance, and which demonstrates Pinter's characteristic aptitude for obfuscation.

SWANN. Since you have known me have you . . . known any other men?

ODETTE. I knew it was that kind of question from your face. No, I have not. Why would I want other men, you silly? I have you.

Pause.

SWANN. What about women?

ODETTE. Women?

SWANN. You remember once Madame Verdurin said to you: "I know how to melt you, all right. You're not made of marble."

ODETTE. You asked me about that ages ago.

SWANN. I know—

ODETTE. I told you it was a joke. A *joke*, that's all.

SWANN. *Have* you ever, with her?

ODETTE. I've told you, no! You know quite well. Anyway, she's not like that.

SWANN. Don't say "You know quite well." Say "I have never done anything of that sort with Madame Verdurin or with any other woman."

ODETTE (*automatically*). I have never done anything of that sort with Madame Verdurin or any other woman.

Silence.

SWANN. Can you swear to me on the medal round your neck?

ODETTE. Oh, you make me sick! What's the matter with you today?

SWANN. Tell me, on your medal, yes or no, whether you have ever done those things?

ODETTE. How do I know? I don't even know what you mean. What things? Perhaps I have, years ago, when I didn't know what I was doing. Perhaps two or three times, I don't know.

Pause.

SWANN. How many times exactly?

ODETTE. For God's sake! (*Slight pause.*) Anyway it's all so long ago. I've never given it a thought. Anyone would think you're trying to put ideas into my head—just to get me to do it again.

SWANN. It's quite a simple question. And you must remember. You must remember with whom . . . my love. The last time, for instance.

ODETTE *relaxes, speaks lightly.*

ODETTE. Oh, I don't know. I think in the Bois . . . on the island . . . one evening . . . you were dining with those Guermantes. At the next table was a woman I hadn't seen for ages. She said to me, "Come round behind the rock there and look at the moonlight on the water." At first I just yawned and said, "No, I'm too tired." But she swore there'd never been any moonlight to touch it. "I've heard that tale before," I said to her. I knew quite well what she was after. [Pp. 24-26]

Except for three lines of initiating banter, I have quoted this scene in its entirety. Clearly, from its rhythms of deceit, its reliance on cliche, and its origins in extortion, we can put little stock in Odette's confession. The savvy ring of her story, however, and her general evasiveness suggest the truth of her complicity with other women. The two impressions coincide without reconciliation, as they do in later scenes between Marcel and Albertine and between Marcel and Andree. Pinter, furthermore, implies Marcel's surveillance of the preceding scene between Odette and Swann later in the script, by rebroadcasting the words, "I knew quite well what she was after," over a later image of Swann, clearly viewed through the eyes of Marcel.

Swann's inability to verify his suspicions of Odette's misbehavior receives articulation in an earlier scene, as well. After Odette rebuffs Swann, who appears at her door unexpectedly, Swann returns later to ascertain the truth of her excuse. In his anxiety over her suspected deceptions, he confuses her house with another and assaults two old men whose voices he presumes are those of Odette's secret consorts. Humiliated and unenlightened Swann notes the inscrutable darkness of Odette's actual residence, and returns home. This image of Swann's dismay recurs later in the screenplay, when Marcel encounters signs of Albertine's deceptiveness. It follows a bitter confrontation between them, during which Marcel accuses her of lying to him and all but confirms his dread of her mendacity. The conclusion of this incident in the image of Swann's retreat from Odette's dark, silent house indicates Marcel's association of his predicament with that of Swann, suggesting

Marcel's doubts over his perception, and that even the obvious might issue from paranoid delusion.

Homosexuality obscures the motives of both sexes in the screenplay. Mlle. Vinteuil's piano lessons, Charlus's interest in Marcel, the activities of Albertine and Andree, and, indeed, a predominance of Marcel's experience form pretexts for the exploitative maneuverings of homosexual interest. Characteristically, Pinter capitalizes on the concealed motives and frustrated inquests surrounding this motif, amplifying it into a metaphor for typical human experience. Marcel's uncertainty acquires the proportions of a nightmare, as whatever tentative decisions he affords himself are inevitably contradicted by some development of "fact."

The dynamics of his affair with Albertine, in its interminable circle of truths and falsehoods, form the chief example of his whiplash between uncertainty and contradiction. Already filled with anxieties over the omnipresence of homosexuality, Marcel agonizes from the outset of the affair over Albertine's conspicuous female affiliations. Between his initial meeting of her at Balbec, where she gambols with the band of mysterious girls, and his reunion with her in Paris, where he is confined to his sickbed, Marcel experiences and witnesses the ubiquitous infestation of homosexuality in both sexes. He undergoes a lengthy infatuation and disillusionment with Charlus, and he observes the tragedy of Saint-Loup's lover's defection to the network of sexual aberration. However, when Albertine visits the bedridden Marcel in Paris, she favors him sexually for the first time, and he consequently embarks on a thick, if uneasy, involvement with her.

Plagued by suspicions and images of her deviance, Marcel interrogates Albertine relentlessly over her activities, but he can turn up nothing conclusive. She eludes all his accusations and questions in a fashion that only exacerbates his certainty of their truth. An excellent example of Pinter's structural compression of Marcel's entrapment by contradiction occurs when Marcel returns to Balbec, three years after his first visit. Marcel encounters his grandmother's physician, Dr. Cottard, and the two retire to the Casino for a chat.

246. INT. CASINO. BALBEC. BALLROOM.
    There are no men in the room.
    A few girls sit at tables, drinking. A girl is playing a waltz on a piano.
    About half a dozen girls are dancing together.
    ALBERTINE *and* ANDREE *dance together.*
    MARCEL *and* COTTARD *stand watching at the door.*
MARCEL. They dance well together, don't they? Girls?

COTTARD. Parents are very rash to allow their daughters to form such habits. I'd never let mine come here. (*Indicating* ALBERTINE *and* ANDREE.)

Look at those two. It's not sufficiently known that women derive most excitement from their breasts. Theirs are completely touching. Look at them.

ALBERTINE *and* ANDREE *dancing close together.*
ANDREE *whispers to* ALBERTINE. ALBERTINE *laughs.*
They ease the contact. [P. 99]

In the succeeding shot, Andree and Marcel are sitting together at a table in the ballroom, having the following dialogue:

MARCEL. What are you looking at?

ANDREE. Those women.

MARCEL. Which?

ANDREE. Over there. Do you know who they are?

MARCEL. No.

ANDREE. Lea, the actress. And her friend. They live together quite openly. It's a scandal.

MARCEL. Oh. . . . You've no sympathy with that kind of thing, then?

ANDREE. Me? I loathe that kind of thing. I'm like Albertine in that. We both loathe that kind of thing. [P. 100]

Marcel nonetheless attacks Albertine with his suspicions in the next scene, announcing that he loves Andree, rather than her, and explaining:

MARCEL. I have a profound disgust for women . . . tainted with that vice.

Pause.

MARCEL. You see, I have heard that your . . . accomplice . . . is Andree, and since Andree is the woman I love, you can understand my grief.

ALBERTINE *looks at him steadily.*

ALBERTINE. Who told you this rubbish?

MARCEL. I can't tell.

ALBERTINE. Andree and I both detest that sort of thing. We find it revolting.

MARCEL. You're saying it's not true?

ALBERTINE. If it were true I would tell you. I would be quite honest with you. Why not? But I'm telling you it's absolutely untrue.

MARCEL. Do you swear it?

ALBERTINE. I swear it. [P. 102]

Albertine subsequently seduces him, weakening her already too glib denial with further protestations against his accusation as she goes. Marcel's suspicions and grounds for them mount throughout the long course of their relationship, until finally he asks her to move out of his house. Albertine, however, coaxes him out of his resolve and wins a several-week reprieve. The next morning, the servant Francoise announces to Marcel that Albertine has packed and left, apparently satisfied with emerging victorious from the stormy affair.

Marcel's anxiety does not subside with her departure. After he receives the telegram proclaiming Albertine's death, articulated in the screenplay by a second image of the horse galloping riderless, here pulling back to reveal the crumpled body of a girl, Marcel turns to Andree for resolution of his nagging doubts. In a sequence of six brief scenes, which alternate between day and night to log the passage of time, Andree confirms Marcel's suspicions by night, but denies them by day, finally accusing him of Albertine's betrayal, and leaving him to despair worse than ever. The following series of quotes provides a sampling of her equivocation, culminating in her ultimate accusation.

> I never did anything with Albertine. (DAY)
> She was so passionate. Remember that day you lost your key, when you brought home syringa? You nearly caught us. It was so dangerous, we knew you would be home any minute, but she needed it, she had to have it. I pretended she hated the scent of syringa, do you remember? She was behind the door. She said the same thing, to keep you away from her, so that you wouldn't smell me on her. (NIGHT)
> You *want* me to say it, don't you? But I won't say things which aren't true. Albertine detested that sort of thing. I can swear it. I can swear that I never did that sort of thing with Albertine. (DAY)
> She and Morel understood each other at once. He procured girls for her. He would seduce the girl first, and then, when the girl was absolutely under his control, he'd hand her over to Albertine, and they'd both enjoy her.
> . . . Lea had her many times at the baths at Balbec. I remember once being with her and some laundresses—oh quite young—by the banks of the river by Balbec. I remember one girl—very sweet she was too—and she cried out: "Oh how heavenly." "Oh how heavenly" . . . quivering, naked, on the grass. (NIGHT)
> The people who have told you these stories about Albertine were lying to you . . . can't you understand that? (DAY)
> She hoped that you would rescue her, that you would marry her. She loved you. She felt in her heart her obsession was a sort of criminal lunacy. I think she might possibly have killed herself, out of despair. (NIGHT) [Pp. 154-56]

The pattern of Marcel's uncertainties and contradicted certainties repeats in his relationship with Charlus, whose dignity and irresistible eccentricity parry every stand against his decadence and deviance that Marcel can make. Marcel's final and most shocking reversal occurs during the war, when he discovers a *Croix de Guerre* in an extraordinary Parisian brothel, run for Charlus by his lover, Jupien. We discover in the following scene that the *Croix de Guerre* belonged to Saint-Loup, whose friendship Marcel had struck up at Balbec, whose charm and innocence have prevailed in the screenplay, who has married Marcel's childhood passion, Gilberte, and whose death Marcel now mourns.

GILBERTE. Two days after Robert was killed I received a package, sent anonymously. It contained his Croix de Guerre. There was no note of explanation, nothing. The package was posted in Paris.

Pause.

GILBERTE. Isn't that strange?

MARCEL. Yes.

GILBERTE. He never mentioned, in any letter, that it had been lost, or stolen.
[P. 162]

With this final development, Marcel's nightmares of panoramic decadence and perversion are nearly confirmed. The "nearly," however, represents the crucial hinge of this situation; Marcel has no irrefutable fact on which to base any conclusion. All of his evidence, considerable as it may be, lies open to interpretation; and all matters of interpretation invoke the problem of perception.

We have previously noted that Marcel entertains doubts about the validity of his perceptions in his discursions from the novel on the natural mobility of things that the mind immobilizes and on the nonexistence of things that the mind creates. This theme receives repeated attention by Proust, and several of its dimensions possess centrality to Pinter's cinematic adaptation. Marcel, for example, dwells over and over again on the image of the three church steeples seen from a moving carriage during his childhood, and on the lifelong impact this image has had on him. Pinter captures this incident and its persistent repercussions by repeating the image of the steeples at several points in the film script, and by describing its main occurrence as follows:

MARCEL'S P.O.V. FROM MOVING CARRIAGE

The twin steeples of Martinville church and, in the distance, a third steeple from another village.

At first the distance between the Martinville steeples and the other is clear, definite. But as the road winds and in the sun's reflection they seem to change position. The third, although rising from higher ground in the distance, suddenly appears to be standing by their side, to be one of them.

Further views of them, as the carriage progresses:

Only the Martinville steeples seen; the third not in sight.

The third very dim, quivering.

The Martinville steeples almost blotted out; the third startlingly clear, luminous.

The three steeples apparently side by side, dancing together in the last rays of the sun.

94. C.U. MARCEL'S FACE, ALIVE. [P. 29]

At the heart of this vision lies an optical illusion, a perceptual trick. Wholeness, it suggests, remains a function of point of view, and even then, like all other impressions of any phenomenon, it is bogus, freakish, and ephemeral. The disposition and condition of the beholder control perception; "A thing is not necessarily either true or false; it can be both true and false." Marcel's perceptions and conclusions regarding the sexual practices of his acquaintances enjoy no exemption, even in his consciousness, from this principle. The steeple montage, in fact, caps the protracted and accelerating sequence of episodes regarding lesbian intrigues. Pinter's matrixing of these events, substantially reordered from the original text, highlights the crisis of indiscernable sexuality and refers the entire issue to the caprice of perception, to the dance of the steeples.

If the significance of the reiterated steeple image contains so much subtlety as to elude some viewers, Pinter reinforces its statement with the similar episode of the three trees. Here, the impression of the trees following the carriage as it moves away from them alternates with shots of "MARCEL'S FACE, ALIVE" and the steeples at Martinville. Beyond these two incidents, both repeated throughout the film, Pinter employs the previously noted contextual tricks, several shots of watchers watching watchers, and numerous views through mirrors, windows, and reflections, each of which suggests the primacy and peril of perception.

The second of these techniques, which the following excerpt exemplifies, often materializes through a diffused sequence of shots, each altering context by adding or subtracting a witness, and anticipating the climactic sequence of an onlooker in Stahr's "making pictures" monologue from *The Last Tycoon*. The montage cited here, unlike many of the others, occurs in tight consecutive sequence.

98. EXT. CHAMPS-ELYSEES GARDENS. PARIS. 1897.
GILBERTE (17) *whispering with girlfriends in the bushes. A girl's voice laughing,* "Oh, Gilberte!"
99. MARCEL WATCHING GILBERTE.
100. SWANN IN FOREGROUND STANDING BY A TREE, WATCHING MARCEL WATCH GILBERTE.
MARCEL *is unaware of* SWANN'S *presence.* [P. 30]

Shot #106 duplicates shot #100, except that Swann is absent from this otherwise identical moment. Pinter's intended effect here seems to depend on actual screen representation for full clarity, but this much is clear from the screenplay: the layered contexts of observers and observed that recur frequently in the film invoke the refractive nature of observation as a major subject in the script. And the numerous instances of views captured through screening substances, framing obstacles, and reflecting surfaces contribute to the presence and to the statement of this theme.

Flaws inhabit not only the original experience of phenomena, but also its mental recreation, here. In the final sequence of the screenplay, which, as we have noted, repeats the opening sequence (albeit with more explication), Marcel, newly released from the sanatorium and now forty-one years old, attends an afternoon gathering at the home of the Prince and Princesse de Guermantes. We begin to recover images from the opening sequence as he walks towards the house, in the following series of shots:

395. EXT. PRINCE DE GUERMANTES'S HOUSE. AVENUE DU BOIS.
MARCEL *walking towards it.*
Carriages, cars, crowds of chauffeurs.
A car is driving towards the house. MARCEL *steps in front of it. The chauffeur shouts.* MARCEL *steps back, trips over uneven paving stones.*
He sways, recovers balance, puts his foot back on the lower paving stone.

396. *Very dim quick flash of Venice.*

397. MARCEL'S *face.*

398. EXT. PRINCE DE GUERMANTES'S HOUSE.
MARCEL *stands still.*
He sways back again and forward.
In background chauffeurs regarding him curiously, with amusement.
MARCEL *sways back.*

399. *Blue glow.*

400. *Chauffeurs.*

401. *Blue mosaics in Saint Mark's Church.*

402. MARCEL'S *face.* [Pp. 165-66]

Proust makes Marcel's endeavor in this and similar repeated bits of action clear; the sensation has provoked some vague ghost of memory in Marcel, and he strives to indulge its formulation by repeating the action that summoned it.

Every time that I merely repeated this physical movement, I achieved nothing; but if I succeeded, forgetting the Guermantes party, in recapturing what I had felt when I first placed my feet on the ground in this way, again the dazzling and indistinct vision fluttered near me, as if to say: "Seize me as I pass if you can, and try to solve the riddle of happiness which I set you." And almost at once I recognized the vision: it was Venice, of which my efforts to describe it and the supposed snapshots taken by my memory had never told me anything, but which the sensation which I had once experienced as I stood upon two uneven stones in the baptistery of St. Mark's had, recurring a moment ago, restored to me complete with all the other sensations linked on that day to that particular sensation, all of which had been waiting in their place—from which with imperious suddenness a chance happening had caused them to emerge—in the series of forgotten days.[8]

Pinter, who cites moments such as this one and the triggering effect of the garden gate bell as his favorites in Proust's work, establishes the connection between the paving stones and St. Mark's Church by the subtlest of means. He takes Marcel's earlier comments on the dangers of recollection and the need for sensory withdrawal as the key to the paving stone moment.

373. INT. SAINT MARK'S CHURCH.
Sounds of two pairs of feet walking over the cobbles.
They stop.
The camera pans up to the blue mosaics of the church. [P. 157]

In the *Village Voice* interview, Pinter explains his intention for the scene.

You see? He sways backward and forward. . . . Then he's still. Nothing happens. He sways back again, desperately trying to get the damn thing, to recapture the damn thing. And you notice that he simply sways back the last time and remains still, concentrating. And then, what I think is good, the chauffeurs. The world of the chauffeurs. In the direction of the film you'd have him aware of them earlier, but then all of the sudden he's oblivious to them. Blue glow.

The nature of Marcel's effort is twice removed at two levels; he *repeats* the moment that *recalls* the image that *reconstructs* the original image. The dissimilarity between the two movements, one genuine and one replicated, implies the flaws inherent in recollection; the second is fabricated, forced, manipulated, and without substance. Pinter's cherished chauffeurs accentuate Marcel's habit of withdrawal from the immediate, the operation of point of view (in their laughter), and the ascent of a usurping world. Marcel has chosen; he has denied his life in order to withdraw into the world of fiction, order, and creation; in order to recapture the past and fix it in art.

As Marcel awaits admittance to the drawing room in the library, the cuing incidents and their consequent images from the opening acquire a lucidness that they lacked previously. The clarity of their mechanism and significance derives partly from our accumulated familiarity with and sensitivity to them, and partly from a more conspicuous relationship between cue and recollection; both ourselves and Marcel have grown more adept at this pattern of invocation. The recollections themselves become more articulated, so that the waiter's inadvertent striking of a spoon against a plate summons again the view of countryside from a railway carriage, but also the sound of a hammer tapping one of the train wheels, linking the image to its cue. The starched napkin with which Marcel wipes his mouth prompts the same frame of sea and sky from a high window, but here we observe a starched towel being replaced on the towel rack in the foreground. The shrill noise of water running through the pipes in the library evokes the image of the dining room at Balbec, with a steamer sounding in the distance. The silent sound track of the opening, with its occasional concessions to the hubbub of the "present," has at last yielded its secret, and Marcel has perfected his communion with the absent past.

This final theme of Marcel's escape into the cherished illusion of memory is accompanied by the characteristic rise, as suggested by the chauffeurs, of a usurping group. The casting off of the old and its replacement by the new, a theme familiar from *The Pumpkin Eater, Accident,* and *The Go-Between*, becomes the subject of the remaining portion of Pinter's script. The last volume of Proust expresses this process most eloquently in the letter that the aging Marcel receives from Gilberte.

> As for the short cut up the hill which you were so fond of and which we used to call the hawthorn path, where you claim that as a small child you fell in love with me (whereas I assure you in all truthfulness it was I who was in love with you), I cannot tell you how important it has become. The huge field of corn upon which it emerges is the famous Hill 307, which you must have seen mentioned again and again in the bulletins. [P. 46]

Pinter goes beyond the utilization of color stock for black and white filming of this crucial sequence at the Guermantes's to force the issues of decrepitude and usurpation. He describes Marcel's entrance into the drawing room in the following direction:

419. INT. DRAWING ROOM. PRINCE DE GUERMANTES'S HOUSE. 1921.
The drawing room doors open.
Camera enters with MARCEL, *who hesitates.*
Hundreds of faces, some of which turn towards him, grotesquely made up, grotesquely old.
He walks into the room. Voices. Faces. The wigs and makeup, combined with the extreme age of those who with difficulty stand, sit, gesture, laugh, give the impression of grotesque fancy dress. [P. 168]

The once youthful eccentricities and banter of the group appear likewise macabre in this setting and condition. All of the living figures of Marcel's past are there, like the ludicrous corpses of an attenuated world, ravaged by disease, drugs, and decay. Even the network of sin and deviance has lost its potency in this milieu, and new evidence of its reach (to Gilberte) passes without comment or impact. Then, in the midst of all this death and chatter, Pinter initiates his closing sequence, discovering for the first time a youthful presence in the room.

443. MARCEL STANDING ALONE.
  GILBERTE *approaches* MARCEL *with a* YOUNG GIRL *of sixteen. She is very lovely.*
  GILBERTE. This is my daughter.
    MLLE. DE SAINT-LOUP *smiles and inclines her head.* MARCEL *gazes at her.*
    Suddenly all of the sounds in the room die. MLLE. DE SAINT-LOUP *speaks silently, smiling.*
    Over this shot we hear the garden gate bell at Combray, "resilient, ferruginous, interminable, fresh and shrill."
    The bell continues over the following shots.
444. *The vast room, the multitude of people talking. No sound.*
445. MLLE. DE SAINT-LOUP *smiling.*
446. *The trees at Hudimesnil.*
447. *The steeples at Martinville.*
448. *Flash of yellow screen.*
449. *The river Vivonne at Combray.*
450. *The roofs of Combray.*
451. *The garden at Combray in the evening.*
452. *The bell at the garden gate.*
453. SWANN *opening the garden gate and departing.*
454. MARCEL *as a child looking out of his bedroom window. The bell ceases.* [Pp. 175-76]

The emergence of Mlle. de Saint-Loup to instigate and preside over Marcel's descent into the world of the past, this triumph of the innocent over the impotence of the disillusioned, remains typical of and necessary for Pinter's conclusion. The retirement of the disenchanted into their orderly webs of artifice forms a consistent feature of conclusion in all of Pinter's screenplays. Here it deviates only in lacking the pessimistic vacuousness that has characterized all previous ascending representatives. If Pinter has brightened the nature of the usurping corps, however, he remains relentless in his assault on the overthrown, depicting Marcel's final epiphany (despite his admitted sympathy for its sentiment) as precisely what it represents: a preference for the accessible immobility of fiction over the incomprehensible chaos of life.

Pinter's intended plan for the screenplay, the simultaneous development of two patterns, "one, a movement, chiefly narrative, toward disillusion, and the other, more intermittent, toward revelation, rising to where time that was lost is found, and fixed forever in art," emerges powerfully from his schematic presentation of the material from Proust's work. As Brater has suggested, "Revelation and disillusion have been rendered visually through cinematic time rather than verbally through fiction."[9]

Pinter's utilization of the yellow screen operates toward fulfillment of both dynamics. In the former, the movement toward disillusion, the close-up view is linked to two disturbing moments in the screenplay, involving repellent magnifications of the faces of Odette and Albertine. Both instances occur as the women draw closer for a kiss, occasioning identical descriptions from the viewpoints variously of Swann and Marcel; *"Her cheeks, smooth and flushed, come closer to his eye and show a coarser grain"* (p. 22 and p. 87).

The suggestion here that close proximity results in a contamination of the formerly distant finds an emphatic parallel in Pinter's rendition of Marcel's infatuation with the Guermantes. Marcel's worship of this noble family evolves, after he finally penetrates into their graces, into his disgust for their triviality. Two incidents, involving first his grandmother and then Swann, clarify this revulsion. The first transpires following his grandmother's retreat, during a walk with Marcel in the park, into a public lavatory, where she apparently conceals an attack of stroke. When she emerges from the building, dazed and disheveled, she remarks with great difficulty to Marcel on the insensitive conversation between two park attendants, who had been chatting outside the lavatory; "I heard what she was saying. Could anything be more like the Guermantes, the Verdurins? Exactly the same" (p. 47). Marcel's encounter with Swann at the Guermantes's house, during which Swann's attempts to communicate the imminence of his death pass unnoticed in the Guermantes's frenzy over a dinner engagement, provides the second accentuation of Marcel's disenchantment with the Guermantes. This scene concludes as the Duc delays their departure for dinner by sending the Duchesse upstairs to change her shoes: a delay he refused to tolerate when it was motivated by her concern for Swann's health.

The yellow screen functions to identify the movement toward revelation through its association with Marcel's epiphanic visions of the steeples, the trees, and his past, and with his ecstatic appreciation of Vinteuil's music. These moments are linked together through both montage and sound track, suggesting Marcel's transcendance of his mounting disillusionment by means of withdrawal into art. His escape into Vinteuil's music, immediately subsequent to his apprisal of Albertine's probable deceitfulness, exemplifies this theme and its technique. After noting that, *"In all shots of the audience at this stage, the sound of the music is dominated by those of fans, feet shifting, yawns, coughs,"* Pinter indicates the following sequence of shots:

318. MARCEL, LISTENING.
(NOTE: *The septet continues over the following shots, which are now all silent, the music quite pure, no extraneous sounds. During the course of this sequence the music will cross-fade to the climax of the third movement of the septet.*)

319. MARCEL.

320. THE MUSICIANS.

321. THE AUDIENCE.

322. MARCEL.

323. YELLOW SCREEN.

324. THE MUSICIANS.

325. THE AUDIENCE.

326. MARCEL.

327. YELLOW SCREEN.

In this shot of the yellow screen the music reaches its sustained climax.

328. MARCEL.

Applause around him.
He sits still, joyous.

329. FLASH OF THE STEEPLES AT MARTINVILLE.
SILENT.

330. M. VINTEUIL WALKING TOWARD CAMERA.
SILENT.

In background MLLE. VINTEUIL *and* FRIEND *playing the piano.* [Pp. 138-39]

The accumulation of these images, which climax in the yellow screen and culminate in the vision of Vinteuil and his scandalous daughter, formulates a statement of the triumph by art over mundane, inscrutable reality. In this sense Pinter establishes the dual nature of Marcel's retreat from life as a simultaneous secession from and transcendance over intolerable, incomprehensible experience, "rising to where time that was lost is found, and fixed forever in art." The patch of yellow wall, Pinter's emblem of inscrutability, estrangement, discrepancy, insignificance, and disillusionment, becomes also his invocation of revelation. Thus, he describes the final shot of the screenplay:

455. *Vermeer's* View of Delft.
Camera moves in swiftly to the patch of yellow wall in the painting.
Yellow screen.
MARCEL'S VOICE OVER. It was time to begin. [P. 177]

From all points of view—theme, action, and image—the circle is complete.

Pinter's growing fascination by the subjects of past, time, and memory obtains similar modes of expression in his screenplays for *Accident* and *The Go-Between,* in which the themes of an obdurate past also conclude in a reprise of their inciting mechanisms. This fondness for circularity as a structural manifestation of our efforts at characterizing the past is evident also in Pinter's original plays of this time period. In *Old Times,* which he wrote immediately preceding his work on Proust, three characters struggle to control each other by alleging opportunistic and irreconcilable versions of the past. The role of memory, especially as a manipulative fabrication, figures centrally in the action, and the action itself conjures temporal dislocation through the initial mysterious presence of an ostensibly absent character. Suggestions of circularity occur also in the initiation of opening dialogue (an answer to an unposed question), in the descriptions of the two settings (mirror images of each other), and in the final action of the play (an enactment of a story told earlier in the play). Together with the screenplays for *Accident, The Go-Between,* and the Proust, *Old Times* implies that the search for the past is not only problematic, but also endlessly circuitous.

During an interview with Mel Gussow before *Old Times* opened in New York, Pinter commented, "The whole question of time and all its reverberations and possible meanings really does seem to absorb me more and more."[10] The question of time recurs conspicuously in Pinter's two major plays following *The Proust Screenplay* (1972): *No Man's Land* (1974) and *Betrayal* (1978). In the former the past resumes its "artistic" nature, existing only as the characters constitute and reconstitute it according to their immediate objectives. According to Peter Hall, who directed *No Man's Land* for London's National Theatre, Pinter stubbornly defended a line in the script that characterized the present as "unscrupulous." Hall, who questioned the meaning of this usage, describes Pinter's clarification as follows: "He chose the word unscrupulous because it shows the ruthlessness of the present, and its ability to lead as it were a life of its own. His sense is simply 'the present will not be changed.'"[11] Consequently, efforts at shaping or escaping from the immutable present occur through recitations of the variable past. Time, although structurally intact, suffers thematic fractures and generally concedes to a milieu in which the imagination prevails, or at least attempts to prevail, over linear reality. In this respect the major characters in *No Man's Land,* both poets, strive for an ordination of subjectivity similar to the one sought by Marcel and to the one that will be sought in *The Last Tycoon* by Monroe Stahr. With *Betrayal,* however, the past becomes concrete; the play's structure works backward in time, revealing the fallibility of memory and a maze of deceit as it regresses. Enoch Brater has attributed Pinter's use of this strategy to his work on the film adaptations, identifying the play as cinematic in its temporal pattern and in its manipulation of images.[12] Despite Pinter's objective revelation of the past through this conceit in *Betrayal* (which he subsequently adapted for film), its concerns remain, even more plainly, with the deceptions that are formulated in the "present." Such verification is a clearly intended artifice; in real time the past is conveniently erased, revised, and rewritten. However much "the past is not past,"[13] its empirical disposition is palimpsest.

The Last Tycoon

[The industrial spying] made his work secret in part, often devious, slow—and hard to describe as the plans of a general, where the psychological factors become too tenuous and we end by merely adding up the successes and failures. But I have determined to give you a glimpse of him functioning, which is my excuse for what follows. It is drawn partly from a paper I wrote in college on A Producer's Day *and partly from my imagination. . . . As for me, I was head over heels in love with him then, and you can take what I say for what it's worth.[1]*

Pinter's screen adaptation of F. Scott Fitzgerald's *The Last Tycoon* also poses special problems: it does not exist in published form. Since Elia Kazan's direction of the film is a first-time collaboration, the degree of his fidelity to Pinter's text seems uncertain, and the film alone is consequently untrustworthy as a reflection of Pinter's work. For my comparison I shall work from a copy of the shooting script, made available by the American Film Institute in Los Angeles, and a text of the novel (itself an uncompleted work).

Fitzgerald died before he was able to finish the novel from which Pinter's screenplay derives. The published text, therefore, contains writing and ideas that sometimes lack precision, conciseness, and coherence. In a foreword printed with Scribner's edition of the unfinished novel, Edmund Wilson makes some noteworthy observations regarding the state of the text.

Scott Fitzgerald died suddenly of a heart attack (December 21, 1940) the day after he had written the first episode of Chapter 6 of his novel. The text which is given here is a draft made by the author after considerable rewriting, but it is by no means a finished version. In the margins of almost every one of the episodes, Fitzgerald had written comments . . . which expressed his dissatisfaction with them or indicated his ideas about revising them. His intention was to produce a novel as concentrated and as carefully constructed as *The Great Gatsby* had been, and he would unquestionably have sharpened the effect of most of these scenes as we have them by cutting and by heightening of color. He had originally planned that the novel should be about 60,000 words long, but he had written at the time of his death about 70,000 words without, as will be seen from his outline, having told much more than half his story.[2]

Judging by Fitzgerald's projections for the length of the work and by the rambling diffuseness of the extant portion itself, much of this draft was due for excision. Thus, Pinter inherits from this source greater latitude and greater urgency for his work. Furthermore, rather than reach beyond the elucidated portion of the novel into second-half episodes suggested by Fitzgerald's outline, Pinter restricts his scope to the first-half draft, refocusing the themes and material into an independent unity. Despite the unusual demands of this undertaking, Pinter's alterations of the original work remain minimal for, like the sources of his previous screenplays, Fitzgerald's novel plays directly into his hands.

The situation of Fitzgerald's narrator, Cecilia Brady, resembles that of the third-party figure whom Pinter extracted from *The Servant*. Cecilia, however, enters even less into Fitzgerald's action (as far as it goes) and possesses fewer facts and connections with respect to it. As she does in the quote that opens this chapter, Cecilia must frequently admit her penchant for fantasy in order to excuse accounts of which she could have no conceivable knowledge. Once again the necessity for fabrication in the absence of hard information comprises a chief theme in the work.

Aside from Cecilia's plethora of narrative disclaimers, numerous anecdotes in the novel espouse this idea. In our first solid impression of Monroe Stahr, the central character of the story, he is chatting with an airplane pilot in the cockpit. Cecilia recounts the dialogue between them from gossip she accumulates years later.

> He [Stahr] was looking down at the mountains.
> "Suppose you were a railroad man," he said. "You have to send a train through there somewhere. Well, you get your surveyors' reports, and you find there's three or four or half a dozen gaps, and not one is better than the other. You've got to decide—on what basis? You can't test the best way—except by doing it. So you just do it."
> The pilot thought he had missed something.
> "How do you mean?"
> "You choose some way for no reason at all—because that mountain's pink or the blueprint is a better blue. You see?" [P. 23]

In the concluding episodes of Fitzgerald's draft, Stahr expresses this idea more succinctly: "You have to say, 'it's got to be like this—no other way'—even if you're not sure. A dozen times a week that happens to me. Situations where there is no real reason for anything. You pretend there is'' (p. 158). Choices, decisions, recountings, must transpire without the facts because, in many cases, the facts quite simply are not accessible.

The preeminence of the imagination and illusion, as a corollary to this condition, also forms a major theme in the novel. Fitzgerald had contrived to write about the declining reign of a Hollywood studio head (fashioned after Irving Thalberg) during the golden age of moviemaking, but he managed before his death to describe only the first harbinger of Stahr's incipient demise: the rapid flower and decay of his romance with the mysterious Kathleen. The very backdrop of the movie business supplies a tension between fact and fiction that mirrors the self-recriminations of the narrator. Both Cecilia's imaginative deviations and the film industry's generic fabrications provide metaphoric affirmation of the preponderance of fantasy.

Pinter includes Cecilia in his screenplay, but, since he strips her of her narrative function (see the first chapter and preceding screenplay discussions for his probable reasoning in this), she seems a rather superfluous appendage to the story. Two screenplay episodes, through which Pinter explores Cecilia's character and connects it to both the themes and action of the main plot, were deleted from the film, and the surviving sequences, which serve only to develop her circumstances (for example, her discovery of her studio executive father making love to his secretary in the office), would probably confuse anyone unfamiliar with Fitzgerald's novel. Cecilia operates in the film primarily as a reflection of Stahr's situation: both of them desire the one thing they cannot, despite their overwhelming power, have. Stahr is obsessed with Kathleen, and Cecilia is obsessed with Stahr.

Pinter utilizes Cecilia to indicate another of the novel's concerns, a contrasting of Hitler's activities with those of Hollywood, in a scene between a screenwriter, Wylie, and her. This scene, which was excluded from the film, occurs in Wylie's car, as the two cruise Sunset Boulevard. As Wylie pesters Cecilia with his unwelcome affections, she fiddles with the radio dial and improvises a scenario for her next meeting with Stahr. A broadcast chorus of ''Sieg Heils'' accompanies Wylie's protestations that Cecilia's romantic delusions are plagiarized from one of his scripts.[3] Such confounding of fiction with real experience is epidemic in the screenplay. Here, Wylie and Cecilia simply tune out the inevitability of Hitler in order to pursue their separate dreams and to assert the authority of their wills over the phenomenal world. For them, Hitler may be manipulated as easily as a retake of a flawed scene. The supremacy of fictional whimsy over factual exigency reflects in

Wylie's comment to Cecilia, "We don't use that line this year," in response to her description of her devotion to Stahr. Cecilia will subsequently repeat Wylie's remark to Stahr as a reaction to his own feelings, echoing this application of fictional values to experiential circumstances, and another screenwriter, Boxley, will exhibit similar disorientation in a later scene when, after a drunken confrontation with Stahr, he yells, "I want copyright protection for that scene I just wrote! About the drunken writer and the producer!" (p. 76). Stahr's predicament consists precisely in this confusion of subjective and objective worlds, but Cecilia's thematic relevance to this issue is diminished by the absence of the Sunset Boulevard scene from the film.

The screenplay also includes a less successful attempt to involve Cecilia in the main action of the story by describing a scene in which she, overcome by a fit of jealous curiosity, visits Kathleen's unoccupied house. This scene, derived from one of Fitzgerald's efforts to justify Cecilia's uncanny familiarity with Kathleen's circumstances, was also eliminated from the film, probably because it fails, once divorced from its role as narrative espionage, to accomplish any plausible connection of her with the principal action. Although we can stretch for instances of foils and parallels, the inclusion of Cecilia fails overall to integrate with the primary lines of the story and constitutes the film's weakest link.

From the opening sequence of the screenplay, however, Pinter capitalizes skillfully on the movie industry metaphor, which now assumes the self-referential role vacated by Cecilia. Setting aside the first chapter of Fitzgerald's work, which chiefly chronicles the thoughts of Cecilia on a transcontinental air flight that appears to represent one half of an intended frame for the novel, Pinter begins his adaptation with two inventions of his own. The initial cinematic sequence consists in a black and white (more accurately sepia) period scene that transpires in a restaurant and depicts a gangland style attack. (This scene has been denounced, with marginal relevance, as untypical of Thalberg's "prestige" films.[4]) After some moments an offscreen voice interrupts the scene's progress, and the camera switches instantly to color film, pulling back to reveal a screening room and the criticisms by its occupants. (In his screenplay for *The French Lieutenant's Woman,* Pinter will employ a similar device, reversing the sequence of artifice and "reality" in his opening segment.) As our first impression crumbles into the menial exertions of technicians and equipment, a second one emerges to provoke a whirligig; a studio tour guide has hardly completed his explanation of camera-simulated earthquakes when an "actual" 'earthquake occurs in the "nonfiction" action of the film. Here, as Pinter introduces

Stahr and other chief figures of the story, we mentally review the tour guide's demystifying spiel, becoming, even in our smugness, a little mystified by the abrupt vortex of realities.

In the aftermath of the quake, the contrasting domains of "reality" and illusion acquire striking dimensions. Pinter and Kazan meticulously transform the scene, which Fitzgerald describes as follows: "Under the moon the back lot was thirty acres of fairyland—not because the locations really looked like African jungles and French chateaux and schooners at anchor and Broadway by night, but because they looked like the torn picture books of childhood, like fragments of stories dancing in an open fire" (p. 32). As Stahr surveys the quake, fire, and flood damage, "reality's" toll on the back lot illusions, the outsized head of the Goddess Siva appears adrift in the flood, some distance away. The workers remark on the Indian idol with pragmatic banality (" 'De Mille needs that head next week' "), while the thing "earnestly waddles and bumps its way down the current of an impromptu river," and Stahr fixes intently on two women who are trapped aboard the head. One of the women, we later learn, bears an uncanny resemblance to Stahr's dead wife, Minna Davis. While Cecilia provides this background and insight in the novel, Pinter includes the tragic Minna Davis myth and image as a part of the tour's itinerary, and in both versions Stahr articulates the likeness during later episodes.

This initial vision of Kathleen, as the workers rescue her from the ravages of nature and the sanctuary of artifice, has significance on several planes. Stahr's impression of her occurs in a dizzying muddle of illusion and reality. Pinter's manifestation of Stahr's attraction to Kathleen repeats a technique familiar from *The Proust Screenplay*; two silent shots of Stahr and one of Kathleen from his point of view interrupt the pandemonium of the rescue operations, suggesting a transcendant negation of reality by the imagination. Beyond the circumstances of bewildering milieu, he confuses her identity with that of his dead wife, so that his obsession with her grounds in delusion at two levels of perception. Kathleen, in fact, persists in her mysteriousness throughout their relationship, becoming almost a figment of his mental circuits. Her motives and past never yield to his curiosity; whatever information she provides about herself seems contradicted by her actions, and, even during the most intimate episodes, she exhibits a peculiar distance from him.

Stahr, however, in his appetite for and habituation with the cinematic world of the ideal, worships her elusiveness. In the novel he betrays his thinking by remarks he makes to his writers, disparaging their characterization of a film's heroine. "In the first place he wanted to tell them what kind of girl she was—what kind of girl he approved of here. She was a perfect girl with a few small faults. . . . She stood for health, vitality, ambition and love. . . . That was the kind of story this was— thin, clean and shining. No doubts" (p. 53). Pinter retains the substance of this speech, but alters its circumstances to combine it with a stroll through the studio back lots, during which we glimpse Busby Berkeley girls, flood reparations, western towns, and Polynesian villages. Against this background of incongruities and facades, Stahr upbraids Wylie over the writer's maligning of the girl.

> STAHR. You've given her a secret life. She doesn't have a secret life. You've made her a melancholic. She is not a melancholic. . . . The girl stands for health, vitality, love.
>
> WYLIE. So how do you want the girl?
>
> STAHR. Perfect. [P. 32–33]

The film will repeat Stahr's demand for a perfect girl as a voice-over during the closing sequence.

Kathleen is a harbinger of Stahr's demise. As Fitzgerald describes him and as Pinter depicts him, Stahr's featured attribute lies in his ability to remove himself from the debris of living; he observes situations through the eye of the camera. Cecilia notes this in the first chapter of the novel.

> He had flown up very high to see. . . . Beating his wings tenaciously— finally frantically—and keeping on beating them, he had stayed up there longer than most of us, and then, remembering all he had seen from his great height of how things were, he had settled gradually to earth. . . . You could say that this was where an accidental wind blew him, but I don't think so. I would rather think that in a "long shot" he saw a new way of measuring our jerky hopes and graceful rogueries and awkward sorrows. [P. 24]

Like Teddy, the impassive philosopher who loses his wife in *The Homecoming,* Stahr operates "on things and not in things." His chief peril in this practice consists in any slip-up that might expose the flimsy basis for his decision-making. Stahr's power depends on his ability to sustain remoteness and the appearance of conviction and correctness in his orders. His affair with Kathleen renders him fallible in all of these respects: he participates, he equivocates, and he miscalculates. He blunders even in his initial attempt to locate the mysterious girl after the flood, insisting to the bloodhounds on his staff that the girl wore a silver belt. This clue leads him to the wrong girl and reveals the flaw, the slight misapprehension of fact, the misstep of his mind, that will bring his ruin. The tricks of the past, memory, and perception will spell his tragedy. At this point Stahr attempts to forsake the search, but the mistaken girl maneuvers him into the presence of Kathleen, and he loses his capacity for objectivity: he becomes irrationally obsessed with Kathleen.

Without the footing of fact and comprehensibility, Stahr pushes farther and farther into the climes of make-believe, invoking criteria from the fictive world of the movies. His effort to affix the lifeless forms of fiction to the chaotic conditions of living meets the same fate that such efforts have met in all of Pinter's previous screenplays. Like Tony, Jo, Quiller, Leo, and Marcel, Stahr becomes a victim of his own perspective, as his interpretations and hence his expectations fail to account for a recondite, but vindictive, reality.

The dynamics of Stahr's struggle ramify in various emblems and situations that develop in the novel and in the film. Perhaps the central symbol of the completed portion of the novel, and one that makes a perfect Pinter fit, consists in Stahr's half-constructed new house. The old house, to which Stahr returns each night to repeat the lonely rituals of the past, comes to represent, particularly in Pinter's treatment, attenuated forms. The new house, to which Stahr absconds with Kathleen, signifies the unready, impossible future. It stands roofless by the ocean, a protectionless skeleton, whose only articulated feature (a projection booth) suggests a replication of the past and an escape from the future into illusion. Ping pong tables, some props, and freshly purchased "real" grass have been furnished by the studio for a recent party on the premises. Here, in this half-formed retreat, imperiled by nature and fortified by the trappings of Hollywood, Stahr enacts his ill-fated, storybook romance with the incarnation of his dead wife: Kathleen.

The friction betwen reality and illusion dominates Stahr's professional experiences as well as his personal ones. Beyond the panoramic instances of double-vision images, such as the one of "Abraham Lincoln" in the studio cafeteria with his fast-food snack, in both the novel and the screenplay, the technical machinations of film production provide some uncanny juxtapositions and self-referential perspectives. Actors' personalities repeatedly clash with those of their roles, special effects give way to the incongruity of their manufacture, and Stahr contributes some notable demystifications of screenwriting. In the last respect, Pinter lifts from the novel some dialogue between Stahr and the screenwriter, Boxley, which seems to describe precisely his own writing technique. Here Stahr spells out for the stumped Boxley an approach to creating a film script.

STAHR. Suppose you're in your office.
You've been fighting duels all day.
You're exhausted.
He sits.

This is you.

He stands.

A girl comes in.

He goes to the door, opens it, comes back in, shuts it.

She doesn't see you. She takes off her gloves, opens her purse and dumps it out on the table.

He mimes these actions.

You watch her.

He sits.

This is you.

He stands.

She has two dimes, a nickel and a matchbox. She leaves the nickel on the table, puts the two dimes back in her purse, takes her gloves to the stove, opens it and puts them inside.

He mimes all this while talking.

She lights a match. Suddenly the telephone rings. She picks it up.

He mimes this.

She listens. She says, 'I've never owned a pair of black gloves in my life.' She hangs up, kneels by the stove, lights another match.

He kneels, mimes lighting another match, then quickly jumps up and goes to the door.

Suddenly you notice there's another man in the room, watching every move the girl makes. . . .

Pause.

BOXLEY (*intrigued*). What happens?

STAHR. I don't know. I was just making pictures. [Pp. 49–51]

Pinter's craft, from what we have seen in the screenplays and from what he himself claims, reduces perfectly to the activity of "making pictures," of cauterizing opaque images that speak all that can be told. He retains this anecdote from Fitzgerald, providing it a bit of trimming and two twists. Fitzgerald ends the encounter with the following dialogue:

"What was the nickel for?" asked Boxley evasively.

"I don't know," said Stahr. Suddenly he laughed. "Oh yes—the nickel was for the movies."

"What in the hell do you pay me for?" Boxley demanded. "I don't understand the damn stuff."

"You will," said Stahr grinning, "or you wouldn't have asked about the nickel." [P. 43]

Pinter reproduces this exchange intact, with one significant modification: his Stahr refers the question of the nickel's destination to an attending secretary, who offers the movie hypothesis. In this Pinter seems to insist that anyone's guess is as good as his, authorizing a range of responses to his own writing, and recalling Stahr's earlier comments on the nature of interpretation and choice. The second twist occurs near the end of the film, where Pinter demonstrates his fondness for this piece of dialogue in an unusual and stunning screen direction. Alone in his office, Stahr abruptly faces the camera and repeats the same scenario directly to the audience. The omnipresence of impenetrability becomes his final epiphany.

In the symbol of the unfinished house, we have already observed how Fitzgerald's work, even in its choices of detail, suits Pinter's sensibility. Another of the novel's motifs sympathetic with Pinter's concerns consists in its depiction of communication. The novel contains a dozen references to "thundering silences" or similar lapses in speech, and the meetings between Stahr and Kathleen constitute tributes to the inarticulate. Their conversations never transcend the banal (which Pinter captures masterfully), and the wordlessness of their emotions and experiences is a frequent alibi in Cecilia's laborious narration (which Pinter discards as unnecessary).

The conditions of speechlessness in Stahr and Kathleen render their motives and actions still less comprehensible, as her decision to make love to him and his to risk losing her materialize abruptly and inexplicably. Fitzgerald elucidates Stahr's dilemma, the internal crisis that prevents him from acting to cement the relationship, and again we note the abrasive juxtaposition of the world of illusion with the world of reality.

> He knew he could have said it then . . . for he knew it was, he knew he could not let her go now; but something else said to sleep on it as an adult, no romantic. And not to tell her till tomorrow. . . .
> He was very busy the next morning, Saturday. At two o'clock, when he came from luncheon, there was a stack of telegrams—a company ship was lost in the arctic; a star was in disgrace; a writer was suing for one million dollars. Jews were dead miserably beyond the sea. The last telegram stared up at him:
> *I was married at noon today. Goodbye:* and on a sticker attached, *Send your answer by Western Union Telegram.* [Pp. 149–50]

All that survives in the film from this is our advance knowledge that Kathleen has previous plans for marriage, Stahr's failure to request interruption of these, and the telegram. To Stahr's incessant and noncommittal declarations, "I don't want to lose you," Kathleen stubbornly repeats her demand, "I want a quiet life" (p. 71). She expresses no interest in the movie industry or its product, and is immune to, even put off by, Stahr's impressive stature in the eyes of the world.

STAHR. Do you ever go to the movies?
KATHLEEN. Oh . . . not much.
STAHR. Why not?
KATHLEEN. Should I?
STAHR. Millions of people do.
KATHLEEN. Why?
STAHR. Because movies are necessary to them. I give them what they need.
KATHLEEN. What you need.
They stand still.
STAHR. It's my life. [Pp. 64–65]

Her awareness of Stahr's need for authorial power and her disinterest
in his fame and fortune make Kathleen even less accessible and more
attractive to Stahr. Despite her apparent implacability, she reveals a
certain vulnerability to Stahr's personal charm, and several times signals her willingness to commit herself to him. Stahr, however, misses
his chances either through misinterpretation of her invitation or through
an obstinate belief in his own ability to dictate eventualities.

KATHLEEN. We're getting married.
STAHR. Are you in love with him?
KATHLEEN. Oh yes. It's all arranged. He saved my life.
Pause.
KATHLEEN. I just wanted to see you once more.
Pause.
KATHLEEN. It's all arranged. [P. 88]

Although Kathleen's hesitant, elliptical speech here plainly offers Stahr
an opportunity to assert his feelings for her, he remains silent. Shortly
afterwards, during the moment which Fitzgerald describes preceding
Stahr's receipt of the telegram, Stahr attempts and fails to proclaim his
intentions. The film dialogue for this critical exchange, Stahr's missed
proposal that results in his loss of Kathleen, proceeds as follows:

STAHR. Are you leaving California?
KATHLEEN. We might . . . I might . . . I don't know.
Pause.
KATHLEEN. Are you going away . . . for a holiday?
STAHR. No.
He stops the car, suddenly.
STAHR. Listen—
KATHLEEN. What?
Pause.
STAHR. Nothing. [P. 90]

Here, in the subtextual labyrinth of communication, Pinter conveys the concealed thoughts and dimensions of his characters, constructing his dialogue from detectable interior truths rather than from primarily narrative criteria. Thus, Stahr's hopes and flaws emerge with equal clarity in his fateful omission.

Pinter's characteristic concern with dominance and subservience, particularly evident in his playwriting and in his screenplay for *The Servant,* likewise obtains secure roots in Fitzgerald's novel. Although Stahr's weakening status becomes a focused issue only in the last pages of the draft portion, Fitzgerald's outlines and notes indicate that the problem of power was to become central to the work. The carefully guarded motives and maneuvers of film industry potentates receive frequent attention in Cecilia's narrative, and she observes in a metaphorical vein that her father's office building resembles a "perpetual tightrope" (p. 28). Stahr has apparently discovered the potency of obfuscated motive in real as well as fictional worlds; his dramaturgical method profits him in both spheres of activity. He delegates no authority; as a "paternalistic employer," he knows all the ropes, calls all the shots, and keeps all the secrets to himself. "There was nothing to question or argue. Stahr must be right always, not most of the time, but always—or the system would melt down like gradual butter" (p. 75). He dwells in an exile of solitude and disguise, and everything hinges on his first false step.

The contours of threat materialize gradually around Stahr; early references in the novel to the possibility of socialist revolution transform into union uprisings that challenge his paternalistic hierarchy. "She has never heard the word labor troubles," Stahr sighs as he describes the perfect girl for his writers (p. 53). This threat, however, remains a thin motif until after Stahr's receipt of the telegram announcing Kathleen's marriage. Now the "labor troubles" begin to solidify as Stahr turns on them as a scapegoat for his frustration: "I want you to arrange something, Cecilia—I want to meet a Communist Party member" (p. 153). Brimmer, the Communist, thus assumes for Stahr the dimensions of The Intruder. The weakening executive's sublimated hostility—his deliberate solicitation of a target for his frustrations and his confusion of Brimmer's identity with that of "the American" whom Kathleen has married—clarifies long before he engages the Communist in a fist fight, and mistakes the man outright in the fog of regaining consciousness. Cecilia persuades Brimmer to leave, and then she turns to the outstretched Stahr.

> After a moment he came awake with a terrific convulsion and bounced up on his feet.

"Where is he?" he shouted.
"Who?" I asked innocently.
"That American. Why in the hell did you have to marry him, you damn fool." [Pp. 165-66]

Stahr's mental exhaustion, exacerbated by unaccustomed drunkenness, has become so acute that he mistakes not only Brimmer for "the American," but Cecilia for Kathleen. Stahr, like Pinter's threesome in *Old Times,* has invested too heavily in the comfortable clarity of fantasy and has plunged headlong through its barriers, into its perils. Where in *Old Times* fraudulent allegations acquire the ominous power to transform reality, in Stahr's case they clash openly with empirical fact; his stab at the darker blue of the blueprint has revealed itself.

In yet another example of the novel's consonance with Pinter's devices, Stahr's fall from power finds expression in the inevitable party game, here ping pong. He challenges Brimmer to a match shortly before the fist fight, but eventually retires from the game, after flouting its rules by "batting a whole box of new balls across to Brimmer" (p. 164), to drink and watch the others play. Again the game captures perfectly in a metaphor the dynamics of Stahr's demise, and Pinter reproduces it faithfully in his script.

Fitzgerald's draft terminates at this point, as Stahr recovers from his decking by Brimmer and suggests that he and Cecilia spend the night at Doug Fairbanks's ranch. In order to unify and conclude the story at this point with dispatch, Pinter aborts the journey to Doug Fairbanks's ranch and manipulates the confrontation with Brimmer into greater significance.

Early on, Pinter focuses the tensions between Stahr and the members of the company board of directors over unwarranted expenditure. Stahr's insistence on retakes for perfection and his support for the making of money-losing "quality films" provoke visible, but carefully masked, opposition from the board. Pinter also insinuates disquiet among the rank and file (an idea that receives more attention in the screenplay that in the film); when Brimmer appears, he intrudes apparently at the request of the writers, not by Stahr's invitation. Cecilia hosts their meeting, and Stahr arrives fresh from the news of Kathleen's telegram. Pinter rapidly delineates the difference between the two men, inventing several exchanges between them to accomplish this task. The initial small talk between Stahr and Brimmer in the film establishes that Brimmer is a Tennessee Baptist and Stahr is a New York Jew: a singular contrasting of identities. Having already reassigned Brimmer to the role of a genuine intruder, Pinter writes deliberately against a typified Communist image in his characterization of him, moving the figure toward a more generalized symbol of usurpation. We learn, for example, that Brimmer possesses a better education than Stahr.

> CECILIA (*TO* STAHR). You have done well by water. (*to* BRIMMER) And you by land.
> STAHR. Sorry?
> CECILIA. *Anthony and Cleopatra.* Did you recognize it?
> STAHR. Shakespeare? No. I didn't get much Shakespeare at school. How about you, Mr. Brimmer?
> BRIMMER. Oh, a little. [P. 100]

For Pinter, Brimmer assumes representation of the ascending tide; he is educated, homogenized, and empty. Stahr, in some dialogue derived from the novel, accuses Brimmer of lacking belief even in Communism.

> STAHR. I don't get to meet Reds very often. Are you a real Red?
> BRIMMER. A real one.
> STAHR. I guess some of you believe in it.
> BRIMMER. Quite a few.
> STAHR. Not you.
> BRIMMER *frowns.*
> BRIMMER. Oh yes.
> STAHR. Oh no.
> BRIMMER *laughs.*
> BRIMMER. Oh yes. [P. 102]

Pinter's Stahr associates Brimmer's presence with a grab for power ("It looks to me like a try for power. I'll give them money but I won't give them power. . . ."), and, although Brimmer speaks only on behalf of the writers, Stahr imagines a much greater constituency for him. Bowing out of the ping pong match, he addresses Cecilia: "I'm going to beat up Brimmer. . . . This fellow has an influence over you. Over all you young people. You don't know what you're doing" (p. 107). As Fitzgerald denotes, Stahr then attempts a physical attack on Brimmer, who easily knocks him unconscious.

After Stahr regains consciousness, Pinter is on his own. Stahr, according to the film, stays the night, ill, at Cecilia's house. We observe the silhouette of Cecilia's high-ranking board member father, Mr. Brady, observing from the window as Stahr staggers into the house. In the morning Stahr receives a message that the board will convene immediately in an emergency session. Stahr, arriving late and in dark glasses to conceal his bruised eye, has clearly become the odd man out from the moment of his entrance into the tensely silent conference room. Brady addresses him thickly:

BRADY. They've [the New York office] asked me to be the spokesman of this board in all further discussions. (*He sips his coffee and smiles.*) They don't consider that trying to beat up the writers' representative is in the best interests of the company. I just want to tell you that this board endorses these views. We also recommend that you go away for a long rest. Take a break. Go to Tahiti or somewhere.

STAHR *stares at* BRADY.

STAHR. This studio will fall without me.

BRADY (*sympathetically*). Take a break, Monroe.

STAHR. This is a waste of time. I'll be talking to New York.

BRADY. They'll be glad to speak to you. Any time. Oh, they said to be sure to go see a doctor about your eye. [Pp. 112-13]

Except for the parting conciliation of another board member ("Mr. Stahr . . . we'll see the studio doesn't fall"), this speech comprises the last unrepeated dialogue of the film. As Stahr walks toward his office and closes himself inside, the screenplay prescribes a montage of fragments from previous scenes intercut with highly contrived clips from movie sequences.

144. *INT. CORRIDOR.*

> STAHR *walks down the corridor, passing the photographs of stars on the walls.*
> *He swallows a pill.*
> *A watchman is testing locks.*
> STAHR *passes him, gets to his office, goes in.*

145. *INT. STAHR'S OFFICE.*

> STAHR *standing in the middle of his office.*
> *Sudden cuts of:*

146. *A COWBOY RIDING INTO A WESTERN TOWN.*

147. *A CARTOON.*

148. *DIDI.*

DIDI. Nobody likes me or something.

149. *TWO MEN FIGHTING IN A STORM.*

150. *BRIMMER, LAUGHING.*

BRIMMER. Oh yes.

151. *HUNDREDS OF NEGROES PLAYING WHITE PIANOS.*

152. *CECILIA.*

CECILIA. We don't use that line this year.

153. *GARBO IN 'CAMILLE.'*

154. *DOCTOR.*

DOCTOR. Any pain?

155. *THE SAN FRANCISCO EARTHQUAKE.*

156. *STAHR IN HIS OFFICE. HE IS STANDING.*

> *This set-up is exactly the same as that in scene 66 with* BOXLEY, *except that* STAHR *is talking directly into the camera.* [Pp. 113-14]

The film substituted voice–over references to the "perfect girl," Stahr's failing health, and Kathleen's wish for "a quiet life" for this montage, but both screenplay and film terminate their sequences in Stahr's abrupt confrontation of the camera and repetition of the screenwriting anecdote. During Stahr's reiteration of his monologue, Pinter intersperses shots of Kathleen performing some of the activities that Stahr describes: she burns Stahr's letter while secretly observed by a man, presumably her fiance. Her inaccessibility and ambiguity become exactly the filmic reality that Stahr has declared, except that she is not susceptible to his authority. The world now reflects his divination of its impregnability, but it does not yield to his efforts to penetrate and control it. He ends by repeating his earlier answer to the bewildered screenwriter.

> BOXLEY (V.O.). What happens?
> STAHR. I don't know. I was just making pictures. [P. 117]

In these final moments of the film, Stahr dictates what now becomes his prevailing statement of the condition of existence: exhaustion, opacity, and surveillance.

As the board members drive away in their limousines, Stahr leaves his office and walks through the film lots in silence. He finally disappears into the vaulted cavern of a sound stage, which echoes his final words in a stunning effect which, due possibly to technical incapabilities, does not occur in the film.

> *EXT. SOUND STAGE. OVER STAHR.*
> *The door to the sound stage is open. Black inside.* STAHR *walks into the blackness.*
> *He disappears. The sound of his steps.*
> *Over this, the echo of 'I don't want to lose you.'* [P. 117]

The temple of fantasy reverberates with and mirrors Stahr's futile sentiment, establishing at once his passage through the looking glass into the unyielding world of his own fabrication: his absorption by a cave of fiction that can only repeat to him his own bleak commandments while ironically converting them into an ambiguous lamentation of his fall from command. Stahr's exile into the spheres of fiction is simultaneously complete, unavailing, and impotent. The studio pragmatists have seized the power.

The themes of Stahr's predicament are conspicuous in the two major Pinter plays that precede his work on *The Last Tycoon* (1975): *Old Times* (1970) and *No Man's Land* (1974). In both of these plays, the characters strive to define and manipulate each other through the contrivance of stories and conceits. Although Deeley, Kate, Anna, Hirst, and

Spooner tend to disguise their fabrications as memories, their quest for authority and their strategy for attaining it are similar to those of Stahr. If Stahr, however, is preempted by a reality that escapes his control, the characters in the stage plays become victims of their own over-empowered games. Here Pinter seems to suggest that, even when the empirical world recedes, all essays into artifice will be contested at least by contradictory allegations, and that such impositions will prove ultimately unsatisfactory as techniques for surviving in milieux of fact or fancy.

Although he narrates technically neither novel nor film, Stahr represents a form of narrator, who invents plot-lines for his own life and for the lives of others. His position of power in the film industry makes an ideal and irresistible vehicle for this practice; it stimulates in him an appetite for fiction, and it confers on him the leverage to exercise his inclination. As a producer of films, he dictates a world of unilateral dimensions, controlling the composition and outcome of all the stories, whether they belong to the fictions of cinema or to the realities of his subordinates. Stahr legislates all the variables in his professional dominion. Inevitably, however, the world beyond Stahr's jurisdiction tempts him with its promises of risks and stakes capable of rendering deeper satisfaction; but his effort to maneuver in these autonomous provinces is doomed because he cannot escape the habits and appetites of a movie tycoon. The perimeters of fiction and fact disintegrate in Stahr's mind; he finally becomes trapped in a story of his own initiation, and it manipulates him according to its own unfathomable teleology.

Like Barrett in *The Servant*, Stahr wages his living in games; but Barrett's knowledge of the phenomenological subjective perspective proves accurate in his situation, and he succeeds in controlling reality through game-like strategies. Stahr, however, overbids and miscalculates his hand, and he becomes the victim of unreckoned forces. If Barrett's success at manipulating Tony depended on Tony's susceptibility to definition and on Barrett's evasion of intractable roles, then Stahr's misfortune is assured in both respects. The servant successfully insinuates his scheme, and the tycoon tragically ordains his myths: each according to the perspectives indigenous to his status. Pinter's discovery of the self-referential value of movie-making as a metaphor for the dynamics of this interplay between chosen and unchosen phenomena will figure prominently in his subsequent adaptation of *The French Lieutenant's Woman*.

144

The French Lieutenant's Woman

*I do not know. This story I am telling is all imagination. These charac-
ters I create never existed outside my own mind. If I have pretended
until now to know my characters' minds and innermost thoughts, it is
because I am writing in (just as I have assumed some of the vocabulary
and "voice" of) a convention universally accepted at the time of my
story: that the novelist stands next to God. He may not know all, yet he
tries to pretend that he does. But I live in the age of Alain Robbe-Grillet
and Roland Barthes; if this is a novel, it cannot be a novel in the modern
sense of the word.[1]*

A taste for narrative contrivance similar to the ones that afflict Marcel
and Monroe Stahr produces a recurrent tension between John Fowles
and his story in *The French Lieutenant's Woman*. Despite all his procla-
mations, concessions, and apologies, Fowles harbors an ill-concealed
proclivity for the innocence of pre-*nouveau roman* fiction. His un-
easiness, however, with the conventions and attractions of omniscient
narration weaves the fundamental webbing of the novel; he formulates a
diachronic narrative that superimposes his modern perspective over the
Victorian action. Throughout the novel Fowles intersperses documents
from the Victorian era and commentary from twentieth-century viewpoints. These interruptions of the story's progress, together with his
lamentations over the artifice of fiction and with the narrative contor-
tions produced by his misgivings, estrange the action in Brechtian fa-
sion. Periodically, Fowles takes time out from his story to inventory his
dilemmas. As he suggests in the passage that keynotes this chapter,
Fowles shares Pinter's mistrust of presumptuous writers, and the reflec-

tions that follow this passage are particularly reminiscent of Pinter's sensibilities; "Perhaps you suppose that a novelist has only to pull the right strings and his puppets will behave in a lifelike manner; and produce on request a thorough analysis of their motives and intentions" (p. 81). The characters and their actions, according to Fowles, will occasionally assert themselves contrary to the novelist's fixed plan because, however diverse or impure the motives of a writer, "Only one same reason is shared by all of us: *we wish to create worlds as real as, but other than the world that is.* Or was. That is why we cannot plan" (p. 81). Thus the tension between artist and creation dominates the novel, focusing the author's role as fabricator and underscoring the issues of freedom and choice.

The issue of choice, its significance for Fowles, his characters, and even his readers, evolves finally into a pair of alternate endings for the story: the first of which prescribes a fairytale reunion of Charles and Sarah, and the second of which observes their autonomous defiance of this imposed narrative convention. In the second ending, Fowles reflects on his own artifice, accentuates the capricious nature of his characters' chosen fates, and confronts his readers with ambiguities for resolution through their own prejudices. This last effect returns to the reader a responsibility for enclosure of the story, since Fowles provides only possibilities and leaves the reader to select from these according to his or her own subjectivity. Because this device functions to envelop the reader in the thematic crisis of the story, and because it coincides so perfectly with Pinter's own aesthetics, the screenplay needed to make some accommodation of this final narrative ambiguity. By selectively including, excluding, and, ultimately, transforming the structural and thematic preludes to Fowles's dual endings, Pinter manages to approximate the problem of contingency intrinsic in the story's conclusion.

Fowles's adoption of this structural conceit, however labored its anachronistic evocations of Thackeray, remains consistent with the concerns of the story. The problem of choice is central to the novel, both within the story and outside of it, as a persistent theme in the narrator's commentary. Indeed, the principal contrast between the Victorian Age, during which the action of the novel transpires, and our own era, from whose perspective Fowles writes, consists in the displacement of authority by freedom; in writing, as in life, choice has become prominent where obedience to convention served in the past. Although Fowles's story examines the beginning of this movement toward freedom, his ultimate subject lies in the modern ramifications of our emancipation from Victorian conformity and order. These ramifications are rendered in Fowles's external narrative, a component that is at once indispensable to the character of the novel and unsuitable to the medium of film. Neither Fowles nor anyone who became associated with the proposed filming of the novel would encourage an adaptation that could not account for the refractive significance of the narrative.

> Another problem with *The French Lieutenant's Woman* was what one critic called its stereoscopic vision, the fact that it is written from both a mid-Victorian and a modern viewpoint. None of the directors who worked on it ever wanted to dodge the 'diachronic' dilemma, though they came up with many different solutions. Nor, incidentally, did any of the producers. As one studio head of production put it to me, he was profoundly uninterested in buying a latterday Victorian romance when there were hundreds of the genuine article—and from the most formidable corpus of writers in English fiction—lying about out of copyright and to be had for nothing.[2]

Conceding that the inclusion of a narrator figure in the film version proved a popular solution of this problem and that he had once subscribed to this proposal, Fowles finally rejected the idea as unfeasible; on screen, such a device would prove awkward and time-consuming. Consequently, the challenge of translating the novel into film lay in devising some radically divergent scheme that would compress the novel's bulk and express its format in cinematic language.

In its accommodation of these requirements, Pinter's screenplay is ingenious. His adaptation, possibly inspired by his work on self-referential incongruities in *The Last Tycoon*, preserves the diachronic tension through an original and uniquely cinematic conceit that contrasts the relationship of the Victorian characters with that of the actor and actress who portray the roles. In his foreword to the published screenplay, Fowles approves this approach; "I do not think of the present script as a mere 'version' of my novel; but as the blueprint . . . of a brilliant metaphor for it" (p. xii). Through the alternating episodes of Pinter's dual storylines, the "stereoscopic" impact of the novel retains its force and implications. Every component of the film exists simultaneously in two "realities"; temporal doublevision presides over our perceptions of character, plot, and setting. The nature of Pinter's construct draws attention not only to the temporal themes of the novel, but also to the artificial mechanics of craft, remaining true in both of these respects to Fowles's work.

Pinter's adaptation animates and intensifies certain facets of Fowles's text while diminishing the presence of others. His embellishments and his deletions, naturally, correspond to the inherent qualities of his medium and to the peculiar inclination of his own aesthetic. Thus, Pinter capitalizes on Fowles's repeated indications that the characters wear manipulative masks and that they contrive their words and actions for particular effect on others. From this theme and from the self-conscious quality of the narrative, Pinter invents the specific device of the film-within-a-film to convey the temporal refraction of the novel. The artifice of *acting* saturates every moment of the film: extending, by virtue of its conspicuousness, even into the scenes between the "actors," Mike and Anna, whom we recognize as distinct from the actors, Jeremy Irons and Meryl Streep. In its simultaneous evocation of three levels of reality, this whirligig recalls the earthquake sequence from *The Last Tycoon* and leads us directly into the phenomenological vertigo of Genet. Everything is pretense; we are condemned to see only constructs of reality. The self-referential episodes of both novel and film reveal the presence of artifice and suggest its complicity on all levels of the action. Ultimate reality is hidden from all; just as the present qualifies the past, the author qualifies the book, the actor qualifies the role, and the self qualifies itself and other, we can see one thing only through the context of another. This condition is the substance of Pinter's world, where nearly everything becomes a product of guesswork and invention, and almost nothing exists as autonomous fact.

In the first words of his novel, Fowles reduces the process of scrutiny to the game of speculation; "a person of curiosity could at once have deduced several strong probabilities about the pair who began to walk down the quay at Lyme Regis" (p. 9). From his vantage point, far away in time and space, the narrator takes careful stock of the various deceptions of viewing angles and distances: deceptions that are characteristic of Pinter's style. The problems of insight and verification extend even into the narrator's perception of himself, inducing momentary objectification of his own person, even as he reconsiders some tentative deductions about the strange pair; "On the other hand he might, focusing his telescope more closely, have suspected that a mutual solitude interested them rather than maritime architecture" (p. 10). This diagnosis of relationship, gleaned through the lens of a telescope, posits a condition of mystery and impenetrability that afflicts each of the major figures in the novel. Indeed, the emblematic telescope will become closely associated with Charles, a paleontologist, who is presently an object of its scrutiny. Finally, the difficulties posed by the act of interpretation receive emphasis in the last paragraph of the opening chapter, as the telescopist notes the presence of a third figure on the quay, whose actions are less explicable and whose nature less scrutable than those of the mysterious pair.

Beyond his advancement of the theme of inscrutability, Fowles devotes his first chapter to an exegesis of the phenomenal world of Lyme Regis. The extraordinary geological and botanical composition of the coast, along with the temporal permutations of its inhabitation, provide a significant background for the action. This setting, as Fowles explicates it, acquires emphatic features of geography and time, due not only to its peculiar topography and his temporal doublevision, but also to its paleontologic wealth. Presiding over the story, this amplified setting establishes a context and scale for human struggles. Our first glimpse of the diminutive figures, Charles, Ernestina, and Sarah, equates them with their environment through the opaque quality of Fowles's rendering, while it simultaneously subordinates them in relation to the magnitude of their surroundings and to his apportionment of text, here. In his description of Lyme Regis, Fowles initiates a thematic counterpoint between the dynamic of inexorable change and the continuance of underlying nature. Thus, he stresses the relative immutability of the geography in contrast with the innumerable alterations of the town. Relative, however, is the operative word, as Fowles unifies the counterpoint in the shared characteristic of inertia. Degeneration is omnipresent in the novel; the planet as well as its civilization undergo a gradual process of decay.

The Cobb, "a long claw of old gray wall that flexes itself against the sea" (p. 9), becomes the initial emblem of a conflict between human and natural forces. "Primitive, yet complex, elephantine but delicate," the magnificent rampart has endured seven hundred years against English history and the sea, but it stands in marked contrast with the fickle, declining village and the massive, precarious cliffs of the coast; "It is in this aspect that the Cobb seems most a last bulwark—against all that wild eroding coast to the west" (p. 10). This heroic artifact has survived centuries of inconstant seas and disintegrating shoreline to protect generations of civilization against the course of nature. In Fowles's view, however, the Cobb warrants attention not because it exemplifies, but because it defies the dynamic of its environment.

Erosion and chaos reach epidemic proportions in the narrative, attacking the fabric of Victorian society and the face of the phenomenal world. However apparent his parallels between the course of civilization and the process of inertia, Fowles sees human activity as a strategy for escaping this condition. "Time was the great fallacy; existence was without history, was always now, was always this being caught in the same fiendish machine. All those painted screens erected by man to shut out reality—history, religion, duty, social position, all were illusions, mere opium fantasies" (p. 165). As Charles enumerates them here, each of these conventions exists as an instrument in the human quest for stability and comprehension in a world that remains finally unstable and incomprehensible; "For it was a less profounder reality he seemed to see than universal chaos, looming behind the fragile structure of human order" (p. 192). Phenomenal mysteries pervade all layers of the novel, becoming manifest not only in the narrative proper, but also in prefatory excerpts from Darwin and in Charles's thoughts and activities as a paleontologist. Through these reiterations Fowles conjures a view of his subject that transcends the bifocal myopias of his one century temporal eclipse.

Thus Fowles's subject is not merely the erosion of Victorian morality glimpsed from the perspective of modern disenchantment, but the gradual decay of all configurations, noumenal and phenomenal, under the force of an inscrutable teleology. The Victorian era, in all its formal and fragile ordering, serves as a metaphor for the artifice of civilization through all ages. Environments in the novel alternate between two prototypes: treacherous, chaotic exteriors and suffocating, composed interiors. Later in the story, when Charles stands at Dr. Grogan's window, Fowles observes, "He felt himself in suspension between the two worlds, the warm, neat civilization behind his back, the cool, dark mystery outside" (p. 123). All human impositions of structure, the novelist's conventions, society's restraints, selfhood, otherhood, and Dr. Grogan's study, become false devices for insulation against nature. Fowles's particular choice and particular depiction of the Victorian period on the precipice of collapse accentuates his concern with the contrivance of fictions in all these aspects of existence.

The limitations of the cinematic medium forced Pinter to abandon this transcendant dimension of Fowles's temporal amplifications. Locations failed to produce terrain capable of expressing the novel's geologic arguments, and the lengthy narrative invocations of Darwin proved unaccountable on film. Presumably because he found no adequate accommodation of this dimension by his medium, Pinter diminished its presence to occasional contextual shots of animals and landscapes, and to minimal depictions of Charles as a paleontologist. Although he partly sacrifices Fowles's rendering of changes as simultaneously sweeping and inconsiderable, significant and insignificant, Pinter evokes a comparable sensation from the connotations of the filmmaking process; he erases the gaps between the two periods of his action (the story of the characters and the story of the "actors") by revealing the identical constitution of their natures. The parallax view of the same things from two vantages in time receives fresh significance from Pinter's conceit. Altered only by superficial adaptations, the same settings and beings comprise both worlds; the past becomes absorbed in the present, an effect merely of its trappings. Thus, the irony of Fowles's long view undermines all the shocking juxtaposition between the two time periods, but Pinter has converted its medium into the currency of cinema.

The ramifications of Pinter's innovation, his contribution of the film-within-a-film conceit, are manifold. We have noted that it faithfully materializes a legacy of problematic concerns from the novel: the scrutiny of subject from two points in time, the self-referential attention to matters of craft and medium, the obfuscations of behavior produced by the artifice of human role-playing, the portrayal of the past as a construct of the present, and the compression of a century's elapse in time. A closer examination of Pinter's screenplay, its conformations with and deviations from the Fowles source, will reveal its operation in these and further respects.

Pinter devotes his first set-up to establishment of the film-within-a-film conceit. Through his first shot, *"A clapperboard. On it is written:* THE FRENCH LIEUTENANT'S WOMAN. SCENE 1. TAKE 3'' (p. 1), he focuses the mechanics of cinematic illusion, directing attention to the behind-the-scenes labors of technicians and artifices of process. "[The clapperboard] *shuts and withdraws, leaving a close shot of* ANNA, *the actress who plays* SARAH.'' In the screenplay Anna "is holding her hair in place against the wind," but the film, as directed by Karel Reisz, substitutes a hand mirror as the emblem of her cosmetic efforts. Although the introduction of the mirror cleverly anticipates subsequent uses of mirrors and other devices to convey an omnipresent awareness of mask, both of these initial images of Anna make radical distinctions between her restrained character and that of Sarah, whose solitude and abandon are the subject of the succeeding shot. Later, certain of Sarah's qualities and circumstances will be identified with those of Anna, but the shock of this first impression emerges from their dissimilarity. As Sarah, dressed in black, begins her perilous walk to the end of the Cobb, off screen voices shout the technical jargon of shooting procedure. The sequence concludes in the mysterious image of Sarah, motionless except for the whipping of her garments in the wind, staring out to sea.

Through two devices of structural montage, this initial scene also comes to signify a fragmentation of the narrative that originates in the novel. Fowles's sequence of action is digressive, so that the story emerges largely through leaps forward and backward in the chronology of events. Thus, he compounds the temporal refractions outside the story with temporal liberties within its development. Because Pinter lacks Fowles's resources for complex narrative linkage among events, the screenplay generally rearranges the plot into cause-effect sequence. Karel Reisz compares this restructuring of the novel with the serial progression of Victorian novels: "Our story takes place in fifteen little self-contained leaps, each of which contradicts what happened previously."[3] The predictive, contradictive, contextual, and thematic functions of Fowles's discontinuous action take shape chiefly through Pinter's reciprocity between the Victorian story and its modern counterpart: a topic for subsequent discussion. Principles of montage independent of the film-within-a-film conceit, however, also contribute to Pinter's suggestion of discursive, fragmented time. The juxtaposition of the first scene with the second and the possibility that this opening sequence and a later episode represent continuous action, despite an interval of thirty-six unrelated scenes, resemble the temporal permutations of the novel. Conventional arrangement and experience of linear time are rendered false, replaced by an artifice that exposes the convention as an inadequate expression of artistic and empirical codes.

The second set-up lacks temporal orientation with respect to the first. Pinter transports us, without explanation, into the interior of Charles's hotel room at the Cups, in Lyme. Cinematic convention indicates a simultaneous or sequential time frame in such cases, but Pinter's preceding denotation of time is confounding, and later sequences seem to characterize this sequence as a flashback. In these respects both the first and the second scenes are suspended in time, awaiting future qualification and imitating the novel's temporal dislocations. Period decor, however, suggests that we are now moving deeper into the story of the film, isolating Sarah in her watchful solitude on the Cobb as the omnipresent mystery that she does indeed pose.

Fowles, also, begins the recounting of his story by discarding his telescope and immersing himself in its revealed world. Like Pinter, he strips away the initial artifice and distance, and slips into the confines of the fiction. The novel, however, unveils its story from the scene on the Cobb, withholding until later any account of the backgrounds of these figures who visit it. By interrupting the continuity of the Cobb narrative, Pinter effects a meaningful suspension of Sarah, as well as a hiccup in time that actually revises the sequence of the novel to reflect the chronology of the story.

Pinter's reorganization of the narrative for the sake of cinematic intelligibility includes bolder story perimeters and cause-effect relationships than those in the novel. In Charles's hotel room, Pinter locates a precise beginning for the story, and he expedites formulation of its concerns by interpolating material from later situations in Fowles's account. The screenplay prescribes that Charles, surrounded by scientific instruments and books, examines a fossil through a microscope. This image evokes some degree of the novel's concerns with prehistoric amplification and telescopic magnification, while it additionally associates Charles with practice of paleontology. The paradoxical qualities of the fossil, its rigid and fragile representation of life form, and the paradoxical qualities of paleontology, its constipated and ecstatic view of existence, will be later transferred to Charles, himself. Because Charles remains a rather passive figure in the novel, the screenplay revises his character to render it more dynamic and dramatic. Karel Reisz worried about this change, noting that Charles's initial "chilly, forbidding . . . manners-ridden behavior might alienate audiences from his plight."[4] Charles's aptitude for enlightenment, however, is predicted in our first glimpse of him as, for now, we note that he whistles as he works.

Pinter capitalizes on the situation in this second set-up to introduce another of the novel's significant themes: the deteriorating artifice of social class. A secondary plot, which traces the romance and upward mobility of Charles and Ernestina's servants, Sam and Mary, will become the principal vehicle for this theme in both novel and screenplay, aligning the collapse of class structure with decay on other levels of existence. In this scene Pinter adumbrates the tension between servant and master through Charles's impatience with the inattentive Sam. Unable to summon his servant by calling, Charles must leave his work to search through the window for Sam.

Charles's view from the window, ultimately obtained through a symptomatic telescope, reveals two impressions. The first consists in a preponderance of animals, clogging the marketplace and serving to recall Fowles's invocations of Darwin as well as Pinter's distinctions between the vital past and the sterile present in *The Pumpkin Eater, The Go-Between,* and *The Proust Screenplay.* Our second impression is of Sam, the ambitious womanizer, *"walking between horses, and treading with distaste over horse dung, the bunch of flowers in his hand"* (p. 2). Although Sam claims to Charles that he intended the flowers for the house, we have already witnessed his efforts to press them on a young girl in the market. Charles, however, overlooks these minor insubordinations, and announces his intentions to visit Miss Ernestina.

The montage of scenes that follows this episode depicts Charles's proposal of marriage to Ernestina. Several contrasts emerge from this sequence, including the juxtaposition of Charles's "urban" habitat with Ernestina's open landscapes and the difference between Charles's language addressing Sam and that directed to Ernestina. Again, Pinter takes his cue from Fowles, who remarks on Charles's chameleonic discourse and links this diversity with his multiple masks. "Charles, as you will have noticed, has more than one vocabulary. With Sam in the morning, with Ernestina across a gay lunch, and here in the role of

Alarmed Propriety . . . he was almost three different men; and there will be others of him before we are finished" (p. 118). Ultimately, Pinter will convert Fowles's indications of masked behavior into the artifice of performance evoked by the film-within-a-film; in this instance, however, he materializes Fowles's suggestion through the contrast in Charles's dialogue during the two scenes. Compare, for example, the following speeches, drawn first from Charles's address of Sam and then from his address of Ernestina:

> I'll shave myself this morning. Breakfast! A double dose of muffins. And kidneys and liver and bacon. [P. 3]

> Ernestina, it cannot have escaped your notice that it is fully six weeks since I came down here to Lyme from London. [P. 6]

Pinter follows up this hint of the acting that underlies behavior by providing Charles and Ernestina an audience for their engagement. Sam, Mary, and Mrs. Tranter, Ernestina's aunt, eavesdrop on the scene in the conservatory from various vantage points in the house. Their reconnaissance produces the multiple and self-interested points of view that typically afflict perception in Pinter's work, while it also develops the characters of those involved in the sequence. Mary, who seems to enjoy a superiority over her mistress similar to the kind that Sam exerts over Charles, is now paired with Sam in the kitchen. As they look on in anticipation of securing their own future, Ernestina declares war on two more conventions of the Victorian world; she announces her intention to marry Charles regardless of her father's wishes. This defiance of filial and female subjugation is emphasized in the film, where Pinter's line, "Papa will do what I want" (p. 7), is supplemented by the admonition, "And I will do what I want."

As Charles and Ernestina seal their vows with a chaste kiss, Pinter interrupts them by a piece of shocking montage. Abruptly, the scene changes to a hotel room, early in the morning, in 1979; "*Dim light. A man and a woman in bed asleep. It is at once clear that they are the man and woman playing* CHARLES *and* SARAH, *but we do not immediately appreciate that the time is the present*" (p. 8). The romantic connection between Sarah and Charles will occur much later in the screenplay; they have not even met at this point in the action. By anticipating the relationship between Sarah and Charles through the interpolation of this scene between Anna and Mike, Pinter evokes the future as a context for developments in the Victorian story. This peculiar narrative structure resembles Brecht's habit of revealing plots in advance for the purpose of deflecting audience attention onto situations other than story. Fowles, also, solicits a skewed reading of his novel by complicating the narrative through interpolation, retraction, and prediction of material, and Pinter contrives the screenplay to replicate this process. Both Fowles and Pinter, through different means, plant the attachment of Charles and Sarah long before it occurs; Fowles begins his story by describing Charles's encounter with Sarah on the Cobb, and Pinter inserts this scene announcing the affair between Mike and Anna. In each case the romance between Charles and Ernestina unfolds beneath the prediction of Charles's ultimate attraction to Sarah, although Pinter's predictive mechanism does not violate the chronology of the narrative.

This suggestion that we perceive, or reperceive, information only as it conforms to a known or predictable eventuality comprises a major premise of Pinter's work generally, and it is fundamental to Fowles's novel. Not only does Fowles structure his narrative by repeated reference to various future contexts, but he also occasionally offers the problem as a subject

> Fiction usually pretends to conform to the reality: the writer puts conflicting wants in the ring and then describes the fight—but in fact fixes the fight, letting the want he himself favors win. . . . But the chief argument for fight-fixing is to show one's readers what one thinks of the world around one—whether one is a pessimist, an optimist, what you will. I have pretended to slip back into 1867; but of course that year is in reality a century past. It is futile to show optimism or pessimism, or anthing else about it, because we know what has happened since. [Pp. 317-18]

Thus, as Pinter's idea of the film-within-a-film indicates, the past is always subject to reconstruction according to the nature of the present. Fowles and Pinter stress this condition by their approaches to the story, but they imbed the tendency toward interpretation manipulated by future contexts, attained or predicted, in the core of the story, as well. In this manner Charles's efforts to understand Sarah's behavior are always contaminated by his own expectations or by subsequent events; he is forever misconstruing her actions or reperceiving them in terms of some extrinsic context. Fowles communicates Charles's dilemma through internal monologue; for Pinter this conveyance lies partly in the attempt by Mike and Anna to conform and interpret their relationship according to the prescriptions of the fiction. In turn our cognition of the fiction is partly determined by the predictive activities of Mike and Anna.

In both novel and screenplay, the locus of suspense shifts slightly from outcome to process, since certain future dispositions of the action are forecast. This shift, however, is restricted to developments within the story, as the final resolution is problematic in both versions. Since Fowles provides multiple choice endings for his novel, the action never obtains the clarity of final enclosure. As we have noted, this frustration afflicts the reader with a relevant inability to realign the expatiations of the story according to its ultimate revelation. Pinter also emphasizes the ambiguity of outcome through the device of the present time plot; he endangers suspense by making the choice of an ending for the script a matter of dispute and by depicting the uncertain efforts of Mike and Anna to imitate the idealistic fiction. Neither account, Fowles nor Pinter, provides the assurance of an enclosed construct, although both suggest its primacy to the understanding of events.

Adumbration operates as a principal cognitive device in both renderings of the story. Fowles accomplishes it through leaps ahead in his narrative, and Pinter manages a similar qualification of developments by exhibiting their course in the present time scenes. The screenplay's interruption of Charles and Ernestina's betrothal by this prediction of Charles's infidelity recasts our perception of their relationship. The information not only reforms our impressions of preceding events, but also will alter our assimilation of subsequent developments. Thus, without violating either the chronology or the superficial manifestations of Charles's relationship with Ernestina, Pinter introduces Charles's inexpressible impatience with her triviality and his unconscious need for the profound mystery of Sarah; the betrothal is qualified by a forecast of doom. The pattern of anticipation at this level is consistent with the parallax formed by our view of the past looking forward, framed by the present looking back.

Subsidiary themes emerge from the qualities linked to each of the two periods in time. Fowles, of course, explicates these differences through his narrative ruminations, noting, for example, that the great-great-granddaughter of the servant Mary is one of today's most celebrated movie stars. Such an idea not only harmonizes with Pinter's deployment of movie-making as a metaphor for our era, but it also delineates the sharp contrasts between the rigid castes of Victorian times and the freakish mobility of today. Pinter captures these disparities through the juxtaposition of past and present milieux and of masked and unmasked characters. When the "actor" portraying Sam, for example, and the "actress" portraying Ernestina play a duet on the piano during a party for some of the film's cast, we glimpse an idea of social upheaval that simply compresses Fowles's musings about Mary's great-great-granddaughter.

The initial impact of the hotel room scene is similar; Charles's daring liberty of a chaste kiss with Ernestina is followed instantly by Mike's casual involvement in a sexual relationship with Anna. Although Pinter intends the temporal shift to occur without immediate identification, a modern telephone appliance begins to ring before much can develop from this ambiguity. The telephone, in all its resonance as an index of contemporary technology, anonymity, alienation, and disembodiment, conveys the first jolt of the shift in time. Its efficiency, artlessness, and emptiness find counterparts everywhere in the ensuing scene. Anna and Mike, whose very names have lost the phonetic richness of their Victorian alteregos, Sarah and Charles, are barely articulate; their dialogue proceeds chiefly in monosyllables and expletives.

> *A telephone rings.*
> MIKE *turns, lifts receiver.*
> MIKE. Yes? (*Pause.*) Who is it? (*Pause.*) Yes, it is.
>   (*Pause.*) I'll tell her.
> MIKE *puts the phone down, turns on light, wakes* ANNA.
> MIKE. Anna.
> ANNA. Mmmn?
> MIKE. You're late. They're waiting for you.
> ANNA. Oh God. [P. 8]

The calibre of language in this exchange lends credence to the supposition that Shakespeare dangled Juliet out of Romeo's reach on her balcony at least partly to engender articulate speech. Pinter clearly links bankrupt idiom with the advent of freedom from historical restraints.

From the text of their dialogue, we glean other clues to the character of modern life; an obsession with schedule distinguishes the present time from the past, and an anxiety over appearances unifies the two periods. The former concern, apparent in the hurried pace of most present time scenes, has an explicit source in Fowles's novel.

> The supposed great misery of our century is the lack of time; our sense of that, *not* a disinterested love of science, and certainly not wisdom, is why we devote such a huge proportion of the ingenuity and income of our societies to finding faster ways of doing things—as if the final aim of mankind was to grow closer not to a perfect humanity, but to a perfect lightning flash. But for Charles, and for almost all his contemporaries and social peers, the time signature over existence was firmly *adagio*. The problem was not fitting in all that one wanted to do, but spinning out what one did to occupy the vast colonnades of leisure available. [P. 16]

Automobiles, helicopters, telephones, and schedules dominate the *mise-en-scene* of Pinter's depictions of modern life. In certain respects, however, the two periods exhibit similarities, and Anna's subsequent misgivings over the studio's apparent knowledge of her whereabouts reveal a hint of the Victorian in her as well as the vestiges of a Victorian double-standard in our times. As Harlan Kennedy has observed:

Anna is not an immaculately-conceived feminist striding stridently into the
Eighties but a woman whose sexual and spiritual evolution has been seen and
presaged by us, like striations in a rock, in the story of her "ancestor." . . .
The French Lieutenant's Woman is about the way the Past and its accretions
are impacted in the Present, and how modern freedoms rise on the strata of
bygone tyrannies.[5]

Anna's concern for the mask of appearance reverberates in her profession as an actress; the telephone is summoning her to the set.

When Pinter resumes the Victorian story, we apparently witness
Anna's work on this day. This connection is another of his devices for
predicting developments in the Victorian action; through the "actors'"
anticipations of upcoming shooting calls, location changes, and script
details, we receive advance information about future events in the story.
Thus, Anna's departure for work signals that a scene with Sarah, and
without Charles, will follow.

In this scene with Sarah that does indeed ensue, Pinter compacts her
past and circumstances into their briefest cinematic essence. This episode, in which Sarah sits silently sketching as two laborers move past
her on the stairs, carrying a coffin, is Pinter's invention; it lacks any
counterpoint in the novel (except, perhaps, as a reference to her final
situation as Rosetti's apprentice). This image, however, works in several
respects to materialize the periphrastic revelations of her background by
Fowles's narrative. Again, Pinter requires definitive starting points for
his action, while Fowles's medium permits him to introduce material in
more roundabout fashion. Pinter's contribution of this episode and of
Sarah's preoccupation with drawing capture the spirit of the novel's
implications; it picturizes her solitude, aloofness, and impenetrability.
Increasingly, Sarah's drawings will serve to amplify her interior concerns, particularly when she sketches the various masks of her face,
looking into a mirror. Here, the juxtaposition of creativity and death
signifies Sarah's ascent to replace the old. Her persistence in sketching
this drawing of an old woman on her deathbed, even after the Vicar
appears and addresses her, emphasizes these qualities of isolation. The
Vicar's dialogue clarifies further aspects of her situation.

You realize that you cannot stay here any longer? I happen to know that Miss
Duff has made no provision for you in her will. The place is to be sold.
Pause.
How much money do you possess?
Pause.
When did you last eat? [P. 10]

Sarah's destitution and exclusion are apparent from the Vicar's
words. Fowles's detailed explanations of her background as a transient

and an outcast become unnecessary in Pinter's account of the story. Cinematic codification necessitates immediate statement of some crisis that incites the action of forthcoming developments. Just as Charles commits himself to an improbable marriage with Ernestina, so Sarah enters an intolerable employment during the scenes that introduce her. When the Vicar offers to arrange a position for her in the home of Mrs. Poulteney, Sarah gratefully submits, after ascertaining that the house overlooks the sea. The novel places Sarah with Mrs. Poulteney one year before the events involving Charles and Ernestina. Pinter enlists Sarah in the Poulteney household at this point in the screenplay in order to exploit the episode as a direct cause for her despair and as dramatic communication of her circumstances in life. The ambiguity inherent in Pinter's temporal plot, however, prohibits certainty over the precise sequence of events, and the incident under discussion might be construed as a flashback consistent with the chronology of the novel, although such speculation seems moot. The sequence in which we see events and in which they effect us is not only more arguable, but more significant. In this case Pinter's adaptation serves as a compression of the story and its tensions.

Immediately following the scene between Sarah and the Vicar, Pinter elucidates the interview between Charles and Ernestina's father, Mr. Freeman. Although this confrontation occurs much later in the structure of the novel, its chronological placement precedes Fowles's initiation of the story. Beyond altering the structural location of this episode, Pinter changes the location of its setting and enlarges the scope of its subject; his revision and abbreviation of Charles's financial situation and Mr. Freeman's mercantile alternative are among Pinter's most radical departures from the novel.

Fowles discloses both this interview and the betrothal scene as moments from the past that are summoned by a digression concerning the ascent of the merchant class in Victorian society: a digression that follows his interjection of Mary's great-great-granddaughter's movie stardom. Economic themes assume much greater prominence in the novel than in the screenplay, since Fowles dwells at length on the Marxist implications of class oppression and capitalist consolidation, but Pinter abridges these motifs due probably as much to disinterest as to a need for editing. A victim of the declining aristocracy, Charles deplores Mr. Freeman's bourgeois mercantilism, and his disdain for the Freeman conglomerate is more apparent in Fowles's work, where Freeman's contempt for Charles's belief in Darwinian principles is ironically juxtaposed with Freeman's avid practice of social Darwinism, than in Pinter's adaptation. Fowles's numerous invocations of Marx and Darwin gain further significance as the narrative progresses, when the Marxist view of history as a product of individual choice competes with the Darwinian view of history as a matter of random evolution. Pinter, however, reduces the scope of this idea, beginning with these alterations in Mr. Freeman; the screenplay retains Freeman's emblematic value, despite its elimination of his more intricate function in the plot and theme, by depicting him against a pictorially eloquent background of commercial activity and by interpolating dialogue from elsewhere in the novel.

Occasionally, Pinter deviates from the novel in order to capture details of character or period through the devices of montage and image. These deviations occur generally where Pinter's more urgent need for economy and unity otherwise forces him to forsake such details, despite their significance in the novel. The sequence of this interview provides an example of such revision. Although Freeman owns a department store in the original version of the story, Pinter portrays him as a magnate in the tea importation business. This change reputedly derived from the exigencies of location shooting,[6] but it operates more vividly than a department store to define Freeman as a symbol of bourgeois mercantilism and labor exploitation. The successive milieux of the wharf, warehouse, and office, against which the interview transpires, materialize suggestions of these economic factors, otherwise lost from the novel. Overpowering machinery and swarms of laborers unloading "Freeman's Teas" are visible even from the prestigious vantage of Freeman's office. Both Fowles and Pinter indicate that Freeman approves the engagement due chiefly to his interest in Charles's inheritance and to his eagerness to employ Charles in the firm. Pinter, however, only hints of Charles's discomfort with Freeman's expectations, and the screenplay omits the elaborate process by which Charles loses his inheritance, rendering him at once less appealing to and more revulsed by Mr. Freeman's designs. These omissions by the screenplay focus the nature of Charles's options on the alternatives represented by Ernestina and Sarah.

As if to clarify these two alternatives, Pinter delineates the romantic triangle in the succeeding scene. This episode depicts the events on the Cobb that form Fowles's entry into the story. Pinter's restructuring of the action in this respect implies two ambiguous possibilities; if this scene reverts to continuous time with the first set-up, then the intervening scenes assume a flashback character, or, if this scene follows chronologically from the linear sequence of preceding episodes, then it establishes the recidivistic nature of Sarah's visits to the Cobb. Neither of these possibilities is verifiable, and both are appropriate.

The screenplay closely parallels the novel in its development of this episode, beginning with Charles's account for Ernestina of his meeting with her father. Since Charles describes portions of the interview that occurred "off camera," we learn more about the interview as well as more about the characters and their relationships. Here, Charles reveals a glimmer of his contempt for the Freeman business, and Ernestina appears to share his disdain.

ERNESTINA. Oh dear, don't tell me. Did he talk of his famous 'empire'?

CHARLES. He did.

ERNESTINA. And did he propose that you might one day join him in the ruling of it?

CHARLES. He was most respectful of what he called my position as a 'scientist and a gentleman.' In fact he asked me about my . . . my work. But as I didn't think fossils were his line exactly, I gave him a brief discourse on the Theory of Evolution instead.

ERNESTINA. How wicked of you!

CHARLES. Yes. He didn't seem to think very much of it, I must admit. In fact he ventured the opinion that Mr. Darwin should be exhibited in a cage in the zoological gardens. In the monkeyhouse. [P. 12]

This banter, aside from articulating the thematic subject of Darwin and implicating the irony of capitalist Freeman's opinion, establishes the urbane superficiality of the couple's relationship.

Significantly, a gust of wind interrupts the exchange, causing Charles to recommend retreat and to notice the solitary, imperiled figure of Sarah, at the end of the Cobb. At this point in the novel, Charles questions Ernestina at length concerning the outcast woman, but Pinter reserves most of this inquiry for a later scene. Before approaching Sarah, Pinter's Charles manages to elicit from Ernestina only three commonplace designations of Sarah: two nicknames, "poor Tragedy" and "the French Lieutenant's Woman," and one diagnosis, madness. All three will prove false. Despite Ernestina's discouragement Charles goes heroically to Sarah, who rewards his overture with a sharp stare that petrifies and haunts him. The prescribed montage for this moment exemplifies the pattern of opening up human contexts into geologic ones:

38. Close up. Sarah. Staring at him.

39. Exterior. The Cobb. Long shot. Day.
CHARLES and SARAH *staring at each other.* [P. 13]

In this manner the meeting between Charles and Sarah assumes a broader significance and a linkage with the course of the world.

By postponing Charles's efforts to examine Ernestina about Sarah until after his encounter with Sarah on the Cobb, Pinter suggests, without the narrative devices of a novelist, that Sarah's stare has intrigued Charles. Furthermore, Pinter's relocation of the setting facilitates other ideas difficult to retrieve from the written text. The questioning sequence in the screenplay occurs in Ernestina's sitting room, and it alternates with a simultaneous scene between Sam and Mary in the kitchen. Pinter derives the situation and the dialogue closely from the novel, rearranging only the particular collaboration of components. As if to echo Charles's ominous defection from proper society in the previous episode, this sequence initiates with an act of secret insubordination by the servants; the juxtaposition suggests imminent collapse of the formal social structure, amplifying the significance of Charles's attraction to Sarah. While Sam's attentions keep Mary from delivery of her mistress's tea, Ernestina chafes at the bell pull, and Charles plies her with his questions. In this manner Ernestina's despotic impatience over her tardy maid sharpens the contrast between her spoiled, petty character and that of the enigmatic Sarah, whose secret Charles seeks. Ernestina provides Charles only with insipid gossip about the woman, phrasing her answers to affect her indifference about the subject, her coyness regarding things sexual, and her frustration over Mary's delinquency. The banality of her responses presumably facilitates Charles's calculation of insouciance on his own part; his apparent nonchalance, in the context of his obvious curiosity, seems rather a contrivance to fool Ernestina. By displaying the pettiness of Ernestina's immediate objective against the mystery of Sarah's protracted obsession, however, the situation in this scene yields its argument.

Pinter's transposition of the setting for this dialogue works to fix Charles's growing disenchantment with Ernestina and her lifestyle. The artificial interior of her sitting room reflects and intensifies her trivial, proper nature, and it contrasts these qualities with the environment in which Charles knows Sarah. These pictorial implications become crucial in the screenplay, since Charles's internal monologues, by which he states in the novel his aversions to the prospects of Ernestina and his attractions to the prospects of Sarah, cannot be gracefully recreated on film. Instead, Pinter burdens image and sequence with this revelatory function.

Sarah's circumstances, a matter of distastefulness and blushing for Ernestina, become the subject of Pinter's succeeding sequence. Although he abbreviates the dialogue and adjusts it to convey something of the Vicar's derisive estimation of Mrs. Poulteney (an attitude otherwise omitted from the screenplay), Pinter faithfully reproduces from the novel the interview of Sarah by Mrs. Poulteney. Fowles spends considerable effort on Mrs. Poulteney's villainy, detailing her abuse of her servants and her merciless, hypocritical practice of Christianity; one of the novel's various endings culminates in Mrs. Poulteney's lurid, fantastical descent into hell. Pinter, however, relies on her interrogation of Sarah to establish Mrs. Poulteney's acrimonious zeal.

> MRS. POULTENEY. The post of companion requires a person of irreproachable moral character. I have my servants to consider.
>
> *The VICAR coughs.*
>
> MRS. POULTENEY *looks at him and then turns back to regard* SARAH *in silence.*
>
> You speak French, I believe?
>
> SARAH. I do, ma'm.
>
> MRS. POULTENEY. I do not like the French.
>
> *The VICAR coughs again.*
>
> Perhaps you might leave us now, Mr. Forsythe? [P. 16]

The Vicar's efforts to discourage Mrs. Poulteney's line of questioning derive from the common wisdom that a French lieutenant has stained Sarah's character and then abandoned her to await wretchedly his improbable return; the conspiratorial coughs suggest that Mrs. Poulteney is aware of these circumstances, as she is in the novel, from a preliminary conference with the Vicar. When Sarah submits to all of Mrs. Poulteney's stipulations and demonstrates her ability to read with 'agreeable expression' from the Bible, Mrs. Poulteney takes her in.

In the screenplay Pinter splices a present day clip into the middle of Sarah's Bible reading.

> 47. Interior. Dressing room. Present.
>
> ANNA *is standing in her corset, her back to the camera. Her dresser is unlacing her corset. It comes off.* ANNA *rubs her waist. She sighs with relief.*
>
> ANNA. Christ! [P. 18]

This interlude, which was excluded from the film, serves not only as an amusing contrast between Sarah and Anna, but also as an identification of their plights. Since a second present time sequence follows Sarah's reading, the rapid oscillation between periods was presumably judged confusing, and the corset scene as well as the subsequent reading were deleted. Instead, the film moves directly from Sarah's initiation of reading to a scene between Mike and Anna in Mike's hotel room.

This hotel room episode serves multiple purposes; it reveals the mechanics of acting craft, it predicts events in the film, and it juxtaposes then with now. As Mike reads a newspaper (in the film he solves a crossword puzzle, aptly suggesting modern divestment of language), Anna, wearing glasses, researches her role. When she discovers the popularity of brothels during the Victorian period, she connects this information with the meaning of one of her upcoming lines of dialogue: " 'If I went to London I know what I should become. I should become what some already call me in Lyme'" (p. 19). Mike responds to her recitation of statistics by picking up a calculator, and the scene ends with his remark: "Allow about a third off for boys and old men . . . That means that outside marriage—a Victorian gentleman had about two point four fucks a week" (p. 19). As a helicopter passes overhead, the scene becomes a veritable inventory of technological devaluation of experience, recalling the Madwoman of Chaillot's lament: "They destroy space with telephones and time with airplanes." Two complementary perspectives emerge from the inelegance of this episode; we perceive the coarseness and vapidity beneath the masks of Charles and Sarah, and we perceive the refinement and profundity beneath the masks of Mike and Anna, who rise so capably to their roles. Again, the distinction and the identification are united.

In both novel and screenplay, various forms of mask denote the relationship between Sarah and Charles. Pinter's delineation of Mike and Anna, whose performances are always dimly visible through the dialogue of Sarah and Charles, accounts for only one instance of such contrivance. From Fowles's recurrent treatises on the self-conscious posturing of his characters, their obsessions with mirrors, manners, literature, and effect, Pinter engineers cinematic images that are symptomatic of artifice.

The screenplay, for example, usually displays Sarah carefully posed in some precarious state. When Charles encounters her a second time, she is perched on an almost inaccessible and perilous ledge of the Undercliff: "*On the broad sloping ledge of grass* SARAH *is sitting. The ledge is five feet below the plateau. Below it is a mass of brambles— beyond it the cliff falling to the sea*" (p. 21). As Charles, clad in his fossil-hunting regalia, observes her from the plateau, her position acquires a suspicion of contrivance, or self-conscious manipulation. Pinter, in fact, amplifies this suspicion through an abrupt shift into present time: "Close up. Anna. Caravan. Present. *She takes off her wig, puts it on a table. She shakes her hair loose. She stares at her face in the mirror*" (p. 22). Although this scene was eliminated from the film, again probably for the sake of fluidity, it contributes in the script to an impression of Sarah as a conceit. Thus, Pinter encodes in cinematic language Fowles's various notations that his characters habitually contrive their behavior, that they enact roles.

Mike and Anna, Pinter's principal representatives of this process, strive incessantly to conform their own relationship to the one in the

fiction. Since their personal situations resemble those of their characters, their efforts are rich with irony. They often confound objective and
subjective realities, mixing the qualities and actions of their characters
with the qualities and actions of their selves. In a sequence that was
deleted from the film, Mike and Anna mock their dialogue, using it to
breach a gap between them that is otherwise unbreachable, due to the
circumstances and conventions of their situation. This episode further
confuses their identities, while belittling both the romantic past, as
"acting," and the cynical present, as inarticulate. A later sequence
between Mike and Anna, which does occur in the film, contains similar
innuendos; an awkward rehearsal transforms abruptly into its finished
product. As Mike bends, script in hand, to help Anna up from the floor
of their rehearsal quarters, Pinter sharply converts their ambiguous
relationship into the ambiguous, but scripted, relationship between
Charles and Sarah. Beyond the shocking juxtaposition of the two periods, this piece of montage shoots the artifice of acting through all
dimensions of the moment.

The relationship between Mike and Anna operates both as a replica of
and a foil for the story of Charles and Sarah. Although we learn that
Mike is married to another woman and that Anna is committed to
another lover (a Frenchman in the film), Pinter reveals these parallels at
a point where they oppose the action of the fiction. Thus, as Charles and
Sarah converge, Mike and Anna begin to draw apart, due to Pinter's
introduction of their external commitments. Other circumstances are
similarly reversed; if Mike's marriage to Sonia parallels Charles's engagement to Ernestina, Anna's reluctance to give up David provides a
closer replication of Charles's dilemma. If Anna shares certain qualities
of mystery with Sarah, her opposite qualities of security distinguish her
from her character. In the present day sequences, Mike is anxious, but
Anna is snug; in the "script" their configurations are reversed. Both
storylines, however, depict the woman's freedom as relatively greater
than that of the man, and as Peter J. Conradi notes, "One scene on the
set showing Anna in jeans while Mike is in Victorian costume would
seem (especially as the opposite combination never occurs) to serve to
underline the point."[7] Eventually, Pinter will capitalize on these parallels and deviations to materialize the alternative conclusions of Fowles's
novel.

Like that of Anna, Sarah's inscrutability is partly the byproduct of
concealed ulterior motives. Her frustrations of Charles's overtures are
subsequently revealed as a strategy for attracting his interest. Since
Fowles's medium allows him unique opportunities for disclosing
Sarah's machinations, Pinter must insinuate some aggressive pattern in

her behavior to account for these hidden designs. He accomplishes this task by making Sarah the author of several messages, some of which occur in the novel, imploring Charles to assist her. These opaque communications exhibit a provocative, unyielding quality that is clearly Pinterian. During tea with Ernestina, Aunt Tranter, and Mrs. Poulteney, Sarah furtively slips Charles the first of her letters: " *'I pray you to meet me at nine tonight. St. Michael's Churchyard'* " (p. 36).

In the novel this meeting takes place on the Undercliff, without prearrangement. Pinter, however, locates it *"in the shadow of a large tombstone"* (p. 37), where they risk emphatic prospects of discovery. By including in this scene the line from Anna's earlier preparation, "If I went to London I know what I should become. I should become what some already call me in Lyme," Pinter suggests the artifice behind Sarah's solicitation of Charles's confidence. Thus, Pinter intimates that even Sarah's arrangement of her false confession may amount to a ploy: an effect contrived to snare Charles. To the accompaniment of the church organ, she speaks of her misery and helplessness, pleading for Charles's assistance.

> I want to tell you of what happened to me eighteen months ago.
>
> *The organ suddenly stops.*
>
> I beg you. You are my only hope. I shall be on the Undercliff tomorrow afternoon and the next afternoon. I shall wait for you. [Pp. 38–39]

Charles does not offer to channel aid to her through the intermediary of Mrs. Tranter, as he does here and repeatedly in the novel; Pinter's Charles gives no indication of his intentions at the conclusion of the scene. By revising the impetus, location, and development of this episode, however, Pinter creates a cinematic momentum toward upcoming consequences.

Both Pinter and Fowles postpone the consequences of this rendezvous to introduce Dr. Grogan, whose advice Charles seeks during the pretext of a social visit. Although Pinter simplifies the circumstances of the visit and condenses the role of the doctor, he retains the clumsy change of subject by which Charles reveals his purpose. As the two become acquainted, exchanging pleasantries over Grogan's telescope, the conversation turns to paleontology, a science that Grogan dismisses.

> GROGAN. When we know more of the living it will be time to pursue the dead.
>
> *They sit back with their brandy and cheroots.*
>
> CHARLES. Yes. I was introduced the other day to a specimen of the local flora that rather inclines me to agree with you. A very strange case, as far as I understand it. Her name is Woodruff. [P. 40]

Dissatisfied with Ernestina's impatient, naive explanations and bewildered by his own contact with Sarah, Charles enlists the opinion of the local professional. The circumstances in the screenplay are nearly as conspicuous as the explications in the novel; Charles intends this consultation both to purify his involvement with Sarah and to conceal his interest from Ernestina and her ilk.

Pinter's condensation of Grogan renders the doctor a more immediately sympathetic figure than the mercurial character in the Fowles, but this new affability serves chiefly to accentuate Grogan's inability to provide a convincing diagnosis of Sarah's condition. Dismissing Charles's suggestion that Sarah's mood may be the consequence of the French lieutenant's betrayal, Grogan attributes her predicament to Hartmann's "third class" of melancholia: ". . . obscure melancholia. By which he really means, poor man, that he doesn't know what the devil it is that caused it" (p. 40). Grogan, however, does attempt to explain Sarah's behavior according to familiar patterns of neurosis. Again, he invokes the wisdom of Hartmann: " 'It was as if her torture had become her delight' " (p. 41). Although Pinter deletes, here and later, Grogan's more extreme interpretations of Sarah's behavior as maliciously manipulative, Charles finds it impossible to accept even what remains of these pat explanations. He ignores Grogan's warning that Sarah "does not want to be cured," and determines to hear her confession, hoping that such a confidence will heal her.

Neither Fowles nor Pinter exposes the contrived nature of Sarah's confession until later in the story. Fowles's Sarah, however, does accompany her speech with an activity that becomes retrospectively significant; as she speaks, she fondles and then defoliates a milkwort, a blue flower that Fowles describes as resembling "microscopic cherubs' genitals" (p. 138). Pinter's screenplay includes no such direction, but, in the film, Sarah achieves a comparable effect by seductively undoing her hair as she talks. Also absent from the screenplay are Sarah's lengthy denunciations of Charles's privileges of sex and class, and what Pinter does retain of her attacks on Charles was omitted from the film. By editing this scene to reduce the quantity of vindictive recriminations and background details, Pinter focuses, at least in retrospect, Sarah's manipulative crafting of her story. Typically, Pinter signifies her process of fabrication by indicating pauses in her speech. These pauses occur not only for the purpose of invention, but also for the effect of impact. She describes her fictitious pursuit of the French lieutenant in Weymouth.

SARAH. But he had changed. He was full of smiles and caresses but I knew at once that he was insincere. I saw that I had been an amusement for him, nothing more. He was a liar. I saw all this within five minutes of our meeting.

Pause.

Yet I stayed. I ate the supper that was served. I drank the wine he pressed on me. It did not intoxicate me. I think it made me see more clearly. Is that possible?

CHARLES. No doubt.

Pause.

SARAH. Soon he no longer bothered to hide the real nature of his intentions towards me. Nor could I pretend surprise. My innocence was false from the moment I chose to stay. I could tell you that he overpowered me, that he drugged me. But it is not so.

She looks at him directly.

I gave myself to him.

Silence. [Pp. 44–45]

Sarah's eloquence and control of her audience in this speech become even more remarkable after her falseness is exposed. Retrospectively, the artificial confession serves as alarming evidence that the outward manifestations of one truth, here her machinations, may be mistaken for the signs of another. As Charles views her performance of the speech, it signifies an agonized confession; later, it will add up differently. Hindsight reveals that Sarah actually constructs this memory from her impressions of the present situation, and that she is suggesting things to Charles about themselves.

When Charles manages to suggest only that Sarah flee Lyme to escape her stigma, and when, alarmed by her power of attraction over him, he demands that they never meet alone again, Sarah takes desperate action. Knowing that Mrs. Poulteney will dismiss her if the zealot learns of her excursion to the Undercliff, Sarah deliberately flaunts her return before the eyes of Mrs. Poulteney's henchwoman, Mrs. Fairley, who observes her behavior from the dairy. In the novel Sarah's decision to expose herself is explicit, but the screenplay only implies her deliberate flagrancy: "The dairy field. Mrs. Fairley's P.O.V. SARAH *walking openly towards Lyme*" (p. 46). Sarah's choice of this open path in the film, however, is conspicuous. In all cases the crisis of Sarah's consequent banishment acquires further suspicion of contrivance when Charles receives her threatening letter.

At this point in the novel, Sarah sends Charles two messages, the first of which seems to threaten suicide and the second of which provides directions to her refuge, in French. Pinter combines the sense of these two communications into one note: " '*The secret is out. Am at the barn on the Undercliff. Only you stand between me and oblivion*'" (p. 47).

Despite the deceptive, threatening tone of this letter, Sarah's ulterior design is not yet apparent, either to Charles or to the audience. Rather, her plight remains compassionate and importunate, and her current situation uncertain, since neither Fowles nor Pinter provides any clue beyond the letter to indicate Sarah's new predicament.

Again, and for the same reasons, Charles seeks Grogan's advice. Pinter invents the preliminary scene, in which Charles tracks Grogan to the asylum and arranges to consult with him later, at home. The rationale for the asylum episode seems essentially theatrical, but the milieu does materialize articulated fears that plague Charles at this point in the novel. As wretched female patients whimper and scream for help, Pinter's Charles confronts the physical manifestation of Sarah's alternative future, which Fowles's Charles so dreads in his imagination. The dialogue between Charles and Grogan at the asylum and during the subsequent scene in Grogan's study, however, derives closely from the novel, which sets both segments of the conversation in Grogan's den. As before, Pinter softens Grogan's stance, deleting the doctor's more vehement allegations against Sarah and omitting the case studies of deranged, malicious women that Fowles has Grogan lend Charles. Instead, Pinter recreates Grogan's more playful, sympathetic activities in this chapter.

> GROGAN *goes to a book shelf and takes down a copy of 'Origin of Species.' He puts his hand on it, as on a bible.*

> GROGAN. Nothing that has been said in this room tonight or that remains to be said shall go beyond these walls. Well, now, you ask for my advice.

> *He paces up and down the room.*

> I am a young woman of superior intelligence and some education. I am not in full command of my emotions. What is worse, I have fallen in love with being a victim of fate. Enter a young god. Intelligent. Goodlooking. Kind. I have but one weapon. The pity I inspire in him. So what do I do? I seize my chance. One day, when I am walking where I have been forbidden to walk, I show myself to someone I know will report my crime to the one person who will not condone it. I disappear, under the strong presumption that it is in order to throw myself off the nearest clifftop. And then—*in extremis,* I cry to my savior for help. [Pp. 50–51]

Neither Charles nor the audience can accept this interpretation of Sarah's behavior; at this juncture in the action, the diagnosis seems preposterous, however conceivable it may be as an explanation of her actions. Again, only in retrospect do we grasp that Grogan's perception of Sarah here is completely accurate, and the degree of his accuracy occurs only by virtue of Pinter's omissions. Thus, by tempering Grogan's pronouncements upon Sarah, Pinter intensifies the irony of Charles's inability to credit them. Charles, in fact, mobilizes against

Grogan and in defense of Sarah with much greater force in the screen-play than in the novel, despite Pinter's reduction of Grogan's incite-ment. Fowles strongly suggests Charles's readiness to relinquish Sarah to Grogan, but Pinter employs this scene primarily to focus Charles's growing affection for and commitment to her. In this respect the asylum episode functions to clarify the motives of Charles and Grogan and to lessen the need for explicit reference to this subtext. Typically, Pinter manages to establish the reality and abhorrence of this prospect without violating the articulate capabilities of his characters. Although Charles insists on his intention to wed Ernestina and reluctantly agrees to bear the expense of institutionalizing Sarah, Pinter clearly insinuates, from the events in the asylum and from Charles's adamant defense of Sarah, that this course will change.

The complicated process by which Charles decides, in the novel, to imitate Sarah's freedom by endangering his social position to rescue her is suggested by the film, but not by Pinter's screenplay. In the film, as Charles lies on his bed in a pose that conspicuously duplicates one of Sarah's earlier configurations, he visualizes the challenge in her stare during the Cobb encounter. Then he rises to go to her: an action that both Fowles and the film connect explicitly with this challenge. Pinter, however, weakens this connection, depicting Charles's decision as a purposeful gazing out the window.

Fowles's ruminations during Charles's journey to Sarah also contain several perceptions that Pinter reduces to implicit values in the screen-play. This chapter in Fowles's version initiates with a prefatory quota-tion from Marx, attacking the conscious deceits and illusions of the ruling class. The narrative links these traits with Mrs. Poulteney and, indirectly, with Sarah, revealing the impermanence of their postures and suggesting that external appearance amounts to a mask assumed temporarily to conceal the inner nature of the thing. In the preceding chapter, the beginning of Charles's trek through the Undercliff, Fowles dwells upon the omnipresence of entropy in nature and upon the hiatus between human and natural affairs. Consequently, these deliberations on the mutability of individuals tend to reflect the fundamental condi-tion of the world; the characters, like the universe, are forever chang-ing, breaking down, inscrutable. To these observations Fowles adds that the Victorian view of the world depended upon "positive all-explaining theories" (p. 197), and that this was not the era for dialectics, paradox, or existentialism. In this manner Fowles prepares the shock of the sudden freedom that engulfs Charles and Sarah in the barn.

Pinter invites some of these insights through his prescriptions for "dense birdsong," lush foliage, and flooding sunlight, but the narrative arguments are necessarily absent from the screenplay, except as they inform its intrinsic premises. The encounter between Charles and Sarah in the barn involves only one significant difference from its description in the novel: Pinter omits Sarah's confession of her contrived discovery on the path. Otherwise, the screenplay faithfully depicts Charles's impetuous surrendering to Sarah and his absurd explanation of his circumstances to Sam and Mary, who have witnessed the passionate embrace. His amorous mood checked by the appearance of the servants and by the formality of his account to them, Charles returns stiffly to Sarah and arranges her escape to Exeter.

Through the present time scene that follows the barn episode in the screenplay, Pinter introduces further parallels and contrasts between his Victorian lovers and his "actor" lovers; in both stories the female is leaving and the male is remaining behind, but, although Charles orders Sarah away, Anna abandons Mike. Pinter has already suggested Mike's frustration over Anna's deviations from Sarah; the scene in which Charles receives Sarah's desperate letter was identically duplicated by a preceding scene in which Mike lies alone in his hotel room. Hindsight of this duplicate shot implies that Mike is lamenting his inability to rescue Anna from similar straits.

Anna's departure for London to meet David, which she announces during lunch at a mobile canteen on the set, provides a hermeneutic lead in the story line of the script. Her inadvertent signal that Sarah does indeed leave Lyme diminishes some suspense and eliminates certain prospects from the upcoming story, though it arouses other anxieties and possibilities. Mike's declaration of his intention to see her in London also serves to adumbrate future developments in the Victorian fiction. This shift in the locus of suspense, from *what* will happen to *how* it will happen, imitates the circuitous route of Fowles's narrative: just as the shock of "Mary" at lunch with "Ernestina" materializes Fowles's arguments concerning class and mask.

The succeeding scenes depict Charles's decision and arrangements to leave for London. His discomfiting encounters with Sam, Mary, and Ernestina disclose the vulnerability of his enforced deceit. Because of his indiscretion, Charles has degraded himself before the servants, and his efforts to exert his artificial superiority over them appear foolish and strained, tending mainly to reduce him to their level. Sam questions his authority, Mary questions his bribe, and Ernestina questions his reasons for going to London. The artificiality of his language with Ernestina rings so falsely that even she discerns his pretension.

CHARLES. Ernestina, I know our private affections are the paramount consideration, but there is also a legal and contractual side to matrimony which is—
ERNESTINA. Fiddlesticks! [P. 59]

Charles manages, nevertheless, to win three days leave from Ernestina, and he flees Lyme, where his mask is sagging in the eyes of all, for London, where his image is intact among his peers.

The lawyer, Montague, and Charles's cronies, Sir Tom and Nat, are minor characters in the novel, but Pinter retains them for their cinematic value as foils for Charles. Montague's name already occurred twice in the screenplay; Charles has offered it to Sarah as an intermediary for his money, and he has offered it to Ernestina as an excuse for his visit to London. By substantially enlarging Montague's role, Pinter has altered his source to focus Charles's opponents, in a manner similar to his reworking of Charley in *Accident*. Montague enjoys a social superiority that Charles both envies and, uneasily, rejects. Fowles suggests only that Montague was an acquaintance of Charles at school; but Pinter organizes the vague, rambling doubts and threats of the novel into the figure of this secure, successful lawyer, who represents them in an image: a living index of Charles's eventual sacrifice.

The subconscious contest between them is manifest initially in a savage game of old English tennis, which introduces their relationship. This game, characteristic of Pinter and original in his version of the story, serves as a thickly masked primitive combat, which discloses not only Charles's relationship with Montague, but also Charles's internal state of mind. Pinter describes their rally as *"violent, intense"* (p. 60), and he assigns the victory to Charles. This triumph discharges some of Charles's feelings of frustration and inferiority, and it also provides him with a necessary temporary advantage over Montague; Charles must compromise himself by enlisting Montague's aid in channeling money to Sarah. Montague agrees tersely to forward the allotments and to serve as a barrier between Charles and the whole business, but the exchange marks a further deterioration in Charles's posture.

Subsequent episodes of Sam's mounting insurrection and of Charles's debauchery with Sir Tom and Nat continue this process of decay. Pinter makes several alterations in Charles's encounter of Sir Tom and Nat at his club. The novel includes a visit to Ma Terpsichore's brothel in the trio's itinerary, detailing Charles's flight from this house into the rooms of a prostitute who resembles Sarah. In order to preserve Charles's purity for his affair with Sarah and to focus other aspects of the trio's rendezvous, Pinter breaks this sequence in half, reserving the prostitute for much later in the action. The screenplay concentrates on the grotesque qualities of the club scene, emphasizing the trio's drunken degradation in the presence of the dignified, impenetrable staff of servants. As Charles and his atavistic chums toast deceased hunting hounds, their progressive incoherence and regressive behavior reveal the Darwinian ape behind their aristocratic postures. This incident serves also to amplify Charles's internal crisis and to engage him in competition with his peers; here the amplification and the contest consist of excessive drinking, and Charles loses the bout. Pinter describes their aborted exit for the brothel as follows:

> CHARLES *stands and collapses. They catch him and hold him up between them.*
> *The group staggers across the room and crashes into a table, knocking it over. They ricochet into another table. With cries from* SIR TOM *and* NAT *of 'Whoops!' 'Steady there!' and finally 'Charge!' the group crashes into table after table along the length of the dining room.*
> *Three expressionless waiters watch them.*
> *They all collapse in a heap on the floor.*
> CHARLES' *eyes closed.*
> SIR TOM. I don't think our dear Charley is going anywhere tonight, old boy, do you? [P. 64]

Charles's greater degree of incapacitation becomes still more pronounced in the film, where his companions remain upright, as he performs a solo execution of Pinter's directions.

Sam's attempt to blackmail the hungover Charles will conclude this round of humiliations. By steaming open an envelope addressed to Charles, which arrives the following morning, Sam deduces Charles's continued involvement with Sarah and decides to pursue his own interests. He delivers the letter, which states simply, " 'Endicott's Family Hotel, Exeter,'" to Charles and, as Charles struggles to formulate a negative reply to Sarah's implied invitation, Sam insinuates his proposition. Announcing his intention to open a haberdashery, Sam solicits money from Charles to back the venture, plainly relying on his knowledge of Charles's affairs for leverage in this matter. Charles's reaction to this tactic signifies not only his refusal to be blackmailed by his servant, but also his rejection of the mercantile trap of marriage to Ernestina. Pinter connects the dual ramifications of Charles's response by indicating that Charles accompanies his denouncement of Sam's proposal by ripping apart the letter he was preparing for Sarah. Finally, Charles concludes the confrontation by announcing his intention to leave immediately for Lyme.

Pinter's deviations from the novel become more conspicuous during the London episodes and during those that follow. His embellishment of Montague, his transplantation of the prostitute, and his abridgement of Grogan comprise some of the screenplay's alterations in the latter portion of the story. More significantly, Pinter has rearranged and revised Fowles's material to stress the inevitability of Charles's stopover in

Exeter during the journey to Lyme. For Fowles, Charles's decision to visit Sarah occurs almost as an impulse, and Fowles obscures the choice through complicated circumstances and deceptive narrative. In the novel Charles's experiences in London are not so clearly gauged to provoke his rejection of the privileged lifestyle; only through Fowles's commentary do we learn of Charles's misgivings about his impending marriage and of his growing sensation "that the pursuit of money was an insufficient purpose in life" (p. 233). Fowles further confounds Charles's situation by misleading the reader through a series of false developments in the story; he devotes two chapters to a description of Charles's direct return to Lyme and reconciliation with Ernestina, before exposing these actions as a fantasy.

> I said earlier that we are all poets, though not many of us write poetry; and so we are all novelists, that is, we have a habit of writing fictional futures for ourselves, although perhaps today we incline more to put ourselves into a film. We screen in our minds hypotheses about how we might behave, about what might happen to us; and these novelistic or cinematic hypotheses often have very much more effect on how we actually do behave, when the real future becomes the present, than we generally allow.
>
> Charles was no exception; and the last few pages you have read are not what happened, but what he spent the hours between London and Exeter imagining might happen. [P. 266]

This peculiar retraction not only interrupts the dynamic of Charles's decision, but also suggests the desire to conform life to fiction that Pinter so effectively captures in the screenplay. The complexity of Fowles's narrative through this section of the book, however, eludes cinematic expression, and Pinter converts the sense of these digressions into images, characters, and actions, restructuring these components to exploit the power of his medium. Thus, the screenplay intensifies the dynamics of Charles's dilemma, where the novel indulges in obfuscating this process. Pinter even inserts a present time scene (cut from the film), which follows Charles's announcement of his departure for Lyme, and which ordains the eventuality of his disembarkment at Lyme. Again mingling the reality of his character with the reality of his own experience, Mike teases Anna: "You know what's going to happen in Exeter? I'm going to have you in Exeter" (p. 67). In this manner Charles's decision to remain overnight in Exeter appears not only premeditated, but inexorable.

Two scenes detailing Sarah's activities in Exeter have already intervened at this juncture in the action; in the first Sarah arrives with her suitcases and in the second, she unpacks some purchases. Pinter modifies these activities by dividing them with the Montague episode, where Fowles portrays them intact, and by altering certain aspects of the

174

novel's depiction. By deleting Sarah's porter from the screenplay, Pinter acutely picturizes her determined independence, as she hauls her luggage up the hill toward Endicott's Hotel; by deleting the bandage that Fowles includes among her purchases, however, Pinter diminishes the evidence of Sarah's scheme to entrap Charles. Sarah's procurement of the bandage in advance of her supposed ankle sprain clearly exposes her contrivance of the injury. Pinter, however, relies on a preponderance of other indications that the injury is probably a pretense, and omits the bandage for the sake of subtlety, if not uncertainty. Earlier in the screenplay and novel, Charles has virtually suggested the idea to Sarah, by commenting during one of their encounters on the Undercliff that a turned ankle would place her in grave jeopardy. Pinter stresses this episode in the woods by abruptly cutting to it from the rehearsal scene: simultaneously linking the idea of the injury to the art of deception. Both the novel and the screenplay provide additional evidence of Sarah's strategy through her careful arrangement of her newly purchased nightgown and shawl; when Charles arrives she will replicate the image that she now creates with the apparel.

Sarah's plan works perfectly in the versions of both media, although Pinter makes some alterations in its aftermath. When Charles discovers her elaborate helplessness, he instantly succumbs to her wiles; but, significantly, a true accident participates in Sarah's contrived design, inciting the final momentum in Charles's seduction. A cascade of coal from Sarah's fire ignites her blanket, and Charles's efforts to rescue her culminate in the passion that sends them to her bed. Through this fortuitous cooperation between chosen and unchosen events, Fowles and Pinter suggest that planning can accomplish only so much; accident is also a factor in experience. In the film this incident signifies not only a conspiracy of design and fate, but also a recurrent visual motif of caged fire, here conspicuously liberated from its constraints.

Pinter's significant deviations from the novel occur subsequent to the seduction, where Charles's postcoital regrets are less pronounced and his determination of Sarah's virginity more discreet than in Fowles's text. Although Fowles's Sarah openly admits her entrapment of Charles and clearly rejects the prospect of a future relationship with him, Pinter softens these developments in a tender, affectionate scene that yields only ambiguity. The disclosure of Sarah's virginity greatly complicates the hermeneutics of the story, both in the novel and in the screenplay; it instantaneously recasts as false our principal impressions of the past, and it misleads our expectations for the future by hinting a false promise of a conventional happy ending. The revelation of Sarah's purity and the implication of Charles in her ruin strongly indicate a fruition of their relationship. Although Pinter diminishes Fowles's forecast of doom in the latter part of this scene, the screenplay does reaffirm Sarah's ultimate inscrutability through her refusal to explain her fabrication of the French lieutenant affair: a fabrication that, revealed, intensifies the mystery of her solitude and misery at Lyme. Thus, despite all recognition of Sarah's contrivances, she remains finally mystifying and unpredictable.

Again, Pinter depicts Sarah's flight through the device of his present day interpolations. As Mike hands Anna a cheese and onion sandwich through the window of her waiting train, he begs her to remain overnight. Both Charles and Mike are trapped in the rigors of obligation; Charles must discharge his Victorian duty, and Mike must abide by the shooting schedule. Sarah and Anna, however, are apparently free: Sarah from mores, and Anna from the script. Although Anna's freedom correlates with Sarah's in certain respects, it differs in more significant and consequential ways. A Sartrean nausea afflicts Anna; her freedom is so great that it paralyzes her, and she cannot choose. Unlike Sarah, she cannot defy convention, because convention barely exists. Instead she follows the course of least resistance.

> MIKE. Stay tonight.
> ANNA. I can't.
> MIKE. Why not? You're a free woman.
> ANNA. Yes. I am.
> MIKE. I'm going mad.
> ANNA. No you're not.
> *She leans through the window and kisses him.*
> MIKE (*intensely*). I want you so much.
> ANNA (*with mock gravity*). But you've just had me. In Exeter. [P. 74]

Through this exchange Pinter forecasts Sarah's disappearance while developing his representation of the poverty of modern experience: its absence of stakes, language, passion, rules, choice, and defiance. Beyond our detection of Anna's false freedom, we note also her typical confusion of fictional and real events.

Anna's actions in this scene keynote a pattern of duplicity that subsequently infests nearly all of Mike/Charles's relationships; Ernestina, Sam, Grogan, and Sarah will now betray Charles in rapid succession. The most revealing of these confrontations occurs between Charles and Ernestina, when he attempts to terminate their engagement.

> CHARLES. Ernestina, I have realised, in these last days, that too great a part of my regard for you has always been ignoble. I was far more tempted by your father's fortune than I have cared to admit. Now I have seen that to be the truth—

ERNESTINA. Are you saying you have never loved me?

CHARLES. I am not worthy of you.

ERNESTINA. Charles . . . I know I am spoiled. I know I am not . . . unusual. But under your love and protection . . . I believed I should become better. I would do anything . . . you see . . . I would abandon anything . . . to make you happy . . .

She covers her face.
He stands still.
She suddenly looks at him.

ERNESTINA. You are lying. Something else has happened.

Pause.

CHARLES. Yes.

ERNESTINA. Who?

CHARLES. You do not know her.

ERNESTINA (*dully*). I don't know her?

CHARLES. I have known her . . . many years. I thought the attachment was broken. I discovered in London . . . that it is not. [Pp. 75–76]

Charles's initial tactic, the confession of his avarice, contains at least some degree of accuracy, and Pinter adopts this ploy from the novel to demonstrate that the apparent is always formed by partial truths which conceal other truths that, for various reasons, cannot be articulated. Generally, this scene reproduces the same episode in the novel, except that Pinter has tightened its sinews to accentuate the disguised machinations of the characters. Thus, he exposes Ernestina's duplicity in her abrupt transition from tears of entreaty to accusations of deceit, and he denotes Charles's humiliation through his confessions to circumstances farther and farther from the truth. The scene concludes as Ernestina, stripped of her role as fiancee, reveals a vitriolic stripe concealed by her former mask, and retaliates against Charles: "My father will drag your name—both your names, through the mire. You will be spurned and detested by all who know you. You will be hounded out of England, you will be—" (p. 76). Although Fowles continues this episode to assure that Charles arranges for Ernestina's attendance by Mary and Dr. Grogan, Pinter terminates the scene at this point, noting only that Ernestina swoons, and not that she peeks at Charles, as she does in the novel, when he leaves her. Even her fainting, however, was eliminated from the film, where the action cuts abruptly to Pinter's entirely original depiction of Sam's openly hostile defection from Charles.

As Charles abandons convention, its blessings abandon him; the structures of artifice do not withstand weakening without total collapse, and the choice for freedom invites the disaster of chaos. A subsequent scene between Charles and Grogan, included in both the novel and the screenplay, but deleted from the film, echoes this sentiment. Here,

Grogan also deserts Charles, accusing him of deceit and lust, and alleging that these crimes will infect the remainder of Charles's life. Charles's rhapsodic invocations of his freedom fall flat, and his discovery, in the succeeding episode, that Sarah has fled compounds the contamination of his fragile optimism. To these developments Pinter adds several scenes in which Mike attempts to contact Anna, who has ensconced herself in a London hotel room with David. As Charles scours all of London for signs of Sarah and contends with the legal actions instituted by the Freemans, Anna gads about in a Mercedes, admires herself in costumes, and sips tea with David. Pinter also includes in this section of the screenplay Charles's ill-fated encounter with the prostitute and her infant, a trite, sentimental episode in the novel that Fowles ties to two romantic motifs: Charles's revulsion by whores, and the child he fathers, in one version of the ending, with Sarah. Since neither of these ideas occurs in the screenplay, this sequence was judiciously eliminated from the film.

Pinter's deviations from the novel proliferate throughout the denouement of the story. Where Fowles concerns himself with the good fortunes of Sam and Mary and with Charles's perambulations in Europe and America, Pinter focuses the mounting desperation in Mike and Anna's efforts to transform their destiny into that of Charles and Sarah. Two sequences in the screenplay, both depicting cast parties, develop their efforts in this direction. The first occurs at Mike's home, where he and his wife have invited some of the actors to celebrate the nearing conclusion of the film. The event occasions typically Pinterian exchanges between Mike and David and between Anna and Sonia, Mike's wife. For its multiple implications, the former dialogue warrants special attention.

DAVID. Have they decided how they are going to end it?

MIKE. End it?

DAVID. I hear they keep changing the script.

MIKE. Not at all. Where did you hear that?

DAVID. Well, there are two endings in the book, aren't there? A happy ending and an unhappy ending?

MIKE. Yes. We're going for the first ending—I mean the second ending.

DAVID. Which one is that?

MIKE. Hasn't Anna told you? [P. 95]

The animosity and incisiveness beneath the apparent innocence of this conversation emerge not only through the double significance of the "ending," but also through their elliptical evasions and accusations of each other. Further ironies lie in the muddled characterization of the script as a fixed enigma, in the manifestation of process, and in the fact that neither of the novel's endings will be exactly replicated in either script, "fictional" or "real." Eventually, Anna and David leave the party, without anything conclusive passing between Anna and Mike, except a prediction of their final meeting as Sarah and Charles at Windermere.

In the novel the reunion of Charles and Sarah differs in circumstances, setting, and conclusion from that which occurs in the screenplay. Fowles, who can afford the bulk and complexity of sustained secondary plots, implies that Sam, in order to expiate an earlier betrayal of his master and to clear the debt of his own good fortunes, signals Sarah's whereabouts to Montague. Since Fowles concerns himself in more detail with Sam and Mary's future, and since he ambiguously attributes Sarah's disappearance to Sam's failure to deliver a letter and brooch from Charles to Sarah, this penance seems appropriate in the novel. Sam communicates the information to Montague when, several years after the events in Lyme, Mary reports that she has observed Sarah entering a handsome house on the Thames. Charles returns from America immediately upon receiving the cable from Montague and goes to visit Sarah at this address. In Fowles's version Sarah's situation in this house remains ominously nebulous; we know only that "She is no longer a governess" (p. 346), and that the house belongs to an amorphous collective of nefarious artists and thinkers for whom Sarah serves as a model, secretary, and assistant. The significance of her circumstances, however, lies primarily in their reversal of Charles's "assumption that fallen women must continue falling" (p. 347), and Pinter's alterations contrive to accentuate this point through visual signs.

Thus, Pinter shifts Sarah's location to the idyllic Lake Windermere and denotes her activities as an artist/governess in residence. Although it would be naive to overlook the pragmatic considerations that probably figured in this choice of setting, it would also be fruitless to speculate or comment upon them; the significant content of this shift consists in its clarity as an index of Sarah's happiness and in its enunciation of the fairytale conventions peculiar to fiction. The scene serves also in both versions as an anticipation of modern developments, but, where Fowles accomplishes this progressive quality through narrative, Pinter exhibits it in *mise-en-scène*.

The home on Lake Windermere, which Pinter designates "The New House," is white, full of light, and overrun by children, according to the screenplay. Pinter relieves the ambiguity and complexity in the novel by delineating Sarah's position in the household and by confessing her as the author of her own exposure. By omitting Sam's complicity both in Sarah's disappearance and in her rediscovery, Pinter simplifies the story and emphasizes Sarah's autonomy: a characteristic he also captures in her artistry. Fowles allows sentiment to usurp the role of choice in the characters' actions and treats the existential theme only through narrative commentary, but Pinter lacks this option. Instead, Pinter softens the environment to evoke the fairytale, but hardens the circumstances to focus the act of choice. In the penultimate ending of the novel, Sarah's revelation of their common child brings them together; in the screenplay they are brought together by their freedom. Pinter demystifies Sarah's intentions by rendering her the author of Charles's invitation to the house and by revealing her need to offer herself to Charles not from desperation, but from freedom. Likewise, Charles's decision to accept her derives from her revelation not of a child, but of his freedom; she disarms him, as always, by doing the unexpected.

> CHARLES. To make a mockery of love, of all human feeling. Is that all Exeter meant to you? One brief transaction of the flesh? Only that? You have planted a dagger in me and your 'damned freedom' gives you licence to twist it in my heart. Well, no more!
>
> *He strides to the door. She seizes his arm.*
>
> SARAH. No!
>
> *He flings her away, violently.*
>
> CHARLES. Yes!
>
> *She falls to the floor, hitting her head. He stops. She sits up, holding her head. He stares down at her. She looks up at him. She smiles.* [Pp. 101–2]

In this manner Sarah challenges Charles once again to imitate her freedom, to drop his posture of indignation and permit their unification as a freely chosen option. They transcend their circumstances by casting aside role constraints (in the film Anna seems almost to break character at this moment), but, ironically, this freedom exists only inside the constraints of fiction. Mimicking Fowles's introduction of the love child, Pinter underlines the cliche of the happy ending with his final, and original, image of the couple.

> 234. Exterior. Lake boathouse. Evening.
>
> *A rowing boat is emerging from the darkness of a boathouse on to the lake. SARAH sits in the prow, CHARLES is by the oars. As the boat glides out into the calm evening water CHARLES begins to row slowly.* [Pp. 102–3]

Like Fowles, however, Pinter will now repudiate this conclusion, exposing the fragility of its artifice.

The happy ending that belongs to fiction is both envied and contradicted by real experience. Fowles indicates this condition by pretending to withdraw his narrator, and then describing the actions of Charles and

Sarah in the "absence" of this artifice. In this second version of the ending, Charles abandons Sarah, refusing to be manipulated and protecting his integrity. The novel closes by noting that both endings are equally plausible, "that there is no intervening god beyond whatever can be seen . . . only life as we have, within our hazard-given abilities, made it ourselves, life as Marx defined it—*the actions of men* (and of women) *in pursuit of their ends*" (p. 365). Pinter, of course, achieves this statement through the final divergence of his dual plot lines; Mike and Anna's demand that their lives imitate the pattern of fiction meets with failure, just as Monroe Stahr's similar insistence met a similar doom. The party that celebrates completion of the film also marks a liberation from a scripted future between Mike and Anna, since they had adopted the script as a model and mechanism for their own relationship. Without the dictates of fiction, they find decisive action impossible and allow themselves to continue, in entropic fashion, on the course of least resistance, perpetuating established relationships and lifestyles.

Pinter's depiction of the party that releases the cast and countryside from their fictional postures includes several remarkable directions, some of which were deleted from the film. The licentious, intemperate behavior of the actors, suddenly liberated from their masks of Victorian propriety, is emphatic; the "Prostitute" dances with "Mr. Freeman," "Sam" dances with "Mrs. Poulteney," and "Ernestina" performs a fan dance in a Victorian corset. In the midst of this incongruous debauchery, Mike and Anna still wear their costumes from the previous scene: a sign of their effort to confound fiction with life. A parallax results also from Pinter's choice of location for this scene; the party transpires at "The New House," simultaneously evoking the serenity and promise of its role in the fiction, and converting it into an index of modern disillusionment. Thus, when Mike, detained by social obligations, searches for Anna he duplicates Charles's route to Sarah in the final scene of the fiction. Upon reaching her dressing room, however, he finds only her wig; she has changed from her costume and left. The final shot of the screenplay shows him at the window of the room in which their fictional reunion had transpired, watching her car disappear. His desperate ejaculation, "Sarah!" (p. 104), reverberates, like Stahr's final words, as a demand that life imitate art and as a lament over the impossibility of this prospect.

The problem of freedom, of choosing and acting outside the prescriptions of an ordaining script of some kind, pervades all levels of Fowles's novel. Both the external and internal dynamics of the story feature this process as a dilemma that afflicts both the author and his characters. The Victorian era intrigues Fowles as a period during which duty served as an evasion of absurdity. "I had better here, as a reminder that mid-Victorian (unlike modern) agnosticism and atheism were related strictly to theological dogma, quote George Eliot's famous epigram: 'God is inconceivable, immortality is unbelievable, but duty is peremptory and absolute.' And all the more peremptory, one might add, in the presence of such a terrible dual lapse of faith" (p. 43).

The polarity between execution of duty and exercise of choice parallels the polarity between Darwin's view of history as evolutionary accidents and Marx's view of it as deliberate actions. Sarah, as protagonist, is aligned with the defiant extreme of this spectrum, but Charles oscillates between the two poles; "He had not the benefit of existential terminology; but what he felt was really a very clear case of the anxiety of freedom—that is, the realization that one *is* free and the realization that being free is a situation of terror" (p. 267). Essentially, Charles's recognition of his release from conventions duplicates the conditions of a withdrawn script; he must now choose for himself. Examples of conformity and nonconformity with artificial restraints are ubiquitous and eclectic in the novel, ranging from Fowles's inculcations of his own craft to the paleontological, sociological, economic, behavioral, and philosophical problems intrinsic in the story. In each of these categories, as in Charles's confrontation with the terror of freedom, definition is exposed as an artifice imposed on a profound, inscrutable chaos.

Pinter's metaphor for this situation, the film-within-a-film, evokes a similar statement and describes similar restraints. Except for Sarah, who consistently invents the pattern of her life and who remains, nonetheless, a figment of fiction, each of Pinter's characters, Victorian or modern, obeys the restrictions of some extrinsic artifice. Although the dynamic between Pinter's diachronic plots retrieves and enriches many of the novel's techniques and concerns, its foremost achievement lies in its approximation of Fowles's diametric endings. Both writers, by means of similar pretexts, imply that perfect endings are the stuff of fiction. When Fowles withdraws his "narrator" and when Pinter withdraws his "script," the stories conclude otherwise, accentuating not only the artifices of fiction and imposed definition, but also the mystery of autonomous choice.

For Fowles and for Pinter, the form of the story affirms its themes. In both media the ideas related to time and artifice are reflected in the structural constitution of the text. The double ending becomes particularly significant as a structural effect because it provides formal harmony with the narrative's concerns; an inconclusive, paradoxical conclusion seems only appropriate for this tale of ambiguity and irreconcilable facts. In the novel the initial ending chronicles Charles's preference for the ambiguities of freedom (Sarah) over the amenities of convention (Ernestina); the second ending concedes that even this act of liberation represents only a conformity with the author's ideology. Thus, in Fowles's alternate ending, Charles defies not only Victorian convention, but also narrative convention by resisting the tradition of reunion.

Pinter's expression of this final dichotomy in the story assumes a different form and implication because his treatment of the relation between artist and creation has deviated from that of Fowles. Although both versions of the work include evidence of the individual's unsatisfiable desires to ordain experience in accordance with the prescriptions of fiction and to liberate fiction from the ordinances of experience, the external tensions between artist and creation are reversed; where Fowles endeavors to free his characters from authorial tyranny, Pinter's "actors" struggle to insinuate themselves into fiction. Consequently, the second ending, through which Fowles abdicates and derails his story, becomes for Pinter an abdication and derailment of his "actors'" efforts to emulate art. Through this device of contradictory endings, however, both Fowles and Pinter extend the condition of inconclusiveness beyond the internal action of the story, referring the problem of enclosure, in all its dialectical complexity, to the reader or spectator. This transfer of dilemma from within the story to outside of it announces, in its very hiatus, the final unity of form and content in both renditions of the work.

We have previously noted Pinter's thematic concern, particularly in *The Go-Between, The Proust Screenplay,* and *The Last Tycoon,* with the fictionalization of experience, and we have noted the presence of this enterprise in his original plays, *Old Times* and *No Man's Land.* Consistent with this strategy for controlling and comprehending past or predicted situations, Pinter's characters in these later plays fabricate "memories" as techniques for manipulating each other. One example of such a conceit occurs near the conclusion of *Old Times,* when Kate avenges herself by annihilating her two "suitors," who have sought all evening to appropriate her through contrived memories. Kate's speech, a version of the past that is empirically false ("I remember you dead"), actually operates as a metaphoric summary of the action of the play and, in its calculation for immediate effect on others, closely resembles the manner of Sarah's deceptive recollection of her betrayal by the French lieutenant. What Karel Reisz has said about Sarah is equally true of Kate: "Partly, it's a story she is making up for herself while looking back at us over her shoulder—at us and Charles—to see what effect it's having."[8] Pinter, himself, has made similar comments regarding maneuvers by characters in *Old Times,* suggesting that Deeley enlists "re-membrance" as a tactic for affecting Anna. "The fact that they discuss something that he says took place—even if it did not take place—actually seems to me to recreate the time and the moments vividly in the present, so that it is actually taking place before your eyes—by the words he is using. By the end of this particular section of the play, they are sharing something in the present."[9]

Prevarication about the past for the sake of intrigue in the present is seminal, as we have seen in the comparison between the stories of Aston and Barrett, even in Pinter's early work. Various themes in *The French Lieutenant's Woman* (1981) have evolved demonstrably from Pinter's current concerns and over the course of his career as a writer. We find in *Betrayal* (1978), for example, Pinter's own treatment of the past as it is imbedded in the present, a theme we have observed throughout *The French Lieutenant's Woman.* In the final chapter of this book, we shall examine these and other correspondences between Pinter's work as an adaptor and his original writing.

10

Patterns

The subjects and techniques of the eight novels that Pinter has adapted for cinema exhibit consistencies as a group and with Pinter's original writing. Certain themes figure centrally in each of the novels: the distortion of time, sequence, and the past; the discrepancy between cause and effect or motive and action; the difficulties of both articulation and verification; the tension between the impulse to fix (order) and the condition of flux (chaos); the strategies of dominance and subservience; and the ascendancy of newcomers over the old guard. Each of these thematic factors holds a common ground in Pinter's original work, and each receives emphatic development in his adaptations for the screen.

Several familiar leitmotifs, such as the iconographic "room" or "house," also recur in the novels, and Pinter makes capital use of these in his versions. Prominent among these devices is the game, which assumes both literal and figurative proportions in the bulk of Pinter's literature. From Hide and Seek in *The Servant* to Real Tennis in *The French Lieutenant's Woman,* the artifice of game playing is explicit in the screenplays. As a conspicuous artifice, the games sensitize us to similar dynamics on subtler levels of the action. Such dynamics do, in fact, exist, and they warrant consideration as the formative principle in Pinter's work.

In their rather uneven study of the collaboration between Pinter and Losey, Houston and Kinder also conclude that the idea of games attains pivotal significance in the films undertaken by this screenwriter-director team.

> Human interaction is dominated by competitive games. The goal is always survival, power, or control over one's own experience. The source of this

power (and its rewards) may involve social ascendance, sex, superior knowledge, or aesthetic power. Each work emphasizes a different dimension of gaming, which is indicated by the title and by the literal games being played, and which is developed both narratively and visually.[1]

The application of this thesis to *The Servant* (which Houston and Kinder perceive as a sadomasochistic game of role reversal), *Accident* (which they interpret as a manipulation of misfortune), and *The Go-Between* (which they see as a direct address of a game present in all four collaborations) succeeds in revealing central tensions in these texts, but their appraisal of *The Proust Screenplay* in these terms elucidates only peripheral circumstances and suffers from an apparently weak understanding of both the novel and the adaptation. In the case of *The Proust Screenplay*, the principal game occurs between Marcel and the empirical developments depicted in the screenplay. As the very structure of the adaptation indicates, Marcel's struggle to recreate the past as coherent, as *art*, becomes the game. Houston and Kinder's discussion, in its exclusive delineation of external competitions among characters, overlooks the crucial premise of this epistemological contest between Marcel and his experience. Games in Pinter infest the whole spectrum of existence, and they extend far beyond his collaborations with Losey.

Over the course of his career, the game has become progressively intrinsic in Pinter's original writing, and it has changed in nature to accommodate his evolving vision. The escalation of the game parallels a three-phase erosion of external reality: as Pinter shifts his scrutiny from the dynamics between self and other, to the dynamics between self and self, to the dynamics between self and nothing, game contexts necessarily expand to include more dimensions of experience.[2]

In the first phase of his playwriting, including *The Birthday Party*, *The Dumb Waiter*, and *The Caretaker*, games exist primarily as strategies to obtain or protect sanctuary, and the threat materializes from potential interruptions of the game routine. Games of homemaking are afflicted by games of menace; but, however much these two sets of tactics adumbrate each other, they are distinct, and threat remains fundamentally extrinsic to the protagonist's game. In this phase games attack or defend against a perceived adversary; they neither invent nor contain it.

The extroverted nature of this contest inspires Pinter's focus on interpersonal relationships as vehicles for advancing self-interests. Dominance, sycophancy, menace, intrusion, and exclusion, themes that transmogrify throughout Pinter's work, originate here as games of selfish interaction. In *The Caretaker*, for example, a three-way relationship among two brothers and an old tramp forms the pretext for Pinter's exploration of interpersonal strategies as manifest in the artifice of games. If we disqualify the triangle formed by Stanley, Goldberg, and McCann in *The Birthday Party,* since the latter two operate in tandem during these scenes, then *The Caretaker* advances this game beyond the simplicity of his earlier plays, in which principal relationships occurred in pairs; interference by third-party dynamics appears only in second-ary situations, such as among Meg, Petey, and Stanley in *The Birthday Party* and among Gus, Ben, and "the operator" in *The Dumb Waiter.* This triangular configuration and its familiar games of jockeying and exclusion become the subject, however, in *The Caretaker.* Because these plays invariably proclaim the inefficacy and futility of rela-tio.:ships based on alliance, and because of their shift toward the prob-lem of exclusion, Pinter's subsequent attraction to the individual apart seems predictable and sensible enough.

The danger has relocated inside the game in Pinter's second phase, and the characters of *A Slight Ache* (chronologically, an earlier play, but one that augurs later themes) and *The Homecoming,* for example, out-wit menace only by remaining aloof from the proceedings. In *The Homecoming* Ruth stays with Teddy's family because she can exploit them through her immunity to their game. Teddy leaves because his game neither accommodates nor exempts him from theirs; predeter-mined familial configurations prescribe Teddy's role in the interminable domestic contest, and he can win only by escaping it. Ruth encounters a similar trap in her relationship with Teddy, but she eludes all of the clan's efforts at assigning her a specified role. Her potency derives from her dislocation in the family, from her evasion of codification in this new context. She prefers her ambiguity in this new game to her inaltera-ble casting in the old one with Teddy. The family's desire for Ruth grounds in two motives: they vie for her as a sign of victory in the game with Teddy, and they crave her as a substitute for the disintegrating image of mother Jessie. In the former respect, they lack any structure for accommodating the fact of her person beyond its insignia of tri-umph, and, in the latter, Ruth will clearly thwart their scheme. Her escape of definition produces Max's lamentations and the mood of ten-tativeness at the conclusion of the play.

If, in earlier plays, the games attempt and fail to control eventuality, in this second phase, defeat is inherent and inevitable in the nature of all shared games. Where previous games served to integrate certain strat-egies into common reality, victory now occurs only outside communal experience, in private games of solitaire that immunize and isolate the self. The success of these solitary games depends on their effectiveness at coexistence with the menace of collective games: the protagonist must create myths of existence and of self that are capable of sustaining each other through the contradictions of experience. In *A Slight Ache,* Edward's myth cannot account for the Matchseller, but Flora manages to impose hers without immediate dissonance. Accordingly, Edward fails, and Flora temporarily succeeds, but the characters in *The Homecoming* end in a state of unresolved tension.

All forms of harmonious relationship depend on mutual subscription to myths or codes of living. Pinter's first phase of writing chronicled the disintegration of relationships due to the inevitable breach of such shared faith. His subjects chiefly focused the absence or failure of relationship where it had been presumed or attempted. The shift in his writing that stamps this middle period of plays consequently displaces the dramatic stress from between selves to within them. Having unmasked and depleted the mutually exploitative premises of relationship, Pinter henceforth subordinates interpersonal dynamics to the conflicts and movements within individuals themselves. Electricity has transferred from the external situation to the internal ones. The characters' autistic considerations dictate their courses of action, and relationships among figures operate chiefly as catalysts on these intrapersonal transmutations. As relationships deteriorate the games replace other contexts as a device for interaction and for unification of the situation.

For the characters in *Landscape, Old Times, No Man's Land,* and *Betrayal,* possibilities for victory no longer exist outside the game: nothing does. The games become the solitary exercise and evidence of living in this world where all other forms of action are absent.

The physical and conversational stasis that paralyzes the characters in *Landscape* derives from their obsessions with the past. These figures, immobile throughout the play, have retired from all activity in order to remember, codify, and fix their lives. The futility of relationship and the elusiveness of self have driven them from the threatening exterior landscapes of the volatile present into the secure interior landscapes of the inert past. Here, to the extent that they can escape external contradiction or internal doubt, they enjoy a freedom to embroider "reality" at will. Beth achieves perfect insular harmony because she resolves doubt with "principles" and never refers her versions of the past to external verification ("BETH *never looks at* DUFF, *and does not appear to hear his voice*"). Duff suffers both from doubt, regarding Beth's unconfirmable affair with Sykes, and from an unsatisfiable need for outside validation ("DUFF *refers normally to* BETH, *but does not appear to hear her voice*")[3]; hence his mental landscapes contain an abrasiveness absent in those of his wife. Because no possibility exists in this disposition for any change in the situation through interaction, the play lacks dramatic tension; even Duff's internal chafing must remain exempt from externally produced mutation, inevitably static.

By withdrawing the conditions of almost total insularity that exist in *Landscape,* and by creating characters who, although they dwell in the past, are condemned to self-doubt and to mutual affirmation, Pinter, in *Old Times,* infuses the situation of *Landscape* with the drama of conflict. Here, the episodes of history become actively charged in and by the present. The games among the three characters fuse both spheres of time inseparably, so that the situations, stakes, and weapons of the conflict acquire the dimensions of both periods simultaneously. Without actually shifting the materials of concern and disputation from the past, Pinter plants the locus of tension in the present by endowing the supposedly factual preterite with the threat of mutability and with the potential to confiscate the future.

No Man's Land involves similar games of remembrance and invention that are likewise connected to the characters' efforts to create themselves and their lives. For Spooner nothing remains but the possibility of insinuating himself into the elaborate pageant that sustains Hirst's illusions of vitality and dignity. Although Hirst readily affirms Spooner to the extent necessary for preservation of certain claims about the past, he maliciously denies Spooner's pleas for recognition in the present and in the future. Hirst experiences security in his relationship with Foster and Briggs because of their indifference to him, but he simultaneously craves and loathes Spooner because of the man's interest in him. The potency of such a relationship proves too dangerous to risk, and Hirst ends by literally deleting Spooner from his dream: "I say to myself, I saw a body, drowning. But I am mistaken. There is nothing there."[4] In the schematics of the dream and in the schematics of the play's action, Hirst invents the role, Spooner claims the role, and then Hirst obliterates the role. Hirst specifies the role for a drowning person, but Spooner insists he is not drowned, and Hirst can only revert to his earlier trick of rescinding the situation: of denying Spooner's participation in his dream as he has, when necessary, deleted Spooner from his revisions of the past. In retaliation for this exclusion, Spooner repeats Hirst's lamentation back to him, confirming the old poet's sentence to "no man's land. Which never moves, which never changes, which never grows old, but which remains forever, icy and silent" (p. 95).

Here, as in *Old Times*, the whims of language have inherited omnipotence in the absence of alternative structures for reality, and when Hirst absent-mindedly changes the subject "for the last time," Foster is empowered to announce ever-lasting winter. The metaphoric invocations of winter, its sterile, silent, uninhabitable landscapes, reflect the themes of "no man's land," both place and play, and of Pinter's work, generally. In Pinter's universe regenerative prospects have vanished, and life has entered into a permanent process of decay. Characters erase themselves as they proceed, accumulating only the spectres of remembrance and artifice, and retreating with these into an ambiguous, infinite present. Where the external world and relationship were matters for control by games in Pinter's earlier work, they are matters of invention through games in these recent plays.

No Man's Land reverses Pinter's customary pattern of action. In the two earlier groups of plays, initial situations of precarious stability move toward violence and radical change. In *No Man's Land*, however, the situation commences unstable and develops into permanence; it moves away from intrusion rather than toward it. Pinter condemns his characters to solitude and stasis, where he had previously condemned them to intrusion and upheaval. *Landscape* and *Old Times* exhibit certain features of this reversal, but their progressions lack the suggestion of diminishing possibilities that distinguishes *No Man's Land*; in *Landscape* the situation begins as fundamentally static, but in *Old Times* it remains potentially unsettled. The subjects of conversation, which provided the sole prospect of vitality in a world commissioned by language, become permanently fixed in the final moments of *No Man's Land*, revealing a gradual, and now complete, acquisition by stasis. Remarkably, the subject achieves permanence by expanding to include all possible topics: "There is no possibility of changing the subject since the subject has now been changed" (p. 93). This restriction through expansion parallels Pinter's view of the present, which becomes a simultaneous containment of all things real and imagined, past, present, and future. By validating language as the cardinal signifier of reality, Pinter infuses the finite with the infinite, reduces infinity to zero, and converts potentiality into stasis. In these respects *No Man's Land* marks a distinct turn in Pinter's writing which, while evolving consistently from recent work, posits an unmistakable, if predictable, contradiction of his earlier work; he has moved, like the pendulum, to his opposite.

Although the past is empirically manifest in *Betrayal*, the play does not deviate essentially from these themes. Significantly, its reverse direction of time seems an apt consequence of the temporal stasis in the preceding plays. We have noted previously that the regressive structure operates as a conspicuous artifice that reveals a matrix of deceptions in various moments of time. Because the games, deceits, and ambiguities are resolved only through the theatrical conceit of retrospection, the opacity of the present remains, practically speaking, intact. The play serves only to confirm the inscrutability of the apparent, and to adumbrate future maneuvers and stalemates similar to the ones we have observed in its predecessors. If *Betrayal*, through its backward movement in time, depicts the past imbedded in the present, it also, through this preponderantly one-way time flow, proclaims a condition of stasis and absence that reveals its "no man's land."[5]

The ascendancy of games to the place of action derives also from Pinter's sympathy with sensibilities of pictures, his primary source of inspiration and frustration. In the picture or the photograph, form provides name, appearance provides substance, and nothing exists beneath the masquerade. The frame defines its subject and activity, and duration is absent. Pinter, however, must develop some form of temporal narrative due to the nature of his media: theatre and cinema transpire in time. Gradually, though, Pinter's concept of duration grows to resemble that of a photograph; he comes to view the present as vastly static and unyielding. As his plays lose the evidence of irreversibility and progress that time schemes normally stipulate, all action becomes a function of games. These games provide a suspended context, an exemption from the properties of time, which moves the plays yet closer to the aesthetics of the photograph. Pinter resorts to games as a device for occupying time without actually evoking or exhausting it. In his work for the cinema, as in his conceit for *Betrayal*, Pinter has evolved other structural vehicles for this dissolution of time, although the game remains prominent as an emblem of this phenomenon.

Pinter's appropriation of the game as his chief dramatic technique satisfies the temporal, behavioral, and existential characteristics of his world. The opaque surfaces of the game emerge from subtextual objectives of the characters and, like the photograph, simultaneously reveal and conceal truth. Since the beginning of the twentieth century, the actor's task has consisted largely in discovery and depiction of subtextual truths. Pinter's style capitalizes on this acting process by pursuing to an extreme the logic that dialogue often conceals motive. Himself a seasoned actor, Pinter formulates his dramatic reality from the orientation of an actor; he focuses and exploits the dynamics between text and subtext. The discourse in his plays amounts almost to a game in itself of concurrently skirting and exposing the characters' concerns. The degree of apparent disparity between text and subtext distinguishes Pinter's work from that of other playwrights. We have observed, for example, that much of his work on the screen adaptations consisted in conversion of the explicit into the implicit. Pinter's foremost talent lies in this ability to capture in obliquely articulated images and dialogue the unarticulated spheres of living. In his derivation of this discipline and sensitivity from the craft of acting, itself, Pinter mirrors the trends in other art forms, such as Photo Realism and electronic music, which also elevate matters of craft to matters of subject.

The game-like operations of obfuscated motive evolve not only from professional practices, but from contemporary vision, as well; obfuscation has become a hallmark of modern life. In recent years we have recognized that political, social, economic, educational, and religious policies aim in varying degrees at obscuring actualities. Most theories of psychology now view behavior as a symptomatic and attempt to discern the statements hidden behind various surface patterns. The trend toward artistic replication of an opaque and inscrutable reality has become prominent in contemporary practice of various disciplines. Certain movements in modern literature, painting, film, and criticism have imitated the conclusions of modern scientific theory, focusing scrutiny on the surface characteristics of their subjects, treating the observable with minimal prejudice, interpretation, or insight. Even the observable has obtained a precondition of inaccessibility; art has adopted the stance of Werner Heisenberg, a physicist who postulated that the very process of observation alters the object of its scrutiny. Although Heisenberg's Principle pertains to activity on a subatomic level, it has produced a radical revision of our conception of the universe and our epistemological relation to it. The mandate of impenetrability implicit in this thinking brings surface properties to the fore. It not only implicates them, but also activates them; even the visible is no longer certain, but responsive. The fascination in all this lies not beneath the surface, where no footholds exist for any conclusions, but in the tension between the observable and the hypothetical: in the clues by which the surface surrenders its secrets. Thus people have come to view their lives much as actors view their scripts; the strategy of the visible consists in obfuscation, and the substance of the invisible is inaccessible, except through its surface manifestations. When we add to this condition the contention that even the perceptible suffers contamination by the perceiver, we have described the rudimentary tension and mechanism of Pinter's work.

Looking back to the screenplays, we can anticipate and parallel Pinter's pattern of development as a playwright according to his choices and treatment of source material. The succession of Pinter's alterations and augmentations of the eight novels becomes particularly significant with respect to the themes under discussion. *The Servant*, for example, tallies with Pinter's initial phase of writing; it exhibits the chief characteristic of this period, a focus on relationship, and it correlates generally with other dramatic values in Pinter's early work. Its linear plot corresponds to the more conventional treatment of time and sequence during this period of his writing. Pinter does not choose, in *The Servant*, to deviate from a chronological sequence of events, despite the presence of a narrator in the source work who provides temporal distortion. Instead, Pinter entirely omits the narrative figure and concentrates on the strategies of relationship among the central characters in the novel. The development of games in this film script toward the inclusion of threat and the acquisition of external dimensions of reality, however, anticipates Pinter's later phases of work: Barrett and Tony have initiated a retreat from the world outside.

In *The Pumpkin Eater, The Quiller Memorandum,* and *Accident*, we detect that Pinter's adaptations tend to isolate and focus the individual in a contest with herself or himself. The three novels on which the screenplays are based do indeed facilitate such a shift, but, except for his approach to *The Quiller Memorandum*, Pinter has altered them to place even more stress on the conditions of solitude that afflict the central figures. As we have noted previously, Adam Hall's narrative for *The Quiller Memorandum* posed special problems of interiority, and Pinter's primary task in rendering the work cinematically legible lay in extroversion of the action. Even this extroversion, including the recreation of Inga as ambiguity rather than enemy, however, maintains intact Quiller's fundamental alienation from others: most of his interaction serves only to accentuate his condemnation to solitude.

Pinter's contributions of the two exiled sons and of their two visits home, for example, function to delineate Jo's alienation in *The Pumpkin Eater*, as does his relegation of her to a victim's role in Conway's discovery of Jake's adultery. Jo's utter displacement by the children at the conclusion of the story, also Pinter's invention, completes our sense of her exclusion. Pinter's characterization of Charley, who enjoys close rapport with Stephen in Mosley's *Accident*, but none in Pinter's screenplay, likewise serves to interrupt the bonds between the protagonist and others. Anna and William become, in Pinter's version, similarly remote and inaccessible, as does Stephen's wife. In both of these scripts, Pinter has revamped conditions to underscore the dynamic within the self by diminishing possibilities for relationships with others, just as he has done in his second phase of playwriting.

Furthermore, Pinter now adopts the quirks of temporal development that exist in the source novels. Although he continues to discard the narrator as such, he has discovered a cinematic rendering on nonsequential time. In both *The Pumpkin Eater* and *Accident,* time acquires nonlinear characteristics, but in *Accident* it closely approaches the condition of nonduration that informs the photograph, hence generating the problems of hindsight that dominiate the third phase of Pinter's writing.

All four of Pinter's most recent screenplays belong to the third group of concerns. In both subject and technique, his script for *The Go-Between* marks a conspicuous shift to the matter of recapturing the past. Pinter reshapes Hartley's novel by instituting alterations and overlays of time sequence to draw more pronounced disparities and comparisons between past and present; he maintains the dynamics between the current and the absent continuously in focus. In developing this theme, Pinter takes advantage of temporal values peculiar to the film medium, because, as Noel King observes, "Film renders action in only one tense—the present—and therefore is suited to Pinter's obsession with the presentness of the past."[6]

The past appears in Pinter only as an aspect of the present; its substance remains vulnerable to the whims of current needs or provocations. Otherwise, it no longer exists. As the past progressively hardens and objectifies, the present undermines memory, reconstituting it as a mental embroidery, a function of inhabiting the present. We can readily discern thematic and structural evidence of this process in Pinter's adaptation of Proust, where he converts the substantial narration of the novels into basically a study of its own genesis. Here Pinter excises the preceptual crisis that underlies the lengthy narrative episodes of Proust's work and elevates it almost to the function of plot. Both of these screenplays adopt a temporal scheme that is essentially photographic; they initiate and conclude in an almost identical moment in time, evoking the simultaneous presence and absence of the past: "a kind of ever-present quality in life."[7]

Pinter's version of *The Last Tycoon* deviates in form and in subject from the trends in *The Go-Between* and *The Proust Screenplay*, but it remains consistent with them in nature. As he did for *The Servant*, Pinter chooses against suggestion of narrative circularity, although both novels construct their stories through the device of a narrator from the perspective of a fixed point in time. According to the identification of past with fiction that permeates Pinter's work, the alternative world of movie illusions that exists in Fitzgerald's novel qualifies to replace memory as the source of tension in the action. Pinter deploys the novel's conflict between fabricated and intractable realities as a surrogate for his more typical friction between compliant, inaccessible pasts and incompliant, preemptive presents. Episodes of fiction alternate here with episodes of life to produce a clash between the elusive and the ineluctable similar to the ones that occur in *The Go-Between* and *The Proust Screenplay*. Time slips gears according to the dual dimensions of existence, outside and inside of fiction, that formulate Stahr's routine.

194

In his screenplay for *The French Lieutenant's Woman*, Pinter accomplishes a total identification of past with fiction, merging the statements of *The Go-Between* and *The Proust Screenplay* with that of *The Last Tycoon* to form an explicit condition. The attempt to recapture the past achieves a fundamental unity with the drive to imitate the world of fiction. Past/fiction coincides with present/"non-fiction" as irreconcilable entities, plainly, but inscrutably, derived from each other. Again, we note the self-conscious accentuation of craft that appears also in *The Last Tycoon* and, variously, in *The Proust Screenplay*. The temporal qualities in Pinter's adaptation of the Fowles novel resemble, in their linear complexity, those in his screenplay for *The Last Tycoon*, progressing generally in chronological sequence, but acquiring distortion through the intermingling of fictional and "nonfictional" events. In each of these screenplays, as in his third group of stage plays, Pinter reveals a preoccupation with figures who inhabit a world both outside of and condemned by time.

In his screenplays and in his stage plays, Pinter shifts the locus of menace from the threat of change to the condition of stasis. Insularity has passed from the ideal to the real, and where his characters previously feared challenge, they now invite it: where the posture was formerly invulnerability, it is now vulnerability. As the dominion of human artifice, initially a contrivance for perpetuating stability against the prospect of upheaval and finally a strategy for enduring in time, envelops and cancels out increasing spheres of experience, the human condition and its remedy become interchangeable; and Pinter reverses their natures. His worlds become sealed systems; intrusion becomes an impossible dream. Condemned to an interminable, impregnable monotony, the characters now invent and define their own oppositions. These illusions fail, however, just as the earlier illusions of security failed, when they are tested against the phenomenal world. The attempt to inscribe the controls of fiction on the mysteries of experience is never successful in Pinter's work.

During an interview concerning his work on *The French Lieutenant's Woman*, Karel Reisz stated his views on the subject of screen adaptation:

> That's the hardy perennial: Do you have to be faithful to the novel? My answer is no. You don't have to be faithful to anything, you have to make a variation on the themes of the novel which, a., is a film, not a filmed novel, and b., is a film in which you can put your feelings and your associations. By making the movie, you don't change the novel; it continues to exist! The whole business of being faithful is a nonsensical aim. A novel is capable of taking you inside a person; it gives you their speculations, their feelings, their historic associations and so on. That's something that movies can only hint at.

195

> But the moment you've accepted that fact, then the whole notion of being
> faithful becomes meaningless because in cinema you have to substitute some-
> thing filmic—Surprise, surprise!—for the things you can't do. You can't just
> leave yourself with the things that are left, the fag-end of what the medium
> can absorb. And the moment you realize that, you're out of the business of
> translating and you're into the business of making it mean what you want it to
> mean.[8]

Pinter's achievement as an adapter consists precisely in this transformation of material according to the special dynamics of the film medium and of his personal milieu. Each of the eight scripts testifies to his
skill at converting language into image and to his success at distilling
ideas into essence and form. We have seen that the significance of visual
images has been seminal in Pinter's work for stage and screen throughout his career, and that his aptitude for stating theme in form has been a
consistent feature of his writing. Economy of expression distinguishes
all of Pinter's scripts, and he has acknowledged that, whatever the difference in degree, both stage and screen require a knack for the succinct.
These characteristics commend Pinter to the cinema as a singularly appropriate talent.

> The disciplines are similar, for a writer, in that although you need, let's say, less
> words on the screen than you do on the stage, nevertheless—although I don't
> really believe this to be true—say that you needed twenty words for a particular
> scene on the stage, you can do with six for a similar scene on the screen. The
> point is, that if you write eight for the screen, two words too many, you're
> overloading the thing, and you're breaking your discipline; precisely the same
> discipline, the same economy, whatever the medium you're writing for.[9]

If Pinter's unique bias and method have contributed generously to his
success as a screenwriter, we may also theorize that his screenwriting
has influenced his bias and method. Noel King has attributed Pinter's
redefinition of "menace" to his experience with the temporal values of
film,[10] and Enoch Brater has suggested that Pinter's manipulation of
images and arrangement of time in *Betrayal* reveal "the profound effect
his work in the movies has had on his dramatic technique."[11] Pinter,
himself, while speaking about his adaptation of *Betrayal* for film, spec-
ulated that his work for cinema may have opened new avenues in his
playwriting. "It was originally written for the stage in a kind of cinematic way, with a structure that possibly owes something to the films
I've worked on for the last twenty years. My early plays started at the
beginning and went to the end; they were linear. Then I did more and
more films, and I felt that 'Betrayal'—even the stage version—comes
as much out of film as it does out of the stage."[12]
Whether Pinter's screenwriting experience inspired or was merely

conducive to these developments is impossible, and probably unnecessary, to evaluate; but his work in both media, stage and screen, has progressed along similar lines. Ironically perhaps, Pinter, who spoke on his high school debating team, once supported the resolution that "in view of its progress in the last decade, the Film is more promising in its future as an art form than the Theatre."[13] His own career, in its progressively frequent essays into screenwriting, may attest to the inevitability of that contention. For Pinter, in any case, the penchant for ambiguity that courts subterfuge in some of his stage plays becomes a genuine asset in his approach to the fully evolved works of compatible writers. Where his original writing seems occasionally contrived, the opacity in the screenplays thrives on elaborate underpinnings and sometimes obtains superior resonance and cogency. Pinter's adaptations of these novels into the medium of film are exemplary accomplishments in sensitive, imaginative transmutation of material; he is an incisive maker of pictures.

Notes

Chapter 1: Media

1. Mel Gussow, "A Conversation (Pause) with Harold Pinter" (interview with Harold Pinter), *New York Times Magazine,* 5 December 1971, p. 131.

2. Bert O. States, "Pinter's *Homecoming*: The Shock of Nonrecognition," *Hudson Review* 21, no. 3 (August 1968):474-86.

3. Most of the extant critical studies of Pinter contain practices of this nature. His work is rarely approached from a phenomenological perspective and is, instead, interpreted through the apparati biographical data, allegorical readings, Pinter folklore, extraneous comparison, and various analytic conceits. Katherine Burkman's study, *The Dramatic World of Harold Pinter: Its Basis in Ritual* (Columbus: Ohio State University Press, 1971), includes in its chapter on "Pinter in Production" an excellent argument for a purely phenomenological exegesis of the plays. She, however, diverges from the sensibilities of such a study by imposing a myth-ritual index on the contours of the individual scripts. Occasionally, this artifice produces absurd claims, such as her contention that *Accident* resolves in a "celebration of life" (p. 117). In a recent article on "Pinter's Progress" in *Modern Drama* 23 (1980):246-57, Noel King notes similar fallacies in studies of Pinter's work, disparaging applications of linguistic and psychoanalytic theories to the plays and proposing his own reading of Pinter according to the "overall body" of Pinter's career. Although this study, like Burkman's, includes fine insights into certain aspects of Pinter's work, it also proceeds by contamination of individual pieces through importation of extrinsic ideas. It seems to me that such approaches violate the prevailing theme of Pinter's writing: that, however mystifying, the slice of life is a complete, unified entity that must be addressed in its own terms.

4. Arnold P. Hinchliffe, *Harold Pinter* (New York: Twayne Publishers, 1967), p. 175.

5. Ibid.

6. Arthur Ganz, ed., *Pinter: A Collection of Critical Essays* (Englewood Cliffs, New Jersey: Prentice-Hall, 1972), p. 12.

7. Roland Barthes, *Camera Lucida: Reflections on Photography* (New York: Hill and Wang, 1981), pp. 88-89.

8. Erwin Panofsky, "Style and Medium in the Motion Pictures," in *Film Theory and Criticism: Introductory Readings,* ed. by Gerald Mast and Marshall Cohen (New York: Oxford University Press, 1979), pp. 243-63.

9. Christian Metz, "Some Points in the Semiotics of the Cinema," in Mast and Cohen, p. 175.

10. Panofsky, in Mast and Cohen, p. 246.

11. George Bluestone, "Limits of the Novel and the Film," in Mast and Cohen, p. 415.

12. Robert Scholes, "Narration and Narrativity in Film," in Mast and Cohen, p. 428.

13. John Fowles, Foreword to *The French Lieutenant's Woman: A Screenplay*, by Harold Pinter (Boston: Little, Brown and Company, 1981), p. ix.

14. Ibid., p. x.

15. Ibid.

16. Stephen Menick, "Remembrance of Things Future" (interview with Harold Pinter), *Village Voice* (New York), 12 December 1977.

17. I have adopted this attitude despite general confusion over the states of the various scripts (see *Times Literary Supplement*, "From Page to Screen," 18 June 1971, p. 695). Indeed, possible and indeterminable degrees of script revision through film production exigencies necessitate the convenience of such a stance. Whatever the production-related status of the published scripts (and, judging by their frequent discrepancies with the finished films, they would seem to represent early, and hence relatively pure, versions of Pinter's work—especially with respect to *The Proust Screenplay*, which has not been subjected to the actual process of filming, and to *The French Lieutenant's Woman*, which Pinter has labeled a preshooting script), I have necessarily accepted these texts as definitive.

Chapter 2: *The Servant*

1. Robin Maugham, *The Servant* (New York: Harcourt, Brace, 1949), p. 15.

2. Harold Pinter, *The Servant*, in *Five Screenplays* (New York: Grove Press, 1973), p. 3.

3. Beverle Houston and Marsha Kinder, "The Losey-Pinter Collaboration," *Film Quarterly* 32 (1978):22.

4. William Baker and Stephen Ely Tabachnick, *Harold Pinter* (Edinburgh: Oliver and Boyd, 1973), p. 102.

5. Ibid., pp. 92-93.

6. Jean-Paul Sartre, *Saint Genet: Actor and Martyr* (New York: Pantheon Books, 1963), p. 617.

7. Baker and Tabachnick, p. 95.

8. Baker and Tabachnick, p. 94.

9. For a more detailed analysis of subtextual games in Pinter's plays, see my "Pinterviews: Problems of Observation from the Modern Disposition" (Ph.D. diss., University of California at Berkeley, 1979).

Chapter 3: *The Pumpkin Eater*

1. Penelope Mortimer, *The Pumpkin Eater* (New York: McGraw-Hill, 1962), p. 222.

2. See, for example, Baker and Tabachnick pp. 96-99 and Martin Esslin, *Pinter: A Study of his Plays* (New York: W. W. Norton and Company, Inc., 1970), pp. 206-7.

3. Baker and Tabachnick, p. 99.

4. Harold Pinter, *The Pumpkin Eater,* in *Five Screenplays,* pp. 63-64.

5. Pinter began his career in the theatre as an actor with Anew McMaster's touring company in Ireland (see Harold Pinter, *Mac* [London: Emanuel Wax for Pendragon Press, 1968]), and he has continued to perform occasionally, including roles in both his screenplays and stage plays.

6. Katherine Burkman, *The Dramatic World of Harold Pinter: Its Basis in Ritual* (Columbus: Ohio State University Press, 1971), p. 107.

Chapter 4: *The Quiller Memorandum*

1. Adam Hall, *The Quiller Memorandum* (New York: Simon and Schuster, Inc., 1965), p. 190.

2. Martin Esslin, *Pinter: A Study of his Plays* (New York: W. W. Norton and Company, Inc., 1970), p. 207.

3. Harold Pinter, *The Quiller Memorandum,* in *Five Screenplays,* pp. 185-86.

4. Burkman, pp. 45-46.

5. Baker and Tabachnick, pp. 90-91.

Chapter 5: *Accident*

1. Nicholas Mosley, *Accident* (New York: Coward-McCann, 1966), pp. 42, 92, and 192.

2. John Russell Taylor, "Accident" (interview with Harold Pinter), *Sight and Sound* 35 (1966):183.

3. Harold Pinter, quoted in John Russell Taylor, p. 183.

4. Harold Pinter, *Accident,* in *Five Screenplays,* p. 219.

5. See Houston and Kinder, p. 27, for a discussion of the significance of this remark.

6. Tom Milne, "Two Films (1): *Accident,"* *Sight and Sound* 36 (1967):59.

7. Gussow, p. 128.

8. For a discussion of this point, see Houston and Kinder, p. 27.

9. Milne, p. 59.

10. James R. Hollis, *Harold Pinter: The Poetics of Silence* (Carbondale: Southern Illinois University Press, 1970), p. 120.

11. Gussow, pp. 131-32.

12. Milne, p. 59.

13. Ibid.

14. Ibid.

15. Tom Milne, *Losey on Losey* (New York: Doubleday and Company, 1968), pp. 107-8.

16. Milne, "Two Films," p. 57.

17. Baker and Tabachnick, p. 102.

18. Burkman, p. 166.

19. John Lahr, ed., *A Casebook on Harold Pinter's The Homecoming* (New York: Grove Press, 1971), p. 14.

20. Harold Pinter, *The Homecoming* (New York: Grove Press, 1966), p. 61.

21. Pinter, *The Homecoming*, pp. 52-53.

Chapter 6: *The Go-Between*

1. L. P. Hartley, *The Go-Between* (New York: Alfred A. Knopf, 1954), p. 31.

2. Jean-Paul Sartre, *Critique de la raison dialectique*, preceded by *Question de méthode* (Paris: Gallimard, 1960), pp. 310-12, 384-86.

3. R. E. Pritchard, "L. P. Hartley's *The Go-Between*," *Critical Quarterly* 22, no. 1 (1980):45.

4. Harold Pinter, *The Go-Between*, in *Five Screenplays*, p. 287.

5. Neil Sinyard, "Pinter's *Go-Between*," *Critical Quarterly* 22, no. 3 (1980):33.

6. Sinyard, p. 22.

7. Gussow, pp. 130-31.

8. Sinyard, p. 21.

9. Joseph Losey, Interview with Harold Pinter, *Time*, 9 August 1971, p. 45.

10. Harold Pinter, *The Proust Screenplay* (New York: Grove Press, 1977), p. 177.

11. Sinyard, p. 23.

Chapter 7: *The Proust Screenplay*

1. Marcel Proust, *Swann's Way*, trans. C. K. Scott Moncrieff (New York: Vintage Books, 1970), pp. 34 and 325.

2. Menick interview.

3. Pinter, *The Proust Screenplay*, pp. ix-x.

4. Stanley Kauffmann, review of *The Proust Screenplay*, by Harold Pinter, *New Republic*, 24 and 31 December 1977, p. 22.

5. Enoch Brater, "Time and Memory in Pinter's Proust Screenplay," *Comparative Drama* 13, no. 2 (1979):124.

6. Jean-Paul Sartre, *What is Literature?*, trans. Bernard Frechtman (New York: Harper and Row, 1965), p. 36.

7. Brater, p. 125.

8. Marcel Proust, *The Past Recaptured*, trans. Andreas Mayor (New York: Vintage Books, 1970), p. 130.

9. Brater, p. 124.

10. Gussow, p. 32.

11. Peter Hall, *Peter Hall's Diaries: The Story of a Dramatic Battle*, ed. John Goodwin (London: Hamish Hamilton, 1983), p. 156.

12. Enoch Brater, "Cinematic Fidelity and the Forms of Pinter's *Betrayal*," *Modern Drama* 24 (1981):503-13.

13. Gussow, p. 131.

Chapter 8: *The Last Tycoon*

1. F. Scott Fitzgerald, *The Last Tycoon* (New York: Bantam, 1976), pp. 38 and 88.

2. Edmund Wilson, Foreword to Fitzgerald, *The Last Tycoon* (New York: Charles Scribner's Sons, 1941; rpt. 1970), p. ix.

3. Harold Pinter, *The Last Tycoon* (unpublished script available in the Louis B. Mayer Library at The American Film Institute in Los Angeles, 1975), pp. 16-18.

4. Irene Kahn Atkins, "Hollywood Revisited: A Sad Homecoming," *Literature/Film Quarterly* 5, no. 2 (1977):108.

Chapter 9: *The French Lieutenant's Woman*

1. John Fowles, *The French Lieutenant's Woman* (New York: New American Library, Inc., 1969), p. 80.

2. Pinter, *The French Lieutenant's Woman: A Screenplay*, pp. x-xi.

3. Richard Combs, "In Search of *The French Lieutenant's Woman*," *Sight and Sound* 50 (1980-81):35.

4. Ibid.

5. Harlan Kennedy, "The Czech Director's Woman," *Film Comment*, September/October (1981):27.

6. Ibid., pp. 30-31.

7. Peter J. Conradi, "*The French Lieutenant's Woman*: Novel, Screenplay, Film," *Critical Quarterly* 24, no. 1 (1982):53.

8. Kennedy, p. 30.

9. Gussow, p. 43.

Chapter 10: Patterns

1. Houston and Kinder, p. 25.

2. For a more complete discussion of Pinter's plays in terms of these phases, see my "Pinterviews: Problems of Observation from the Modern Disposition" (Ph.D. diss., University of California at Berkeley, 1979).

3. Harold Pinter, *Landscape and Silence* (New York: Grove Press, 1970), p. 7.

4. Harold Pinter, *No Man's Land* (New York: Grove Press, 1975), p. 95.

5. In his subsequent one-act play, *A Kind of Alaska,* Pinter continues his study of time, memory, and the past through the conceit of sleeping sickness. Here, a hiatus of twenty-nine years operates ironically to bind and to sever the links between past and present, and the disease itself becomes an emblem of petrified time.

6. Noel King, "Pinter's Progress," *Modern Drama* 23 (1980):250.

7. Gussow, p. 131.

8. Kennedy, p. 28.

9. Harold Pinter, interviewed in *Isis*, 1 February 1964, p. 19.

Notes

10. King, p. 250.

11. Brater, "Cinematic Fidelity," p. 597.

12. Leslie Bennetts, "On Film: Pinter's *Betrayal* Displays New Subtleties," *New York Times*, 27 February 1983, sec. H, pp. 1 and 23.

13. Baker and Tabachnick, p. 150.

Bibliography

Writings by Pinter

Betrayal: A Play by Harold Pinter. New York: Grove Press, Inc., 1978.

The Birthday Party and The Room: Two Plays by Harold Pinter. New York: Grove Press, Evergreen Books, 1961.

The Caretaker and The Dumb Waiter: Two Plays by Harold Pinter. New York: Grove Press, Evergreen Books, 1961.

Complete Works: One. New York: Grove Press, Inc., 1976. (This includes *The Birthday Party, The Room, The Dumb Waiter, A Slight Ache, A Night Out, The Black and White, The Examination,* and "Writing for the Theatre.")

Complete Works: Two. New York: Grove Press, Inc., 1977. (This includes *The Caretaker, Night School, The Dwarfs, The Collection, The Lover, Five Revue Sketches: Trouble in the Works, The Black and White, Request Stop, Last to Go, Special Offer,* and "Writing for Myself.")

Complete Works: Three. New York: Grove Press, Inc., 1978. (This includes *The Homecoming, Landscape, Silence, The Basement, Revue Sketches: Night, That's All, That's Your Trouble, Interview, Applicant, Dialogue for Three, Tea Party:* play; *Tea Party:* short story, and *Mac.*)

Complete Works: Four. New York: Grove Press, Inc., 1981. (This includes *Old Times, No Man's Land, Betrayal, Monologue:* TV play; *Family Voices*: radio play.)

Five Screenplays. New York: Grove Press, Inc., 1973. (This includes *The Servant, The Pumpkin Eater, The Quiller Memorandum, Accident,* and *The Go-Between.*)

The French Lieutenant's Woman: A Screenplay. Boston: Little, Brown and Company, 1981.

The Homecoming. New York: Grove Press, Evergreen Books, 1966.

The Hothouse: A Play by Harold Pinter. New York: Grove Press, Inc., 1980.

Landscape and Silence. New York: Grove Press, Inc., 1970. (This includes *Night.*)

The Last Tycoon. Los Angeles: The American Film Institute, Louis B. Mayer Library, 1975.

The Lover, Tea Party, The Basement: Two Plays and a Film Script by Harold Pinter. New York: Grove Press, Evergreen Books, 1967.

Mac. Ipswich: W. S. Cowell Ltd., Pendragon Press, 1968.

Monologue. London: Covent Garden Press Ltd., 1973.

Bibliography

A Night Out, Night School, Revue Sketches: Early Plays by Harold Pinter. New York: Grove Press, Evergreen Books, 1967.

No Man's Land: A Play by Harold Pinter. New York: Grove Press, Inc., 1975.

Old Times: A Play by Harold Pinter. New York: Grove Press, Inc., 1971.

Other Places. New York: Grove Press, Inc., 1983. (This includes *A Kind of Alaska, Victoria Station,* and *Family Voices.*)

Poems. London: Enitharmon Press, 1971.

The Proust Screenplay. New York: Grove Press, Inc., 1977.

Three Plays by Harold Pinter. New York: Grove Press, Evergreen Books, 1962. (This includes *A Slight Ache, The Collection,* and *The Dwarfs.*)

Screenplay Sources

Fitzgerald, F. Scott. *The Last Tycoon.* New York: Bantam Books, Inc., 1976.

Fowles, John. *The French Lieutenant's Woman.* New York: New American Library, Inc., 1969.

Hall, Adam. *The Quiller Memorandum.* New York: Simon and Schuster, Inc., 1965.

Hartley, L. P. *The Go-Between.* New York: Alfred A. Knopf, Inc., 1954.

Maugham, Robin. *The Servant.* New York: Harcourt, Brace, 1949.

Mortimer, Penelope. *The Pumpkin Eater.* New York: McGraw-Hill, 1962.

Mosley, Nicholas. *Accident.* New York: Coward-McCann, 1966.

Proust, Marcel. *Remembrance of Things Past: Swann's Way.* Translated by C. K. Scott Moncrieff. New York: Vintage Books, 1970.

_____. *Remembrance of Things Past: Within a Budding Grove.* Translated by C. K. Scott Moncrieff. New York: Vintage Books, 1970.

_____. *Remembrance of Things Past: The Guermantes Way.* Translated by C. K. Scott Moncrieff. New York: Vintage Books, 1970.

_____. *Remembrance of Things Past: Cities of the Plain.* Translated by C. K. Scott Moncrieff. New York: Vintage Books, 1970.

_____. *Remembrance of Things Past: The Captive.* Translated by C. K. Scott Moncrieff. New York: Vintage Books, 1970.

_____. *Remembrance of Things Past: The Sweet Cheat Gone.* Translated by C. K. Scott Moncrieff. New York: Vintage Books, 1970.

_____. *Remembrance of Things Past: The Past Recaptured.* Translated by Andreas Mayor. New York: Vintage Books, 1971.

Other Works Cited

Atkins, Irene Kahn. "Hollywood Revisited: A Sad Homecoming." *Literature/Film Quarterly* 5, no. 2 (1977):105–11.

Baker, William, and Tabachnick, Stephen Ely. *Harold Pinter.* Edinburgh: Oliver and Boyd, 1973.

Barthes, Roland. *Camera Lucida: Reflections on Photography.* Translated by Richard Howard. New York: Hill and Wang, 1981.

Bibliography

Bennetts, Leslie. "On Film: Pinter's *Betrayal* Displays New Subtleties." *New York Times,* 27 February 1983, sec. H, pp. 1 and 23.

Brater, Enoch. "Cinematic Fidelity and the Forms of Pinter's *Betrayal.*" *Modern Drama* 24 (1981):503–13.

_____. "Time and Memory in Pinter's Proust Screenplay." *Comparative Drama* 13, no. 2 (1979):121–26.

Burkman, Katherine. *The Dramatic World Of Harold Pinter: Its Basis in Ritual.* Columbus: Ohio State University Press, 1971.

Combs, Richard. "In Search of *The French Lieutenant's Woman.*" *Sight and Sound* 50 (1980–81):34–35 and 39.

Conradi, Peter J. "*The French Lieutenant's Woman:* Novel, Screenplay, Film." *Critical Quarterly* 24, no. 1 (1982):41–57.

Esslin, Martin. *Pinter: A Study of his Plays.* New York: W. W. Norton and Company, Inc., 1970.

Ganz, Arthur, ed. *Pinter: A Collection of Critical Essays.* Englewood Cliffs, New Jersey: Prentice-Hall, 1972.

Gussow, Mel. "A Conversation (Pause) with Harold Pinter" (interview with Harold Pinter). *New York Times Magazine,* 5 December 1971, p. 43 and pp. 126–35.

Hall, Peter. *Peter Hall's Diaries: The Story of a Dramatic Battle.* Edited by John Goodwin. London: Hamish Hamilton Ltd., 1983.

Hinchliffe, Arnold P. *Harold Pinter.* New York: Twayne Publishers, 1967.

Hollis, James R. *Harold Pinter: The Poetics of Silence.* Carbondale: Southern Illinois University Press, 1970.

Houston, Beverle, and Kinder, Marsha. "The Losey-Pinter Collaboration." *Film Quarterly* 32 (1978):17–30.

Isis, 1 February 1964, entire issue on Joseph Losey.

Kauffmann, Stanley. Revision of *The Proust Screenplay,* by Harold Pinter. *The New Republic,* 24 and 31 December 1977, pp. 22–23.

Kennedy, Harlan. "The Czech Director's Woman." *Film Comment,* September/October (1981):26–31.

King, Noel. "Pinter's Progress." *Modern Drama* 23 (1980):246–57.

Klein, Joanne. "Pinterviews: Problems of Observation from the Modern Disposition." Ph.D. dissertation, University of California at Berkeley, 1979.

Losey, Joseph. Interview with Harold Pinter. *Time,* 9 August 1971.

Mast, Gerald, and Cohen, Marshall, eds. *Film Theory and Criticism: Introductory Readings.* New York: Oxford University Press, 1979.

Menick, Stephen. "Remembrance of Things Future" (interview with Harold Pinter). *Village Voice* (New York), 12 December 1977.

Milne, Tom. *Losey on Losey.* New York: Doubleday and Company, 1968.

_____. "Two Films (1): *Accident.*" *Sight and Sound* 36 (1967):57–59.

Pritchard, R. E. "L. P. Hartley's *The Go-Between.*" *Critical Quarterly* 22, no. 1 (1980):45–55.

Sartre, Jean-Paul. *Critique de la raison dialectique,* preceded by *Question de méthode.* Paris: Gallimard, 1960.

Bibliography

_____. *Saint Genet: Actor and Martyr.* Translated by Bernard Frechtman. New York: Pantheon Books, 1963.

_____. *What is Literature?* Translated by Bernard Frechtman. New York: Harper and Row, 1965.

Sinyard, Neil. "Pinter's *Go-Between.*" *Critical Quarterly* 22, no. 3 (1980):21–33.

States, Bert O. "Pinter's *Homecoming:* The Shock of Nonrecognition." *Hudson Review* 21, no. 3 (August 1968):474–86.

Taylor, John Russell. "Accident" (interview with Harold Pinter). *Sight and Sound* 35 (1966).

Index

Index

nant's Woman (screenplay), 163, 167–68, 176–77; in *The Go-Between* (screenplay), 85; in *The Homecoming* (play), 75; in *The Last Tycoon* (screenplay), 137–39; in Pinter's writing, 22, 23, 191; in *The Proust Screenplay*, 117; in *The Pumpkin Eater* (screenplay), 33–34, 36

Doubt. *See* Alienation: through incomprehension; Behavior: inscrutability of; Dialogue: as equivocal; as evasive; as smokescreen; Motive: as contradiction of the apparent; inscrutability of; Pinter's dramaturgy: themes and qualities of; Point of view: as problematic; Verification: as problematic

Dumb Waiter, The, 13, 47; as early phase of Pinter's writing, 25, 186–87; sanctuary and intrusion in, 14, 20, 40

Enclosure (*see also* Restructuring: for contadictory enclosure; for enclosure): as problematic, in *The French Lieutenant's Woman* (novel), 146, 155–56, 182–83; (screenplay), 182–83

Esslin, Martin, 44

Film medium: Pinter's valuation of, 2–3, 196, 197

Film-within-a-film. *See* Moviemaking

Films: deviation from screenplays, 8, 200n.17; in *The French Lieutenant's Woman*, 154, 163, 164, 165, 167, 168, 170, 173, 174, 175, 177–78, 180; in *The Go-Between*, 94; in *The Last Tycoon*, 129, 131, 132, 143; in *The Proust Screenplay*, 103–4; in *The Pumpkin Eater*, 29, 34, 39, 40, 41; in *The Quiller Memorandum*, 44, 45

First-person narration. *See* Narration

Fitzgerald, F. Scott. *See Last Tycoon, The*

Fowles, John. *See French Lieutenant's Woman, The*

French Lieutenant's Woman, The: discussion of adaptation, 145–84; (screenplay), 6, 22, 81, 101–2, 200n.17; conceit of moviemaking in, 6, 132, 144; correlated with Pinter's plays, 185, 195

Games (*see also* Order: as conceit; Relationship): escalation of, in Pinter's writing, 73–75, 102, 144, 186–91, 193; of interpretation, in *The Homecoming* (play),

75; in *The Proust Screenplay*, 186; in *The Quiller Memorandum* (novel), 42; as motif, in Pinter's writing, 8, 25, 185–92; as ordering device, in Pinter's writing, 22–23, 185; of playacting, in relationships, 18–19; as revelation, in *Accident* (novel), 63; (screenplay), 63, 70; in *The French Lieutenant's Woman* (screenplay), 172–73; in *The Go-Between* (novel), 91; (screenplay), 92; in *The Last Tycoon* (novel/screenplay), 140; in Pinter's writing, 22–23, 185–86

Genet, Jean (*see also Maids, The*), 18, 148

Go-Between, The: discussion of adaptation, 77–102; (novel), 106; (screenplay), 86, 106, 123, 135, 183; correlated with Pinter's plays, 186, 194–95; time in, 106–7, 107, 127, 153

Gussow, Mel: interview with Pinter, 127

Hall, Adam. *See Quiller Memorandum, The*

Hall, Peter, 74, 127

Hartley, L. P. *See Go-Between, The*

Heisenberg, Werner, 192

Homecoming, The: (film), 1, 41; (play), 48, 73–75; dynamics of games and relationships in, 27, 59, 134, 187–88; sanctuary and intrusion in, 14, 21, 25, 41

Homosexuality. *See* Relationship: homosexual

Houston, Beverle and Marsha Kinder: study of Pinter's films, 12, 185–86

Identification: through intercutting, in *Accident* (screenplay), 68–70; in *The French Lieutenant's Woman* (screenplay), 163, 164–65, 171, 175, 176, 178; in *The Go-Between* (screenplay), 87; in *The Proust Screenplay*, 105–11, 119–20, 125–26; through montage, in *The Go-Between* (screenplay), 83, 96–99

Intercutting (*see also* Adumbration: through intercutting; Contrast: through intercutting; Identification: through intercutting; Time: cinematic intercutting of): of movie clips, in *The Last Tycoon* (screenplay), 142–43. *See also* Time: cinematic intercutting of

Interiors, 82, 135, 162; furnishing as strategy, 14–15, 20, 21, 22, 25; as sanctuary, 20–21, 150; vacant, 11, 29, 39, 40–41